A Proposal for Correcting the ENGLISH TONGUE Polite Conversation, Etc.

JONATHAN SWIFT

A Proposal for Correcting the ENGLISH TONGUE Polite Conversation, Etc.

Edited by
Herbert Davis
with
Louis Landa

BASIL BLACKWELL · OXFORD
1964

First published 1957
Reprinted 1964

PRINTED IN GREAT BRITAIN FOR
BASIL BLACKWELL & MOTT LTD. BY
THE COMPTON PRINTING WORKS (LONDON) LTD. LONDON, N.1.
AND BOUND BY
THE KEMP HALL BINDERY, OXFORD

PREFACE

IN the original plan of this edition, Vols. IV and V were to have contained the three pieces which are now printed here as Part I of this volume, and all the *Journal to Stella*. But since the *Journal* has in the meantime been edited with notes in two volumes by Sir Harold Williams for the Clarendon Press; and since in any case being a series of letters it does not strictly belong to an edition of the *Prose Works*, it has been decided not to include it here.

Instead, I have completed this volume with *Polite Conversation*, for which Swift claimed that he had begun to collect the material as early as 1704, and some undated pieces on manners and education, together with a hitherto unpublished paper in defence of punning, and a collection of other pieces of that sort, which indicate the prevalence of that dangerous practice among Swift and his friends.

The next volume will also contain a miscellaneous collection of autobiographical pieces, Marginalia, and the Abstract of the History of England, etc.; and the final volume will now be given up entirely to provide a full Index to the whole edition.

The editors wish to make due acknowledgement for the permission to reprint here from the Swift Manuscripts in the Pierpont Morgan Library in New York and the Henry Huntington Library in San Marino.

The CONTENTS

ILLUSTRATIONS OF TITLE-PAGES

The INTRODUCTION

PART I

THE three tracts included in Part I of this volume could well be considered as companion pieces to those published in Volumes VI and VIII of this edition. They belong to the same period and have certain obvious resemblances. Nevertheless, they are distinguishable in some respects from the political tracts which Swift wrote during his association with the Harley government. Two of the three, the *Proposal for Correcting . . . the English Tongue* and the *Abstract* of Collins's *Discourse of Free-Thinking*, though by no means free of partisan intentions, were not inspired by immediate political events and are not concerned with the evil activities of politicians or the disruptions of national life by party journalists. Even the obviously partisan *Preface to the Bishop of Sarum's Introduction* was in some measure due to Swift's concern for historical truth, especially in dealing with the events of his own lifetime. His indictment of Burnet's falsification of history may remind us of his opinion of historians as expressed, for instance, in *Gulliver's Travels*, where Gulliver in Glubbdubdrib has his eyes opened to the past, and is able to correct ancient and modern history. 'I was chiefly disgusted with modern history,' Gulliver tells us after he has discovered 'how the World had been misled by prostitute Writers.' And we recall that earlier in *The Battle of the Books* the modern historians are described as '*heavy-armed Foot*, all *Mercenaries*.'

It is interesting that *The Examiner* in October and November of 1713 should have printed several papers paralleling Swift's own ideas of history—of its dignity and value, and of the failure of England to produce great historians, except, of course, Clarendon, whom the Tories liked to contrast with Burnet.[1] I do not suggest that Swift wrote these *Examiners*,

[1] See *The Examiner*, October 9, November 27, November 30, 1713.

though it is possible that he made suggestions for them, particularly for the issue of November 30, where Burnet is pilloried. Here the analysis of the Bishop of Sarum's *Introduction* has striking resemblances to Swift's *Preface*, and the remarks on corrupt historical writing could easily have come from the hand that later penned Gulliver's encounter with historical shades. Furthermore, the *Examiner's* definition of 'parallel' history embodies Swift's conception of Burnet's effort—'those *Histories* which are written not so much out of regard to past Occurrences, as for the sake of exposing the present State of Affairs, under an artful Resemblance to Facts and Incidents of another Date.'[1] Similarly, Collins's *Discourse of Free-Thinking* seemed to Swift not merely a piece of heterodoxy but also a specious use of the past. At the same time that *The Examiner* was exposing Burnet, it gave some attention to Collins, in terms that Swift would approve. The author of the paper of November 6, in fact, ended with a quotation from Swift's *Abstract* after a lengthy attack on the *Discourse* and the ignorance of history and the laws and customs of the ancients displayed by free thinkers. The occasion of this paper was the publication of the second part of Bentley's *Remarks upon a Late Discourse of Free-Thinking*, with its elaborate dissection of Collins's historical errors, among other inaccuracies; and though Swift's indirect method distinguishes his attack from those of Bentley and *The Examiner*, there is no question that his irony veils his conviction that the deist had corrupted biblical and ancient history in a dangerous, if somewhat ludicrous, performance.

Swift viewed these effusions of Collins and Burnet not merely as corruptions of history, but also, as *The Examiner* (November 30) complained of Burnet, a 'Reproach to the Commonwealth of Letters.' Here was not only bad history, but bad writing. Swift was as contemptuous of the bishop's style as he was of his matter. He might, in fact, have drawn illustrations from Burnet to support the view set forth in

---

[1] Swift was himself adept at 'parallel' history; for example, in *A Discourse of the Contests and Dissensions . . . in Athens and Rome* and *The Examiner*, No. 17. See also his comment on this device in *The Examiner*, No. 16.

the *Proposal for Correcting . . . the English Tongue* and other tracts included in this volume, that the language was exhibiting symptoms of decay and needed regulation. *A Discourse of Free-Thinking*, with its solecisms and uninspired writing, could hardly have been less offensive; and we may be certain that the amusing comment in the *Preface* about Burnet would apply equally well to Collins—'that peculiar Manner of expressing himself, which the Poverty of our Language forceth me to call [his] Stile.'[1]

In June 1711 Swift proposed to Robert Harley the formation of 'a society or academy for correcting and settling our language, that we may not perpetually be changing as we do. Harley, Swift wrote to Stella, 'enters mightily into it, so does the dean of Carlisle [Atterbury]; and I design to write a letter to lord treasurer with the proposals of it, and publish it. . . .'[2] The reformation of the language had been the subject of his reflections for some time. In the previous year he had contributed an essay to *The Tatler* (No. 230, September 28, 1710) calling attention to 'the continual corruption of our English tongue' and suggesting that Isaac Bickerstaff constitute himself Censor and compiler of an annual *Index Expurgatorius* for the purpose of expunging all words and phrases offensive to good sense. The letter to Harley was to be a continuation and expansion of this idea. Preoccupied as Swift was, progress was slow. He finally completed and sent the letter to Harley on February 22, 1711–12, who in turn passed it on to Matthew Prior, from whom Swift retrieved it for publication, nearly a year from the time he first mentioned it to Harley.[3] It appeared on May 17, 1712, under the title, *A Proposal for Correcting, Improving and Ascertaining the English Tongue; in a Letter to the Most Honourable Robert, Earl of Oxford and Mortimer, Lord High Treasurer of Great Britain.*[4]

A few days before its publication Swift wrote to Stella: 'I suffer my name to be put at the End of it, wch I nevr did before in my Life.'[5] His willingness to publish the *Proposal*

---

[1] See below, p. 57.   [2] *Journal to Stella*, June 22, 1711.
[3] *Ibid.*, February 22, March 11, 1711–12.
[4] Advertised in *The Post-Boy*, May 15–17, 1712.
[5] *Journal to Stella*, May 10, 1712.

under his own name, and to have it associated with the Tory circles attached to the Harley ministry, is not without significance. Swift clearly wished the enterprise to be thought of as Tory and ministerial. It is true that he disclaimed any political intent. Soon after publication he reported to Stella that two answers had appeared, 'thô tis no Politicks, but a harmless Proposall about the Improvement of the Engl. Tongue.' 'I believe,' he added, 'if I writt an Essay upon a Straw some Fool would answer it.'[1] But in the light of the political overtones in the *Proposal* Swift's disclaimer is disingenuous. In fact, the lengthy panegyric of Harley, the praise of him as one who saved his country from ruin 'by a *foreign War*, and a *domestick Faction*,'[2] as well as other matters, is obviously partisan. It could not conceivably have been interpreted otherwise by contemporaries; nor could Swift have been unaware of the provocative impact on the Whigs. Oldmixon expresses their attitude when he remarks ironically on this part of the *Proposal* that it is 'incomparable, full of most delicate Eulogy in the World.'[3] Swift was well aware that anything signed with his name would at once become a target for the Whigs, even if he wrote, as he said, on a straw. But he was ready to accept the attacks and the wrangling in order to make it quite clear that the merit of founding an English academy belonged to Harley and other Tories, including himself. In the 'institution and patronage' of the academy—his own phrase—there was to be no leaven of Whiggism. On this point he was determined; and the partisan note in the *Proposal* seems deliberately designed to let all the world, and posterity, know where the credit lay.

Nevertheless, if the Whigs were not to have a part in the institution of the academy, there was no intention of excluding them from the original membership. The persons chosen were to be the most capable, he wrote, 'without any regard to Quality, Party, or Profession.'[4] In a list of possible academicians drawn up by Swift and Harley, unfortunately lost,

---

[1] *Journal to Stella*, May 31, 1712.   [2] See below, p. 18.
[3] See *Reflections on Dr. Swift's Letter to the Earl of Oxford about the English Tongue*, London, 1712, p. 32.   [4] See below, p. 14.

'twenty persons of both parties' were included, so Swift told Archbishop King, and there is no reason to doubt it.[1] Even Oldmixon grudgingly remarks that Swift has promised 'the Whigs that they shall come in if they will.'[2] Harley, always placable, would not have wished it otherwise. We need not therefore take seriously, as Oldmixon and other Whigs pretended to do, the list of alleged members printed in *The British Academy* (1712), a list which comprised all or most of the Tory 'Brothers,' the dinner group to which Swift belonged. This group he might find adequate for its avowed purpose, 'to advance conversation and friendship, and to reward deserving persons,'[3] but he would not have accepted it *in toto* for the academy.

The Whig writers began to attack the *Proposal* immediately. Within the week *The Medley* (May 19–23), founded by Oldmixon and Arthur Mainwaring 'to provide an Antidote against the Poison of the Examiner,' made passing reference to 'the very extraordinary Letter to a Great Man' and followed in the next issue with an extended political diatribe, using the *Proposal* as a point of departure. Thus at the very outset the tract was treated as a party document. *The Medley* detected Jacobitism in Swift's preference for the romance languages over the Saxon. This Tory project, the author of the paper declared, took special care

> that we have no new Addition of *Saxon* Words by bringing over the *Hanover* Family, but to hasten as much as they can a new Invasion by the *Pretender* and the French, because that Language has more Latin Words than the *Saxon*, which may be a very great help to us when we come to perform our Divine Worship in the *Roman* Tongue.[4]

At the same time the Whig writers were preparing two pamphlets in answer, both portentously announced in *The Medley* of May 23–26, which referred to Swift as 'a Clergyman of Noise, tho' I can't say of Eminence.' The heralded pamphlets were not published under their proclaimed titles, but

[1] *Corr.* i, 325. [2] Oldmixon, *Reflections*, p. 10.
[3] *Journal to Stella*, June 21, 1711. [4] See the issue of May 23–26, 1712.

they probably are the two answers to Swift which appeared in the next few days, Oldmixon's *Reflections on Dr. Swift's Letter to the Earl of Oxford* and *The British Academy*, this latter of composite authorship, with Mainwaring a principal con-tributor. The tract by Oldmixon is little more than sustained diatribe. Swift is denounced as an irreverent cleric, a bad poet, and a scheming flatterer. Certain details of his *Proposal* are ridiculed, particularly his plan to fix the language for ever, which is asserted to be as visionary as the endeavours to discover the longitude, perpetual motion, and the Grand Elixir. *The British Academy* is less random in its criticism and more urbane in its tone, though it could not resist the customary Whig jeer at 'that Orthodox Divine, who it is well known was never half so witty upon any other Subject, as upon that of Religion.'[1] Swift's plan for an academy was dismissed as the scheme of a Tory faction to secure pensions from Harley and, in return, to celebrate his greatness and perpetuate his memory. The Whiggish disparagement of the *Proposal* was revived two years later by the deist John Toland, who characterized the project as a cunning job of villainy intended to divert 'the most pregnant wits from studying the Prosperity of their Country, or examining into any Mis-management.'[2]

Swift could not claim to be original in suggesting that the language should be fixed by the authority of an academy instituted for the purpose. Even before the founding of the French Academy in 1635 the idea was prevalent in England; but with the French to serve as example and stimulus the English reformers became more hopeful. The Royal Society added its voice, and pleas came from such figures as Evelyn, the Earl of Roscommon, Dryden, and Defoe, all of whom felt that the language needed authoritative control. Swift was therefore following a well-established precedent. He begins the *Proposal* with an historical sketch designed to show that English is less refined than French, Italian, or Spanish because

[1] *The British Academy, being a New-erected Society for the Advancement of Wit and Learning*, London, 1712, p. 10.
[2] *The Grand Mystery laid open*, London, 1714, p. 21.

it has a smaller infusion of the Latin. He then considers the
alteration and corruption of the Latin from the time of
Romulus to that of Julius Caesar and the relative permanence
of the Greek from Homer to Plutarch and of the Chinese,
stable over a period of two thousand years. Since history
teaches by examples, the implication is that the English people
may learn from the past. The English language, not yet
entered into its decline, may be saved, Swift thinks, if ways are
found out to fix it for ever. Thus English authors will have
their chances to gain immortality. He proceeds to an examina-
tion of the corruptions, which date mainly from the Civil War
and have continued ever since. Laxity now was everywhere
observable, among poets, dramatists, courtiers, wits, even
among men of learning. Witness the 'barbarous Custom of
abbreviating Words,' the confounding of etymology, the
general tendency to adopt current modish speech without
regard to its propriety. The wide prevalence of false refinements and corrupt usages demonstrates the necessity for
control over a language perpetually changing. He therefore
submits his proposal for an academy authorized to give
sanction to usage, exhorting Harley to institute such a body
and give it his patronage, a plea so mingled with panegyric
that Oldmixon thought it 'very odd' that Swift should call
panegyric 'the most *barren of all Subjects*.'[1]

Although the *Proposal* reflects Swift's characteristic desire
for order and authority and his suspicion of innovation, he
does not maintain that the English language must remain
static:

I do not mean that it should never be enlarged: Provided,
that no Word, which a Society shall give a Sanction to, be afterwards antiquated and exploded, they may have Liberty to receive
whatever new ones they shall find Occasion for: Because then
the old Books will yet be always valuable according to their
intrinsick Worth, and not thrown aside on Account of unintelligible Words and Phrases, which appear harsh and uncouth,
only because they are out of Fashion.[2]

[1] *Reflections*, p. 13.   [2] See below, p. 15.

He accepted the inevitability of new words entering into the language from many sources, such as new inventions, commerce, navigation, war, and changes in law and religion. Growth, controlled development of the language, this he envisaged, but it was not his main concern. His fundamental aim was to state persuasively the necessity of arriving at and preserving a sanctioned standard language, in order to give permanent life to all written records.

Swift's attack on Anthony Collins was announced in *The Examiner*, January 19–23, 1712–13:

> I hear there is now in the Press, *An Abstract of Mr. C——ns's Discourse of Free-Thinking*. Whether it be written by an Enemy or a Friend, My Author does not say: But in either Case, if the Writer strips that adventurous Piece of its Disguises, and leaves it naked and exposed in full Light, he will amply deserve a perusal, and cannot fail of being Useful or Entertaining.

This was the 'little Whim' suitable for a threepenny pamphlet which Swift had reported to Stella a few days earlier, and which he insisted was 'not Politicks.'[1] A diversion, dashed off in a few days, Swift nevertheless could not resist his natural inclinations to turn even this to partisan advantage. This aspect of his character he himself clearly understood, and later expressed it to his friend Charles Ford in a revealing remark: 'no Cloyster is retired enough to keep Politicks out, and I will own they raise my Passions whenever they come in my way.'[2]

At the moment he was immersed in politics, the most active of the journalistic writers defending the Harley ministry as negotiations leading to the Treaty of Utrecht slowly progressed. But early in 1713 there was a lull in his activities, and he may have felt that his talents were not being put to the fullest use. He had set himself the task of writing a 'large Treatise'—the work eventually published as *The Four Last Years of the Queen*—but at the time this stood 'stock still.' To Stella he wrote that 'some think it too dangerous to publish, and would have me print onely what relates to the

[1] *Journal to Stella*, January 16, 21, 25, 1712–13.
[2] *The Letters of Jonathan Swift to Charles Ford*, ed. David Nichol Smith, Oxford, 1935, p. 82.

Peace.'[1] In the second week of January he took occasion to write an *Examiner*, but he was relatively unoccupied when he conceived the idea of heaping ridicule on the deist Anthony Collins, whose *Discourse of Free-Thinking* had recently appeared. With preferment never out of his thoughts at this time, Swift was perhaps not unwilling to appear as a champion of orthodoxy, possibly to counter some of the shrill attacks on *A Tale of a Tub*. Collins was fair game. His reputation as a free thinker and a controversialist was well established by two earlier works, *An Essay on the Use of Reason in Propositions* (1707) and *Priestcraft in Perfection* (1709), and now with the publication of the *Discourse of Free-Thinking* his dangerous heterodoxy was further confirmed. Along with Toland and Tindal, he was viewed as a leading spokesman for the deists, sufficiently important to come under fire from Hoadly, Bentley, and others.

When Swift's 'little Whim' was published on January 25, he wrote to Stella that 'if it takes . . . you sh[a]ll hear of it.'[2] It is never mentioned again. The omission of the *Abstract* from the *Miscellanies* of 1727 and from those early volumes of Faulkner's edition which came under Swift's attention suggests that it did not take, or that Swift did not himself value it highly. In fact, Faulkner for reasons not evident never printed it, although there was no question of its authenticity since Charles Ford lists it among the pamphlets and papers he held in readiness for Swift when the Faulkner edition was being planned.[3] After its first publication in 1713, it was not reprinted until John Nichols included it in his *Supplement* in 1776. The early biographers of Swift ignore the *Abstract*, but Nichols terms it 'admirable irony' and Temple Scott says that 'it frightened Collins into Holland.'[4] Although Collins departed for Holland when his tract was under attack, there is no evidence that Swift had any special responsibility. Later commentators have shown a disposition to stress the

---

[1] *Journal to Stella*, January 18, 1712–13.
[2] *Ibid.*, January 25, 1712–13.
[3] *Letters to Ford*, p. 159.
[4] See *A Supplement to Dr. Swift's Works*, ed. John Nichols, London, 1776, p. 253n.; *Prose Works*, ed. Temple Scott, III [166].

B

political implications of the *Abstract*, yet at a moment when
every piece by Swift, known or suspected, was being subjected
to attack, it is perhaps significant that this tract apparently
received no attention from the Whig journalists. The political
note may have been thought too far-fetched and ineffective
to merit reply, or quite possibly Swift's authorship was not
detected. In any case, the Whig writers would not wish to
align themselves in any respect with the heterodox Collins;
and in fact the *Discourse* was scathingly criticized not only by
Whig clergymen but also in *The Guardian*, No. 3, an essay
which Steele, if he did not write, at least approved. But Swift
obviously thought it a jest worthy of a moment to associate
Collins and free-thinking in general with the Whigs, and in the
Abstract he resorts to a favourite device, assuming the identity
of his opponents. Here, in the guise of a Whig, he suggests
that his party, having failed to re-establish its power by
political means, should have recourse to a system of divinity
to accomplish its end. The *'irrefragable Discourse'* by Collins
was now happily available, *'a brief compleat Body of* Atheology'[1]
which might be put into 'plain *English*' and thus made intelligible to the members of such Whig clubs as the Kit-Kat and
the Hanover. If the principles expounded by Collins can be
given wide prevalence, then the Whig cause is bound to
benefit: '*For I am sensible that nothing would more contribute to
the* continuance of the War, *and the Restoration of the late Ministry,
than to have the Doctrines delivered in this Treatise well infused into
the People.*' Thus by way of introduction the Whig *persona*
explains his motive for summarizing the *Discourse* in plain
English. Except for passing mention of Latitudinarian and
High Church bishops, and of Holland, with its implications
for Calvinism and nonconformity, there is no further political
substance in the *Abstract*. The identity of interest between
Whig and atheist or free thinker which Swift endeavours to
establish lacks his usual felicitous touch, nor does he return
to the point in the conclusion, when the putative Whig
summarizer reappears for a final comment. The political
element is, then, tenuous and ineffective.

[1] See below, p. 27.

The real blow is struck at deism. Swift took the threat of deism seriously. Before the publication of the *Abstract* extreme rationalistic and free-thinking attitudes had received his attention in *An Argument against Abolishing Christianity* and in the *Remarks* on Tindal's *Rights of the Christian Church*, both written in 1708. Deistic tenets are attacked in three of his few surviving sermons, most elaborately in the sermon *On the Trinity*; and a similar, if casual, preoccupation with the free thinkers may be found in other works, including *The Examiner*, *A Letter to a Young Clergyman*, and the random *Thoughts on Religion*. It is quite true that he never attempted a thoroughly logical and systematic refutation, but this was not to be expected of a writer whose genius lay in irony. Swift in fact showed a strong reluctance to engage in doctrinal polemics; as he once said to Dr. Delany, 'the grand points of Christianity ought to be taken as infallible revelations.'[1] He emphatically rejected the deistic contention that the fundamental Christian doctrines should be justified by means of elaborate dissection and explanation. 'I do not find,' he wrote in the *Letter to a Young Clergyman*, 'that you are any where directed in the Canons, or Articles, to attempt explaining the Mysteries of the Christian Religion. And, indeed, since Providence intended there should be Mysteries; I do not see how it can be agreeable to *Piety*, *Orthodoxy*, or good *Sense*, to go about such a Work.'[2] The deep-rooted conviction expressed in these lines makes comprehensible Swift's contemptuous refusal to meet Collins and other free thinkers by purely logical argument.

Thus it is that Swift relies on a congenial device, the *reductio ad absurdum*, achieved by a slight distortion of Collins's text, a twist of his meaning here or there, and the addition or omission of a word; and often merely by a bald statement drawn from the *Discourse* he manages to convey to the reader a strong impression that the free thinker is illogical, shallow, and intellectually complacent. A surprising number of current issues emerge in the *Abstract*, such matters as the place of reason and mysteries in religion, the controversy over the Trinity, the justification of an established church, the

---

[1] *Corr.* iv, 289.   [2] See vol. ix of this edition, p. 77.

validity of the ancient ethical systems, the contempt of the clergy, the dissensions among the sects. They all emerge, but casually, without anything being elaborately argued or positively resolved, yet these controversial issues, on which the deists relied, are made to seem valueless in providing grounds for their challenge to true Christianity.

The fragment, *Some Thoughts on Free-thinking*, which is printed here following the *Abstract*, is of uncertain date. Its matter, as well as the phrase '*written in* England' in the superscription, suggests that it may belong to the same period as the *Abstract*. It was first printed in Faulkner's *Works*, Vol. XVI, 1767, in the Appendix, along with 'Letters *and* Poems . . . upon *Trifles*.' Rather curiously it is designated a letter, and is said to be '*Copied from the original*.' Its only value is to show Swift pondering a matter that he mentions more than once, the need for stronger restraints on those who publish heterodox religious views under the pretence that they are merely exercising their right to freedom of thought.

A Preface to the Bishop of Sarum's Introduction to the Third Volume of the History of the Reformation of the Church of England belongs to the last months of 1713, when Swift engaged in intensive journalistic activity. In response to urgent appeals he had returned to England from Ireland in September, forgoing reluctantly the relative calm of Laracor and Dublin to take up once again the task of defending the ministry from Whig attacks. The essential details, historical and political, which form the background of Swift's *Preface to the Bishop of Sarum's Introduction* are to be found in Volume VIII of this edition and need not be repeated in full here. Almost immediately he was involved in the violent controversies growing out of the Treaty of Utrecht, signed a few months earlier but creating issues which did not quickly subside. He had barely settled in London when he was confronted with Steele's *The Importance of Dunkirk Consider'd*, to which he replied with *The Importance of the Guardian Considered* on November 2, just as Bishop Burnet's *Introduction to the Third Volume of the History of the Reformation of the Church of England* was being announced. The tracts of Steele and Burnet were part of a concerted Whig endeavour to exploit such significant matters as the long deferred demolition of Dunkirk and fears over the succession to the throne. Less effective than Steele as a political writer, the Bishop of Salisbury was nevertheless a formidable spokesman who over a period of years had ably represented Low Church and Whig principles in the House of Lords and in his prolific writings. Now at the age of seventy, despite a penchant for extreme statement and gloomy prophecies of national disaster, he was little diminished in partisan vigour or influence; and there may well be some truth in Swift's reiterated remark, that behind Steele one can discern the figure of the Bishop of Sarum and his 'shrewd Advice.'[1] If Steele was the chief journalistic enemy in the waning months of 1713, Burnet was by no means an opponent to be ignored. *The Examiner* had devoted the issue of October 9 to the first two volumes of his *History*; and on November 30 it levelled its fire on the *Introduction to the Third Volume*, this last perhaps as preparation for Swift, whose *Preface to the Bishop of Sarum's Introduction* was announced for the following week. It was published on December 7, a second edition appearing within the month (December 25).[2] In turning his attention to Burnet for the moment, Swift did not lose sight of Steele, as the inclusion of caustic comment on *The Englishman* and *The Guardian* indicates.

Burnet's elaborate *Introduction* was sent forth to announce the pending publication, long deferred, of the third volume of his *History of the Reformation of the Church of England*, but it was readily seen to be another of those 'flagrant *Prefaces* of party rage'[3] for which the bishop was notorious among the Tories. He had, in fact, within the year published a third edition of his *Pastoral Care* with a New Preface and had revived some old sermons, to which he added a partisan

---

[1] See *Poems*, ed. Harold Williams, Oxford, 1937, p. 180; vol. viii of this edition, pp. 36, 38, 65.
[2] Announced respectively in *The Examiner*, December 7 and December 25.
[3] The phrase is from Thomas Parnell's poem, *On Bishop Burnet's being set on Fire in his Closet*.

preface,[1] protesting all the while that he desired to heal
rather than open breaches. Tories might well think, as one
writer indicated, that Burnet had reprinted these earlier works
merely for the sake of their prefaces;[2] and Tory writers
ironically noted the strictures on High Churchmen, the
Universities, and the lower clergy, with the imputations that
these groups, as well as the Harley ministry, were under-
mining the Church and the Revolution Settlement. The New
Preface to *Pastoral Care* was a particular irritant, including as it
did a defence of bishops and harsh criticisms of the younger
clergy. This open episcopal antagonism to the inferior clergy
was not overlooked by ministerial writers, such as George
Sewell, who was preparing an answer to Burnet's *Introduction
to the Third Volume* almost simultaneously with Swift and who
makes a curious reference to Gregory Misosarum, the pseudonym under which Swift answered Burnet, as proclaiming
himself '*the only Man who can Answer the said Bishop*.'[3]

In this atmosphere of political animosities Swift's *Preface
to the Bishop of Sarum's Introduction* appeared, taking advantage
of Burnet's vulnerability—his lack of tact, his tendency to
self-justification at the expense of others, his exaggeration of
the dangers threatening the nation. Swift ridicules Burnet
for the portentous manner of announcing the new volume of
his *History* by an *Introduction* in advance and by perpetual
advertisements in the Gazette. He banters Burnet on his style,
urging him 'if it be not too late in his Life, to endeavour a little

[1] *Some Sermons preach'd on Several Occasions; and an Essay towards a New Book
of Homilies*, 1713.
[2] See [John Asgill], *Mr. Asg..l's Congratulatory Letter to the Lord Bishop
of Sarum, upon the Excellent New Preface just publish'd*, 2nd edition, 1713, p. 6.
[3] See his *Introduction to the Life and Writings of G——t Lord Bishop of S——m*,
London, 1714, p. 4. Sewell's tract, an effective attack on Burnet's *Introduction*,
appeared on January 7, shortly after Swift's went into a second edition. He
appears to have been employed regularly by the ministry to answer Burnet.
In this tract he refers to an Advertisement (which I have been unable to locate)
'put into his hands the other day': '*Whereas Mr. G. S. who used to Answer the
Bishop of Sarum, has not been heard of for a considerable Time, and is supposed to be
Dead; This is to give Notice, That I* Gregory Misosarum *am the only Man who can
Answer the said Bishop, and that I will constantly do the Same.*' Sewell then adds:
'Who this *Gregory* is, or whether he has in any manner performed his Promise
I can't tell. . . .'

at mending his Style, which is mighty defective in the *Circum-stances* of Grammar, Propriety, Politeness and Smoothness.'[1] More seriously, he takes Burnet to task for maliciously pro-faning the defenceless dead in the person of Henry Wharton, the learned antiquarian and church historian, who had exposed glaring errors in the earlier volumes of the *History*. These were diversionary matters, less important than a refutation of Burnet's allegation that the ministry, supported by High Churchmen, favoured the Pretender and was intent on restor-ing England to Catholicism. Rumours of Jacobite intrigue and the ministerial Francophile policy at the expense of England's Dutch allies added force to Burnet's customary eloquence on the subject of popery. Swift accuses Burnet of stirring up the people against their governors, of creating wholly imaginary dangers, and of fathering Jacobite opinions on the Tories, declaring that his accusations fasten guilt not merely on the ministry and the lower clergy, but on Parliament, the Queen, and the majority of the nation as well. Fortunately Swift could set down his convictions unhampered by any knowledge of Bolingbroke's intrigue with the Pretender or Harley's devious plans for his own safety regardless of the succession. That perennial topic of dissension, the dis-parity between episcopal affluence and parochial poverty, gave Swift further opportunity for effective rejoinder, as did Burnet's well-known tenderness for dissent—'this Prelate, who can smell *Popery* at five hundred Miles distance, better than *Fanaticism* just under his Nose.'[2] The interest of the tract is increased by some revealing remarks on the Reformation and on church temporalities, the latter a topic of persistent concern to Swift.

Those later commentators who have felt that Swift was not altogether fair to Burnet have perhaps not realized the extent to which Burnet seemed to the Tories a practitioner of the art of political lying. To Swift, the Bishop of Sarum's obvious 'Political Craft mix'd with Divinity' invited not only serious re-futation but ridicule and witty retaliation as well. His experience with this violent Whig churchman was not recent. It went back to the occasion when Swift had come to the defence of the Whig statesmen threatened with impeachment by the Tory House of Commons in 1701. In view of his utter distaste for Burnet's style, it is ironical that *A Discourse of the Contests and Dissensions between the Nobles and the Commons in Athens and Rome* should have been attributed to Burnet, who afterwards told Swift that 'he was forced to disown it in a very public manner, for fear of an impeachment, wherewith he was threatened.'[1] When the real author became known in 1702, Burnet, Somers, and Halifax sought his acquaintance, Swift tells us, 'with great marks of esteem and professions of kindness'. They 'were very liberal,' he adds, 'in promising me the greatest preferments I could hope for, if ever it came in their power.'[2] That preferment, as we know, never came from the Whigs, and Burnet, Swift felt, was among those who had failed him. There is no indication of a warm friendship between the two in those early days, yet in view of Swift's remark that he knew Burnet well, we must believe that their encounters were not merely casual. But whatever the relationship it did not withstand, as with Steele, the violence of party conflict.

The pamphlet controversy between Swift and Burnet spread to Ireland, to become part of a bitter quarrel in progress there. The Dublin edition of *A Preface to the Bishop of Sarum's Introduction*, which appeared early in 1714, is of unusual interest because Swift made a significant textual change relevant to the situation in Ireland, a revision which applied particularly to Burnet's alleged contempt for the lower clergy and for Convocation. Burnet's notoriety with the inferior clergy dated back to 1703, when extracts from a purloined manuscript of his *History of His Own Times* were printed.[3] One of these, reflecting on the clergy, Swift quotes, not quite accurately, in *A Preface to the Bishop of Sarum's Introduction*: 'It is a famous Saying of his, *That he looks upon every Layman to be an honest Man, until he is by Experience convinced to the contrary:*

---

[1] See vol. viii of this edition, p. 119.
[2] *Ibid.*
[3] By Henry Sacheverell in *The New Association*, 1703, and again by Charles Leslie in *Cassandra II*, 1704, and George Hickes in *Three Short Treatises*, 1709. For the extract quoted by Swift, see Sacheverell, p. 23, Hickes, Preface, sig. d².

And on every Clergyman as a Knave, until he finds him to be an honest Man.[1] When, in his *Introduction to the Third Volume*, Burnet continues in this vein by a slighting reference to 'assemblies of clergymen' and the little to be expected of them, Swift seized this assault on Convocations as a further example of the bishop's contempt for the cloth. Burnet, of course, exempted the Whig clergy from his strictures. It was the lower clergy and the Lower House of Convocation, Tory in their views (or Jacobite as Burnet would have it) that came under his interdiction; and in both London editions of his answer we find that Swift has written: 'I am not surprized to see the B——p mention with Contempt all Convocations of the Clergy; for *Toland, Collins, Tindall,* and others of the Fraternity, talk the very same Language.' The Dublin edition has a different reading: the list of names was enlarged to read '*Toland, Asgil, M . . . . th Collins, Tindal.*' When Faulkner reprinted this tract in the *Works*, Vol. VI (1738), he erroneously supplied the omitted letters, to make the name read 'Monmouth,' an error perpetuated by all later editors. The reference in fact was to the noted Irish statesman, Robert, later Viscount Molesworth, to whom Swift addressed the fifth Drapier's Letter in 1724. In 1713, however, Molesworth represented an extreme and dangerous Whiggism. He was then sitting in the Irish Parliament, a member of the Irish Privy Council, and an outspoken critic of the clergy. Swift described him to Harley at this time as 'very bad' and 'the worst' of the Whig Privy Councillors.[2] Earlier, in 1694, he had earned the lasting ill will of the Tory clergy by the Preface to his *Account of Denmark*, violently anti-clerical in tone; and he had fortified their dislike by translating Hotman's *Franco-Gallia* in 1711. As Swift was busily engaged with Steele and Burnet in December 1713, Molesworth once again offended the Tory clergy and became involved in a quarrel with the Lower House of Convocation in Ireland and the Irish House of Lords. The controversy originated in an address by the Irish House of

---

[1] See below, p. 71.
[2] *Corr.* vi, 243; see also *Drapier's Letters*, ed. Herbert Davis, Oxford, 1935, pp. 287–8.

Commons offering to censure Swift's friend, Sir Constantine
Phipps, then Lord Chancellor of Ireland. Phipps, a centre
of partisan wrangling, was accused, among other things, of
dereliction in prosecuting an alleged Jacobite publisher who
had proposed to reprint the *Memoirs of the Chevalier de St.
George.* Convocation came to the defence of the Lord Chancellor. When its representatives appeared in the Presence
Chamber before the Lord Lieutenant, Molesworth was over-
heard remarking that 'They that have turned the world upside
down, are come hither also'.[1] The members of Convocation
took umbrage. They complained that Molesworth had pro-
faned Holy Scripture and had represented them as 'a turbulent
and seditious Body.' They asked the Lords to vindicate
Convocation from this 'wicked calumny,' an affront that cast
odium on the House of Lords as well as the whole clergy.
The Lords, already committed to the defence of the Lord
Chancellor[2] and willing to widen the quarrel with Commons,
at once requested that House, where Molesworth sat, to join
in censuring a piece of behaviour 'impiously profaning the
holy Scriptures.' 'The Lords feel,' the address read, 'the
Commons will show readiness to do Justice . . . from the
Zeal they have observed from the Commons in former
Parliaments, expressed against Toland and Asgil.'[3] Thus
Molesworth was linked to two heterodox figures whose
blasphemous writings had been censured in the Irish Commons
in earlier sessions, Toland for *Christianity not Mysterious* and
Asgill for his controversial book on the subject of death.

Several correspondents kept Swift informed of the tempest
in Dublin, including Archbishop King, who minimized

---

[1] See *Corr.* ii, 118, and issues of *The Flying Post, The Evening Post,* and *The Post-
Boy* from December 26, 1713, to January 26, 1713–14, which regularly carried
reports from Dublin. John Oldmixon, in his *History of England,* 1735, p. 534,
gives the Whig version.

[2] See *The Dublin Gazette,* December 22–26, reporting a resolution of Decem-
ber 18 in the Irish House of Lords, 'that the Words spoken by *Richard Nuttall,*
Attorney, *August* last, *That the Lord Chancellor of this Kingdom . . . was a Canary
Bird and a Villain and had set this Kingdom together by the Ears, and ought to be
Hanged,* are False, Scandalous and Malicious, tending to stir up Sedition, and
highly reflecting upon the Government of this Kingdom.'

[3] See *The Evening Post,* December 29–31; *The Post-Boy,* December 29–31.

Molesworth's behaviour and refused to support an address favourable to Sir Constantine Phipps.[1] At the same time the London periodicals were reporting the contretemps at length, the Whig journalists stating the case for Molesworth and the Commons, the Tory press giving an opposed view. Under a Dublin date line of January 12, *The British Mercury* reported that Molesworth had lost his place as Privy Councillor 'for affronting the Clergy in Convocation.' Three days later *The Examiner* defended Sir Constantine Phipps and attacked Molesworth and the Irish House of Commons. This brought a reply in the form of a signed letter from Steele in *The Englishman* (January 19), whose defence of Molesworth Swift characterized in *The Public Spirit of the Whigs* in the following month as an affront to 'the whole Convocation of Ireland'[2]—a Convocation in which Swift, had he been in Ireland, would likely have served as Prolocutor of the Lower House. The Whig journalists did not spare Swift. *The Flying Post* (January 21–23) remarked that the Irish House of Lords in linking Molesworth to Toland and Asgill might more appropriately have seen the resemblance between these two and the Dean of St. Patrick's. In the next issue, devoted to a defence of Steele, it referred to 'The supposed Writer of the Examiner [as] a reputed Atheist, and Author of a Book, call'd *A Tale of a Tub*, which is a villainous Satyr upon all Reveal'd Religion, and even Morality itself.' At this juncture one of Molesworth's defenders chose to reprint the objectionable Preface to *An Account of Denmark*, with added comment to show that the Tory clergy have been in actual fact those who 'have turned the world upside down'. Swift is mentioned slightingly in the company of the Reverend Francis Higgins, a turbulent and controversial Irish High Churchman;[3] Burnet is praised. Thus by the time Swift was preparing the text of the Dublin edition of his answer to Burnet, the violently partisan quarrel

---

[1] Corr. ii, 116ff.   [2] See vol. viii of this edition, p. 37.
[3] *Mr. Molesworth's Preface, with Historical and Political Remarks, to which is added A True State of his Case with Respect to the Irish Convocation*, London [1714], p. 38. This was published between January 23 and January 28, as internal evidence indicates. Higgins seems to have been no less offensive to Swift than to the Whigs: see *Journal to Stella*, ed. Harold Williams, II, 192, 536, 540.

in Ireland had spread to England and had reached out to include him. Taking a cue from the Irish House of Lords, he revised the text to introduce the name of 'M . . . . th' in distasteful association with such noted heterodox figures as Toland and Asgill, lumping Burnet with all of them as having in common a contempt for the clergy.

Louis Landa.

PART II

I HAVE explained in the preface why a change of plan made it necessary to include a rather miscellaneous collection of pieces of different dates in this volume. But there is perhaps some justification for printing *Polite Conversation*, though it was not finished and published until 1738, together with the *Proposal for correcting the English Tongue*, 1712, and a number of the scraps and trifles, written before as well as after that, here included in the *Appendix*. For *Polite Conversation* is a work which Swift kept by him for a great many years; and it was begun not later than 1704. In a letter to Pope, dated June 12, 1732, giving an account of what he had written in the previous five years, after complaining that 'his poetical fountain is drained' and 'even prose speculations tire me almost as much,' he continues

Yet I have a thing in prose, begun above twenty-eight years ago, and almost finished. It will make a four shilling volume, and is such a perfection of folly that you shall never hear of it till it is printed, and then you shall be left to guess.

It is perhaps unlikely that the 'treatise' which introduces the 'Dialogues' contains much which was actually written as early as 1704. Yet it is Bickerstaffian in tone, and its material was obviously collected in part during the period when Swift was seeing a great deal of London society. The title, moreover, both in the Dublin and London editions refers to the 'most polite Mode and Method now used at Court and in the best companies of England.' And the pseudonym, Simon Wagstaff, though first appearing only in the London edition and therefore possibly added by Mrs. Barber or the London publisher, was obviously intended to recall the famous family of the Staffs of Staffordshire, whose genealogy was given in *The Tatler*, No. 11, for May 5, 1709, and perhaps to remind us of the conversation piece at White's given in the following paper. Indeed, the comments of Acorn and Friendly might be taken as a hint to prepare the way for such a work as Swift was engaged upon:

> *Acorn.* Dear Sir, hold: What you have told me already of this change in Conversation, is too miserable to be heard with any Delight; but, methinks, as these new Creatures appear in the World, it might give an excellent Field for Writers for the Stage, to divert us with the Representation of them there.
> *Friendly.* No, No: As you say, there might be some Hopes of Redress of these Grievances, if there were proper Care taken of the Theatre; but the History of that is yet more lamentable, than that of the Decay of Conversation I gave you.

In the previous generation the plays of Congreve had served the purpose of satirizing 'these new Creatures,' as they appeared in the world and also of showing all the possibilities of the art of conversation. But now, in the decline of the theatre, a new method had to be found to prevent the 'Decay of Conversation.' In the 'several Dialogues' of which *Polite Conversation* consists there is nothing to fix the date precisely; but there is also nothing to suggest that they do not belong to the reign of Queen Anne. And there are good reasons for connecting them with the Castilian trifles and the punning games which are associated with Swift and his friends, Sir Andrew Fountaine, Dr. Howard and Dr. Molyneux, who were acquainted with the Earl of Pembroke in 1707, when he was appointed Lord Lieutenant of Ireland. And when Swift went to London that winter, he stayed with Sir Andrew Fountaine in Leicester Fields and wrote several punning letters thence to his friends in Dublin.

A Dialogue in the Castilian Language, dated 1707, which was first printed by Elrington Ball in 1910, is an interesting early sample which has survived of a conversation piece. Though this had no connection with *Polite Conversation*, it has been pointed out by George P. Mayhew that these punning games and later the Anglo-Latin games in which Swift indulged, contain some phrases which were used in the 'Dialogues.'[1]

But these scraps all seem to date from after 1730, and the note-book, now in the Huntington Library, belongs to the years 1734–36, when Swift was putting the finishing touches to his work. If we may assume that Mr. Simon Wagstaff's account of his labours in preparing this treatise are parallel to Swift's, we may take it that the little 8-page note-book contains the fruit of the 'last six or seven years,' when Swift was not 'able to add above nine valuable sentences to enrich the collection.'[2] In that case the actual conversations must have been almost complete by about 1730, though the work had been begun in the early years of the century and the greater part of the collection gathered before 1714; and then it was 'methodically digested' during the next sixteen years. This introductory account was finished in the early part of 1737, as Lord Orrery took the manuscript to London, in July 1737; and Swift's calculations were then worked backwards from 1736–37.

There are no indications in the *Dialogues* themselves that show the different stages of their composition. We might for a moment be tempted to argue that the reference to 'a new play, written by a lord, . . . called "Love in a Hollow Tree"' suggests a date soon after 1705, when the play was first published; but we might have to accept it as a late addition remembering that the author, William Grimston, was not made a peer until 1719, and further, if we may believe Johnson's story, that it gained greater attention in 1734, when it was reprinted by the Duchess of Marlborough, to make a fool of him.[3] There is one reference to the extension of London and the building of Hanover Square which was

---

[1] *Corr.* i, 375–8; Appendix II. See also *Swift's Anglo-Latin Games and a Fragment of Polite Conversation*, HLQ, vol. xvii, pp. 133f.
[2] *Corr.* vi, 39.   [3] See Boswell, *Life of Johnson*, Clar. Press, 1934, IV, 80.

probably written later than 1726, when Swift after twelve years' absence would have noticed the changes that had taken place. And it is certainly probable that the reference to Sir Isaac Newton, 'an instrument-maker,' who 'was knighted for making sun-dials better than others of his trade' was written after 1724, since it had been in the April of that year that he made his assay of Wood's copper money for Ireland, and reported that 'it was of the same goodness and value with the Copper . . . coined in the King's Mint for England.'[1]

Nevertheless, the impression of the *Dialogues*, as a whole, is extraordinarily timeless and Swift is entirely justified in his boast that

> my collection of discourse hath descended by tradition for at least an hundred years, without any change in the phraseology.

And we may well accept his statement that

> these polite questions, answers, repartees, replies, and rejoinders (had been collected) with infinite labour, and close application, during the space of thirty-six years.

There is further evidence provided in this volume of Swift's constant interest in this subject. The *Hints towards an Essay on Conversation* probably belong to the same time as his contribution to *The Tatler*, No. 230, dated September 17, 1710, on the corruption of the English tongue, followed in 1712 by his *Proposal for Correcting, Improving and Ascertaining the English Tongue*. In each of these papers he is concerned with the problem of maintaining the integrity of the mother tongue for the purposes of writing and conversation. In addressing himself to Isaac Bickerstaff to make his papers 'the instrument of introducing into our style that simplicity which is the best and truest ornament of most things in life' he upholds the same standard in writing which he was later to recommend so cogently in his *Letter to a young Clergyman*. In his *Hints* he suggests an interesting explanation of the degeneracy of conversation since the days which he always considered the point of highest politeness in England—'the peaceable Part of King Charles the First's Reign': for then women had not been

[1] See *Drapier's Letters*, Clar. Press, 1935, pp. 205–7.

excluded from society, and at the houses of several ladies persons of the best understanding of both sexes met together for agreeable conversation. In his appeal to the Lord Treasurer to preserve the language from decay he is moved by a fear of the affectations and modish fashions which seem to him to be symptoms of a deterioration of manners and true politeness. Whatever may be said of the superficiality of some of his views on language, its growth and development, there are few writers who have been so constantly on the alert to warn us against all threats to clarity of expression in writing and in conversation.

The Introduction to *Polite Conversation* shows him in an easy playful mood; but beneath it is the same intention and purpose as in his earlier attacks on pedantry, vanity, ill-mannered raillery and straining after wit. He prepares us for the 'perfection of folly' which is to come in the Dialogues themselves by an ironical celebration of all the dullness and lack of taste in the writings of those of his contemporaries whom he delights for various reasons to ridicule; and he offers his thanks to those who have been of great assistance to him in gathering his fine flowers of wit and repartee from such illustrious writers as those prolific translators, Ozell and Stevens, and such poets as Lord Hervey, Mr. Tibbalds, and the most illustrious laureate, Mr. Colley Cibber.

> Let the Popes, the Gays, the Arbuthnots, the Youngs, and the rest of that snarling Brood, burst with envy at the Praise we receive from the Court, and Kingdom.

The three Dialogues that make up the actual conversations all take place at Lord Smart's house in St. James' Park, with the same small company at breakfast, at dinner, and afterwards at tea with the ladies; Sir John Linger, the Derbyshire squire, appears only in the Second Dialogue, as he joins them for a while at dinner. Nothing is spared us, from the opening greetings on the street to the final leave-takings—all the small-talk, witty remarks, repartees, common proverbs; we might well suppose that Swift had ransacked all the phrase-books and the collections of proverbs, and simply rearranged them in a continuous flow of conversation.[1] It has been suggested that Ray was obviously one of his sources, and it is quite likely that he was acquainted with his work, though he does not appear to have had in his library any edition of the *Collection of English Proverbs*. And if we examine some of the proverbs that do occur, we find that they are usually the more obvious ones which Swift would have had no need to look up in Ray. It is not impossible that his method was that which is carefully described as Mr. Simon Wagstaff's, who was accustomed 'to set down those ingenious sentences which, without my utmost vigilance, had been irrecoverably lost for ever'; and to listen to the discourses of the company 'and then at proper seasons . . . to enter them in my table book, while the company little suspected what a noble work I had then in embryo.' For we do in fact still possess a very large collection of Swift's manuscripts, in which he has set down proverbs and sayings, and turned them into Anglo-Latin, or used them for all those strange word-games with which he continued to amuse himself and his friends throughout a great part of his life.

I have not thought it necessary to include in this edition of his *Works* much of this casual material, which can be found in the Forster collection, the Pierpont Morgan Library, and the Huntington Library. But I have included in the Appendixes to this volume some samples of puns, jokes, and a few Anglo-Latin scraps made out of phrases which occur in these Dialogues. None of the actual manuscripts of *Polite Conversation* seem to have survived, neither the manuscript which was given to Lord Orrery[2] 'to be printed in London for Mrs. Barber's benefit,' nor the copy from which the Dublin edition was printed. This may have contained some variants, or else Swift himself made alterations and additions in the proofs.[3]

Among the manuscripts that have survived one of the most curious is *A modest Defence of Punning*, now printed from the holograph manuscript in the Morgan Library, which is dated

---

[1] See Mackie L. Jarrell: The Proverbs in Swift's *Polite Conversation*. *Huntington Library Quarterly*, Vol. XX, No. 1, Nov. 1956, pp. 15–38.
[2] *Corr.* vi, 39.   [3] *Corr.* vi, 67–8.

c

Cambridge, November 8, 1716. It was written as 'a compleat Answer to a scandalous and malicious Paper called *God's Revenge against Punning*,' which had been published in London on November 7, 1716. The manuscript seems to be a fair copy written out by Swift himself in such form as to be ready for the printer. Perhaps he did not then know who was the author of *God's Revenge against Punning*; and when he discovered who it was he may have decided not to print his Answer. For there can be little doubt that it had been written by Pope,[1] who reprinted it in 1732 in the last volume of their *Miscellanies*, where it follows his papers against Curll. If he had known of Swift's answer, he would probably have included it in the volume. Swift's *Defence* is itself a series of puns, at the rate of one or two a line, carefully underlined so that they will not be overlooked. He deals with all the examples given in the pamphlet, and writing as if from Cambridge, is particularly concerned to vindicate the loyalty of the university which had been recognized and acknowledged by George I's gift of books, which provides Swift with a frightening series of puns:

His Majesty's *Liber*ality in that noble Present of *Books*, as it will make us *Lettered*, so it *Leaves* us *bound* to Him for ever, and we should be *covered* with Gilt, and deserve to be *bound* as Slaves in Turkey, if we failed in our Loyalty; etc.

His final objection that the Devonshire Man of Wit had not broken his neck may not only have served to introduce puns on Brecknock and Necromancer, but may also indicate that he recognized that the writer of *God's Revenge against Punning* had had in mind Gay's recent fall from his horse, when he had broken his fine snuff-box. But there remain some curious problems. This manuscript is preserved among the papers which had been given to Sir Andrew Fountaine, many of which had once belonged to Swift's friend, Charles Ford, editor of the *London Gazette* until September 25, 1714, when, immediately after Lord Stanhope's appointment as Secretary of State, both the editor and the Printer of the *Gazette* were

[1] The arguments in favour of Pope's authorship have been excellently stated by Norman Ault in his Introduction to the *Prose Works of Alexander Pope*, Shakespeare Head Press, 1930, pp. cx–cxiv.

removed. Ford was imprisoned for some months on his return
from France in the summer of 1715, and he was in Dublin
with Swift in July and August 1716. At the beginning of
September he set out on his journey to Rome, arriving in
Paris in October; and he remained abroad for two years,
returning to Dublin in the autumn of 1718. Did he then
receive from Swift the manuscript, a fair copy, prepared for
the printer and dated November 8, 1716, which Swift had
decided not to print? Or is it possible that Swift had already
given him the manuscript in August 1716, with instructions
to arrange for its publication as a reply to *God's Revenge against
Punning*, which was itself concocted between them at the time
they heard of Gay's fall, first mentioned in a letter of Pope's
dated August 7? Was it, in fact, to be a sort of double-
barrelled attack, concocted by Pope and Swift and Gay—
the intermediary being Ford—in August 1716, against Lord
Stanhope, who had been officially responsible for dismissing
Ford as well as for intercepting the letters sent to Swift in
1715 by the Duke of Ormonde; and against Lord Hervey (the
father of Pope's 'Lord Fanny') who had been made Earl of
Bristol in 1714 (cf. the reference to Bristow stones and carbuncles). The young Earl of Warwick, Colonel Frowde,
Eustace Budgell, and Daniel Button were all members of the
Whig group, which was disturbing Pope in his plans for
the translation of the *Iliad*. At any rate, whether *God's
Revenge* was by Pope or not, it was, like Swift's *Modest Defence*,
clearly of Tory origin, as set forth in the ballad, *In Defence of
the Art of Punning*—

> But, dearest NANN, I smell the bottom
> Of all our Anti-punsters (rott'em)
> It is a *Popish-Jesuit* Plot,
> By *Tory Jacobites* begot; . . .
>
> And tho' our Words may squint awry
> Yet they shall know that we can spy
> Their *Popish Plot* with *Half an Eye*.

Did Swift suspect that Ford had written *God's Revenge*, or is the
attempt to prove that he was Sir John Baker, Kt., another game
in which they all took part. He 'usually passeth for a Spaniard

and by the Quarter etc. . . . (his family name was Ford or Forth) a Knight of Malta, a knight of the Port, descended from the famous *Fonsecas*, a Chevalier de *Fond Sec*.' There can be no doubt that this would be taken by his friends as definitely referring to Ford, who was also particularly known as an enemy to punning.

What was Swift's intention, and why his paper was never printed, it is now difficult to determine. But the fact remains, that presumably some time in 1716, Swift wrote out carefully, as if for the printer, an elaborate defence of Punning, in a way which has the effect of repeating the satire in *God's Revenge*. And that makes it all the more difficult to explain why it was that Swift's paper did not appear at the time.

Swift was not content to defend punning; he continued to practise it unceasingly. Several pieces of this kind survive and are reprinted here in the Appendixes to this volume. Most of them have been printed before. An early example is the *Dying Speech of Tom Ashe*, a joke which was sent to the Earl of Pembroke, when he was Lord Lieutenant of Ireland. It can therefore be dated 1707 or 1708; it was first printed in 1765.[1] And there are two others which belong to the same time, here printed from the original manuscript, now in the Morgan Library.[2] I have reprinted also in Appendix F another example of punning, which has not hitherto been included in Swift's works, a trifle, called the *History of Poetry*, which Waters, Swift's first Dublin printer, published as a single half-sheet in 1726.

There are two pieces on the subject of Good Manners which it is difficult to date or to relate to one another. The *Treatise on Good Manners and Good Breeding* was first printed by Dr. Delany in 1754; *Hints on Good Manners* was first printed by Deane Swift in 1765. The Treatise is certainly not an elaboration of the Hints; it seems indeed to have been written first. It is illustrated entirely from Swift's experiences at the Court, 'while he knew it.' He recalls, for instance, the many ridiculous accidents he had witnessed at Court caused by

---

[1] See Swift, *Works*, Dublin, 1765, vol. XIII, pp. 223f.
[2] See *Corr.* i, 375–81; ii. 407.

those who were over-eager to show their politeness, or too much concerned with ceremonial forms; and the impertinencies of ceremonial behaviour 'at those tables, where ladies preside, who value themselves upon account of their good breeding.' He tells the story in particular of Prince Eugene's visit to the Queen in January 1712, and Mr. Hoffman's concern because he was wearing a tie-wig; and in recommending punctuality as a necessary part of good manners, he cannot refrain from a wry comment, remembering how often his own patience had been tried—that 'the greatest minister he ever knew was the greatest trespasser against it.' But in the *Hints on Good Manners* he is less concerned with courts, though he does remark that 'whatever politeness he observed there was not of court growth, but imported'; and it is clearly his later years as Dean that made him protest against that uncomfortable excess of good manners, that 'teazing with civility' which was 'worse in Ireland.' It is pleasant to find one who is generally thought of as proud and masterful noting that the chief ingredients of good manners are modesty and humility; and we may detect something like an apology for quite unintentional lapses from these virtues when he confesses that men of wit and good understanding sometimes cause offence by the most innocent raillery, because they over-estimate the intelligence of those they are talking to. Similarly when he condemns talking in one's own trade as a great breach of good manners, he is careful to include not only members of the professions but also the wits and the poets.

The other unfinished paper which Deane Swift first printed in 1765 with the title 'Of the Education of Ladies' has nothing whatever to do with the 'Hints for an Intelligencer' on that subject.[1] It is indeed possible that it may have been written long before, as it almost seems to be addressed to an English audience. The real subject of it is not how ladies ought to be educated, but rather the question whether it is prudent for 'the bulk of lords, knights and squires' and those of 'the clergy who have tolerably good preferment' to choose wives who may be described as educated women with 'some taste

[1] See vol. xii of this edition, pp. 307–8.

of wit and humour' and a knowledge of their own native literature. Thereafter it is mainly concerned with statistics of the number of men in England who may be considered as 'tolerably educated with a sufficient share of good sense.' He concludes that if we accept the modest estimate of about one thousand, then at least half that number would be forced 'to couple themselves with women for whom they can possibly have no esteem.' And we are left to consider whether it would be a good thing if by some means this matter could be remedied.

There is one more paper which was first printed in 1765, a sort of learned joke, a parody of philological scholarship, entitled *A Discourse to prove the Antiquity of the English Tongue*, showing from various instances that Hebrew, Greek, and Latin were derived from the English. It may have been intended for an *Intelligencer*, as it can be dated after 1727, for it contains an ironical reference to 'our illustrious modern star, Doctor Richard Bentley, with whom the republic of learning must expire as mathematics did with Sir Isaac Newton.' Even after Newton's death Swift could never forgive him for his favourable report on Wood's copper coinage for Ireland. It may have been intended as an extravagant parody of the methods of the etymologists, and a hit at those scholars who claim approbation for the long years of labour which they have undertaken for the benefit of mankind and for the honour of their own dear country. But for the most part it seems to be just a game of playing with Greek and Latin names, in which Epaminondas is interpreted as an *Ape o' mine own days* and Alexander the Great acquires his name because he was fond of eggs roasted in hot ashes, so that when his cooks heard he was come home to dinner, they cried out *Alleggs under the Grate*.

I have included in the Appendixes some samples of these exercises in Anglo-Latin with which Swift and Sheridan amused themselves—such as the *Consultation of Four Physitians*, the manuscript of which was among the papers acquired by Faulkner at the time of Swift's death. I have also printed some fragments of late manuscripts, now in the Huntington Library, which have not appeared in any earlier edition of Swift's *Works*. Some of these are interesting as examples of his interest in English as it was spoken in Ireland, and in what he called 'barbarous denominations in Ireland.'

Finally I have included here 'Further Thoughts on Various Subjects'; that is to say, the additions to those originally published in the *Miscellanies in Prose and Verse*, 1711.[1] That first group was dated October 1, 1706. They were afterwards extended to almost twice their original length, when reprinted in the *Miscellanies*, 1727. A further collection was first published by Dodsby in London in 1745, and reprinted in the Hawkesworth London edition of 1755, with a note:

> These *Thoughts* and the *Bon Mots de Stella* that follow, seem to be part of Sheridan's collection of *Contes à rire* and *bon Mots*, mentioned in Swift's letter to Sheridan, March 27, 1733—'I am confident your collection . . . will be much the best extant; but you are apt to be terribly sanguine about the profits of publishing: however it shall have all the pushing I can give.[2]

Presumably they were never published until the manuscripts were found with Swift's letters to Sheridan after their deaths. The collection is also referred to in a letter of Lord Bathurst, September 9, 1730, in which he quotes from Swift's answer to his previous letter:

> I show all your letters to our Irish wits; one of them is going to write a treatise of English Bulls and blunders.

At any rate, some of these 'Thoughts on Various Subjects' might well be called *Bons Mots*; they are short, pithy, and well-turned:

> Men are content to be laughed at for their Wit, but not for their Folly.
> I never wonder to see Men wicked, but I often wonder to see them not ashamed.
> Very few Men do properly live at present, but are providing to live another Time.

But a good many of them are rather reminiscences of incidents or persons, which belong to Swift's stay in London during the last years of Queen Anne. He makes fun of human vanity in many forms and draws instances from a title-page of

---

[1] See vol. i of this edition, pp. 241–5.
[2] See Swift, *Works*, 4to, vol. VI, pt. ii, pp. 178f.

Pomfret—*Poems by the Author of the Choice*, and from the story
of Dennis, the critic, fleeing back to town, because of his fear
of a French privateer off the coast, which he imagined the
King of France had sent out to catch him; and of Dr. Gee,
Prebendary of Westminster, who disguised himself when
abroad in fear of the Inquisition, because he had written a
small paper against Popery. Or he recalls observations which
he had made to Lord Bolingbroke at that time, or oddities
which had amused him, such as that delightful octogenarian,
the first Earl of Cromarty, who decided to retire to his country
house in Scotland for six years, in order to save some money
to spend in London. These are presumably some of the *Contes
à rire* which Swift had provided for Sheridan's collection.

The pieces brought together in this volume, whether concerned with conversation or the art of writing, whether fragments or trivia, are all the product of Swift's constant concern
with language. He delighted in its possibilities as a weapon for
the controversialist and the preacher, as a trumpet to rouse
men to stand fast in the evil day against the enemies of public
virtue or good sense; but he enjoyed also its possibilities as a
sort of plaything for the mind at leisure. And if it is true, as
he claimed, that he had been collecting material for some of
these treatises since the early years of the century, we may well
consider these activities as the natural occupation of one who
had just finished diverting himself with *A Tale of a Tub*.
For there he had shown all the dangerous possibilities of
indulgence in verbal wit, parodying and imitating the extrava-
gances of the previous age, almost allowing the same devils to
possess him for a moment in order to rid himself of them for
ever; but perhaps not quite succeeding. For, in his Bickerstaffian jokes, in his shameless delight in the game of punning,
in his inventive word-play in English, Latin, and Irish, in his
competitions with Sheridan in verse and prose, he had continued to the end to indulge as a jester in this playing with
baubles, while at the same time he brought to perfection for
serious use in irony and satire a prose of utter simplicity,
lucidity, and power—completely controlled, concise, and clear.

HERBERT DAVIS.

PART I

A Proposal for Correcting, Improving and Ascertaining the English Tongue

A PROPOSAL

FOR

Correcting, Improving and *Ascertaining*

THE

English Tongue

IN A

LETTER

To the Most Honourable

ROBERT

Earl of Oxford and Mortimer,

Lord High Treasurer

OF

GREAT BRITAIN.

LONDON:

Printed for Benj. Tooke, at the
Middle-Temple-Gate, Fleetstreet. 1712.

A

PROPOSAL

FOR

Correcting, Improving and Ascertaining the ENGLISH TONGUE:

IN A

LETTER to the Most Honourable *ROBERT* Earl of *OXFORD* and *MORTIMER*, Lord High-Treasurer of GREAT-BRITAIN.

To the Most Honourable ROBERT *Earl of* OXFORD, *&c.*

My Lord,

WHAT I had the Honour of mentioning to your Lordship some Time ago in Conversation, was not a new Thought, just then started by Accident or Occasion, but the Result of long Reflection; and I have been confirmed in my Sentiments by the Opinion of some very judicious Persons, with whom I consulted. They all agreed, That nothing would be of greater Use towards the Improvement of Knowledge and Politeness, than some effectual Method for *Correcting, Enlarging,* and *Ascertaining* our Language; and they think it a Work very possible to be compassed, under the Protection of a Prince, the Countenance and Encouragement of a Ministry, and the Care of proper Persons, chosen for such an Undertaking. I was glad to find your Lordship's Answer in so different a Style, from what hath been commonly made use of on such like Occasions, for some Years past; *That all such Thoughts must be deferred to a Time of Peace:* A Topick which some have carried so far, that they would not have us by any Means think of preserving our Civil or Religious Constitution, because we are engaged in a War abroad. It will be among the distinguishing Marks of your Ministry, My Lord, that you had a Genius above all such Regards; and that no reasonable Proposal for the Honour, the Advantage, or the Ornament of your Country, however foreign to your more immediate Office, was ever neglected by you. I confess, the Merit of this Candour and Condescension is very much lessened; because your Lordship hardly leaves us Room to offer our good Wishes; removing all our Difficulties, and supplying our Wants, faster than the most visionary Projector can adjust his Schemes. And therefore, my Lord, the Design of this Paper is not so much to offer you *Ways and Means*, as to complain of a *Grievance*, the Redressing of which is to be your own Work, as much as that of paying the *Nation's Debts*, or opening a Trade into the *South-Sea*; and although not of such immediate Benefit, as either of these, or any other of your glorious Actions, yet perhaps in future Ages not less to your Honour.

My Lord, I do here, in the Name of all the learned and polite Persons of the Nation, complain to your Lordship as *First Minister*, that our Language is extremely imperfect; that its daily Improvements are by no Means in Proportion to its daily Corruptions; that the Pretenders to polish and refine it, have chiefly multiplied Abuses and Absurdities; and, that in many Instances, it offends against every Part of Grammar. But lest your Lordship should think my Censure too severe, I shall take leave to be more particular.

I BELIEVE your Lordship will agree with me in the Reason, why our Language is less refined than those of *Italy*, *Spain*, or *France*. It is plain, that the *Latin* Tongue in its Purity was never in this Island; towards the Conquest of which, few or no Attempts were made till the Time of *Claudius*: Neither was that Language ever so vulgar in *Britain*, as it is known to have been in *Gaul* and *Spain*. Further, we find that the *Roman* Legions here, were at length all recalled to help their Country against the *Goths*, and other barbarous Invaders. Mean time, the *Britons* left to shift for themselves, and daily harrassed by cruel Inroads from the *Picts*, were forced to call in the *Saxons* for their Defence; who consequently reduced the greatest Part of the Island to their own Power, drove the *Britons* into the most remote and mountainous Parts; and the Rest of the Country in Customs, Religion, and Language, became wholly *Saxon*. This I take to be the Reason why there are more *Latin* Words remaining in the *British* Tongue than in the old *Saxon*; which, excepting some few Variations in the Ortho-graphy, is the same in most original Words with our present *English*, as well as with the *German* and other *Northern* Dialects.

EDWARD *the Confessor* having lived long in *France*, appears to be the first, who introduced any Mixture of the *French* Tongue with the *Saxon*; the Court affecting what the Prince was fond of, and others taking it up for a Fashion, as it is now with us. *William the Conqueror* proceeded much further; bringing over with him vast Numbers of that Nation, scatter-ing them in every Monastery, giving them great Quantities of Land, directing all Pleadings to be in that Language, and endeavouring to make it universal in the Kingdom. This, at least, is the Opinion generally received: But your Lordship hath fully convinced me, that the *French* Tongue made yet a greater Progress here under *Harry* the Second, who had large Territories on that Continent, both from his Father and his Wife; made frequent Journeys and Expeditions thither, and was always attended with a Number of his Countrymen, Retainers at his Court. For some Centuries after, there was a Constant Intercourse between *France* and *England*, by the Dominions we possessed there, and the Conquests we made: So that our Language, between two and three hundred Years ago, seems to have had a greater Mixture with the *French* than at present; many Words having been afterwards rejected, and some since the Time of *Spencer*; although we have still retained not a few, which have been long antiquated in *France*. I could produce several Instances of both Kinds, if it were of any Use or Entertainment.

To examine into the several Circumstances by which the Language of a Country may be altered, would force me to enter into a wide Field. I shall only observe, that the *Latin*, the *French*, and the *English*, seem to have undergone the same Fortune. The first, from the Days of *Romulus* to those of *Julius Cæsar*, suffered perpetual Changes; and by what we meet in those Authors who occasionally speak on that Subject, as well as from certain Fragments of old Laws; it is manifest that the *Latin*, three Hundred Years before *Tully*, was as unintelligible in his Time, as the *English* and *French* of the same Period are now: And these two have changed as much since *William the Conqueror*, (which is but little less than seven Hundred Years) as the *Latin* appears to have done in the like Term. Whether our Language, or the *French*, will decline as fast as the *Roman* did, is a Question that would perhaps admit more Debate than it is worth. There were many Reasons for the Corruptions of the last: As the Change of their Government into a Tyranny, which ruined the Study of Eloquence; there being no further Use or Encouragement for popular Orators: Their giving not only the Freedom of the City, but Capacity for Employments, to several Towns in *Gaul*, *Spain*, and *Germany*, and other distant Parts, as far as *Asia*; which brought a great Number of foreign Pretenders into *Rome:* The slavish Disposition of the Senate and People; by which the Wit and Eloquence of the Age were wholly turned into Panegyrick, the most barren of all Subjects: The great Corruption of Manners, and Introduction of foreign Luxury, with foreign Terms to express it: With several others that might be assigned: Not to mention those Invasions from the *Goths* and *Vandals*, which are too obvious to insist on.

THE *Roman* Language arrived at great Perfection before it began to decay: The *French*, for these last Fifty Years, hath been polishing as much as it will bear; and appears to be declining by the natural Inconstancy of that People, as well as the Affectation of some late Authors, to introduce and multiply *Cant* Words, which is the most ruinous Corruption in any Language. *La Bruyere*, a late celebrated Writer among them, makes use of many new Terms which are not to be found in any of the common Dictionaries before his Time. But the *English* Tongue is not arrived to such a Degree of Perfection, as, upon that Account, to make us apprehend any Thoughts of its Decay: And if it were once refined to a certain Standard, perhaps there might be Ways to fix it for ever, or at least till we are invaded, and made a Conquest by some other State: And even then, our best Writings might probably be preserved with Care, and grow into Esteem, and the Authors have a chance for Immortality.

BUT without such great Revolutions as these, (to which we are, I think, less subject than Kingdoms upon the Continent,) I see no absolute Necessity why any Language should be perpetually changing; for we find many Examples to the contrary. From *Homer* to *Plutarch*, are above a Thousand Years; so long, at least, the Purity of the *Greek* Tongue may be allowed to last; and we know not how far before. The *Grecians* spread their Colonies round all the Coasts of *Asia Minor*, even to the *Northern* Parts, lying towards the *Euxine*; in every Island of the *Ægean Sea*, and several others in the *Mediterranean*; where the Language was preserved entire for many Ages, after they themselves became Colonies to *Rome*, and till they were overrun by the barbarous Nations, upon the Fall of that Empire. The *Chinese* have Books in their Language above two Thousand Years old; neither have the frequent Conquests of the *Tartars* been able to alter it. The *German*, *Spanish*, and *Italian*, have admitted few or no changes for some Ages past. The other Languages of *Europe* I know nothing of; neither is there any Occasion to consider them.

HAVING taken this Compass, I return to those Considerations upon our own Language, which I would humbly offer your Lordship. The Period wherein the *English* Tongue received most Improvement, I take to commence with the Beginning of Queen *Elizabeth*'s Reign, and to conclude with the great Rebellion in Forty-two. It is true, there was a very ill Taste both of Style and Wit, which prevailed under King *James* the First; but that seems to have been corrected in the first Years of his Successor; who, among many other Qualifications of an excellent Prince, was a great Patron of Learning. From that great Rebellion to this present Time, I am apt to doubt whether the Corruptions in our Language have not,

D

at least, equalled the Refinements of it; and these Corruptions very few of the best Authors in our Age have wholly escaped. During the Usurpation, such an Infusion of Enthusiastick Jargon prevailed in every Writing, as was not shaken off in many Years after. To this succeeded that Licentiousness which entered with the *Restoration*; and from infecting our Religion and Morals, fell to corrupt our Language: Which last, was not like to be much improved by those, who, at that Time, made up the Court of King *Charles* the Second; either such who had followed him in his Banishment, or who had been altogether conversant in the Dialect of those *Fanatick Times*; or young Men, who had been educated in the same Company; so that the *Court*, which used to be the Standard of Propriety, and Correctness of Speech, was then, and I think hath ever since continued the worst School in *England*, for that Accomplishment; and so will remain, till better Care be taken in the Education of our young Nobility; that they may set out into the World with some Foundation of Literature, in order to qualify them for Patterns of Politeness. The Consequence of this Defect upon our Language, may appear from the Plays, and other Compositions, written for Entertainment, within fifty Years past; filled with a Succession of affected Phrases, and new conceited Words, either borrowed from the current Style of the Court, or from those, who, under the Character of Men of Wit and Pleasure, pretended to give the Law. Many of these Refinements have already been long antiquated, and are now hardly intelligible; which is no Wonder, when they were the Product only of Ignorance and Caprice.

I HAVE never known this great Town without one or more *Dunces* of Figure, who had Credit enough to give Rise to some new Word, and propagate it in most Conversations; although it had neither Humour nor Significancy. If it struck the present Taste, it was soon transferred into the Plays, and current Scribbles of the Week, and became an Addition to our Language; while the Men of Wit and Learning, instead of early obviating such Corruptions, were too often seduced to imitate and comply with them.

THERE is another Set of Men, who have contributed very much to the spoiling of the *English* Tongue; I mean the Poets, from the Time of the Restoration. These Gentlemen, although they could not be insensible how much our Language was already overstocked with Monosyllables, yet to save Time and Pains, introduced that barbarous Custom of abbreviating Words, to fit them to the Measure of their Verses; and this they have frequently done, so very injudiciously, as to form such harsh unharmonious Sounds, that none but a *Northern* Ear could endure. They have joined the most obdurate Consonants, without one intervening Vowel, only to shorten a Syllable: And their Taste in Time became so depraved, that what was at first a poetical Licence, not to be justified, they made their Choice; alledging, that the Words pronounced at length, sounded faint and languid. This was a Pretence to take up the same Custom in Prose; so that most of the Books we see now-a-days, are full of those Manglings and Abbreviations. Instances of this Abuse are innumerable: What does your Lordship think of the Words, *Drudg'd, Disturb'd, Rebuk'd, Fledg'd,* and a Thousand others, every where to be met in Prose, as well as Verse? Where, by leaving out a Vowel to save a Syllable, we form so jarring a Sound, and so difficult to utter, that I have often wondered how it could ever obtain.

ANOTHER Cause (and perhaps borrowed from the former) which hath contributed not a little to the maiming of our Language, is a foolish Opinion, advanced of late Years, that we ought to spell exactly as we speak; which beside the obvious Inconvenience of utterly destroying our Etymology, would be a Thing we should never see an End of. Not only the several Towns and Counties of *England,* have a different Way of pronouncing; but even here in *London,* they clip their Words after one Manner about the Court, another in the City, and a third in the Suburbs; and in a few Years, it is probable, will all differ from themselves, as Fancy or Fashion shall direct: All which reduced to Writing, would entirely confound Orthography. [It would be just as wise as to shape our Bodies to our Cloathes and not our Cloaths to our bodyes.] Yet many People are so fond of this Conceit, that it is sometimes a

difficult Matter to read modern Books and Pamphlets; where
the Words are so curtailed, and varied from their original
Spelling, that whoever hath been used to plain *English*, will
hardly know them by Sight.

SEVERAL young Men at the Universities, terribly possessed
with the Fear of Pedantry, run into a worse Extream; and
think all Politeness to consist in reading the daily Trash sent
down to them from hence: This they call *knowing the World*, and
reading Men and Manners. Thus furnished, they come up to
Town; reckon all their Errors for Accomplishments, borrow
the newest Set of Phrases; and if they take a Pen into their
Hands, all the odd Words they have picked up in a Coffee-
House, or a Gaming Ordinary, are produced as Flowers of
Style; and the Orthography refined to the utmost. To this
we owe those monstrous Productions, which under the Names
of *Trips*, *Spies*, *Amusements*, and other conceited Appellations,
have over-run us for some Years past. To this we owe that
strange Race of Wits, who tell us they write to the *Humour of
the Age*. And I wish I could say, these quaint Fopperies were
wholly absent from graver Subjects. In short, I would undertake to shew your Lordship several Pieces, where the Beauties
of this Kind are so predominant, that with all your Skill in
Languages, you could never be able either to read or understand them.

BUT I am very much mistaken, if many of these false
Refinements among us, do not arise from a Principle which
would quite destroy their Credit, if it were well understood
and considered. For I am afraid, my Lord, that with all the
real good Qualities of our Country, we are naturally not very
polite. This perpetual Disposition to shorten our Words, by
retrenching the Vowels, is nothing else but a Tendency to
lapse into the Barbarity of those *Northern* Nations from whom
we are descended, and whose Languages labour all under the
same Defect. For it is worthy our Observation, that the
Spaniards, the *French*, and the *Italians*, although derived from
the same *Northern* Ancestors with our selves, are, with the
utmost Difficulty taught to pronounce our Words; which the
Swedes and *Danes*, as well as the *Germans* and the *Dutch*, attain

to with Ease, because our Syllables resemble theirs, in the
Roughness and Frequency of Consonants. Now, as we struggle
with an ill Climate to improve the nobler Kinds of Fruits;
are at the Expence of Walls to receive and reverberate the faint
Rays of the Sun, and fence against the *Northern* Blasts; we
sometimes by the Help of a good Soil equal the Productions
of warmer Countries, who have no need to be at so much Cost
or Care: It is the same Thing with respect to the politer Arts
among us; and the same Defect of Heat which gives a Fierce-
ness to our Natures, may contribute to that Roughness of our
Language, which bears some Analogy to the harsh Fruit of
colder Countries. For I do not reckon, that we want a *Genius*
more than the rest of our Neighbours: But your Lordship
will be of my Opinion, that we ought to struggle with these
natural Disadvantages as much as we can; and be careful
whom we employ, whenever we design to correct them; which
is a Work that hath hitherto been assumed by the least qualified
Hands: So that if the Choice had been left to me, I would
rather have trusted the Refinement of our Language, as far as it
relates to Sound, to the Judgment of the Women, than of
illiterate Court-Fops, half-witted Poets, and University-Boys.
For, it is plain, that Women in their Manner of corrupting
Words, do naturally discard the Consonants, as we do the
Vowels. What I am going to tell your Lordship, appears very
trifling; that more than once, where some of both Sexes were
in Company, I have persuaded two or three of each to take a
Pen, and write down a Number of Letters joined together,
just as it came into their Heads; and upon reading this Gibber-
ish we have found that which the Men had writ, by the frequent
encountering of rough Consonants, to sound like *High-Dutch*;
and the other by the Women, like *Italian*, abounding in Vowels
and Liquids. Now, although I would by no Means give Ladies
the Trouble of advising us in the Reformation of our Language;
yet I cannot help thinking, that since they have been left out
of all Meetings, except Parties at Play, or where worse Designs
are carried on, our Conversation hath very much degenerated.

In order to reform our Language; I conceive, my Lord,
that a free judicious Choice should be made of such Persons, as

are generally allowed to be best qualified for such a Work, without any regard to Quality, Party, or Profession. These to a certain Number, at least, should assemble at some appointed Time and Place, and fix on Rules by which they design to proceed. What Methods they will take, is not for me to prescribe. Your Lordship, and other Persons in great Employment, might please to be of the Number: And I am afraid, such a Society would want your Instruction and Example, as much as your Protection: For I have, not without a little Envy, observed of late the Style of some great Ministers very much to exceed that of any other Productions.

THE Persons who are to undertake this Work, will have the Example of the *French* before them, to imitate where these have proceeded right, and to avoid their Mistakes. Besides the Grammar-part, wherein we are allowed to be very defective, they will observe many gross Improprieties, which however authorized by Practice, and grown familiar, ought to be discarded. They will find many Words that deserve to be utterly thrown out of our Language; many more to be corrected, and perhaps not a few, long since antiquated, which ought to be restored, on Account of their Energy and Sound.

BUT what I have most at Heart, is, that some Method should be thought on for *Ascertaining* and *Fixing* our Language for ever, after such Alterations are made in it as shall be thought requisite. For I am of Opinion, that it is better a Language should not be wholly perfect, than that it should be perpetually changing; and we must give over at one Time or other, or at length infallibly change for the worse: As the *Romans* did, when they began to quit their Simplicity of Style for affected Refinements; such as we meet in *Tacitus* and other Authors, which ended by Degrees in many Barbarities, even before the *Goths* had invaded *Italy*.

THE Fame of our Writers is usually confined to these two Islands; and it is hard it should be limited in *Time* as much as *Place*, by the perpetual Variations of our Speech. It is your Lordship's Observation, that if it were not for the *Bible* and *Common-Prayer-Book* in the vulgar Tongue, we should hardly be able to understand any thing that was written among us an

Hundred Years ago; which is certainly true: For those Books
being perpetually read in Churches, have proved a Kind of
Standard for Language, especially to the common People.
And I doubt whether the Alterations since introduced, have
added much to the Beauty or Strength of the *English* Tongue,
although they have taken off a great deal from that *Simplicity*,
which is one of the greatest Perfections in any Language.
You, my Lord, who are so conversant in the sacred Writings,
and so great a Judge of them in their Originals, will agree,
that no Translation our Country ever yet produced, hath come
up to that of the *Old* and *New Testament:* And by the many
beautiful Passages which I have often had the Honour to
hear your Lordship cite from thence, I am persuaded that the
Translators of the Bible were Masters of an *English* Stile
much fitter for that Work, than any we see in our present
Writings; which I take to be owing to the *Simplicity* that runs
through the Whole. Then, as to the greatest Part of our
Liturgy, compiled long before the Translation of the *Bible* now
in use, and little altered since; there seem to be in it as great
Strains of true sublime Eloquence, as are any where to be
found in our Language; which every Man of good Taste will
observe in the *Communion-Service*, that of *Burial*, and other
Parts.

BUT, where I say that I would have our Language, after
it is duly correct, always to last; I do not mean that it should
never be enlarged: Provided, that no Word, which a Society
shall give a Sanction to, be afterwards antiquated and exploded,
they may have Liberty to receive whatever new ones they shall
find Occasion for: Because then the old Books will yet be
always valuable according to their intrinsick Worth, and not
thrown aside on Account of unintelligible Words and Phrases,
which appear harsh and uncouth, only because they are out of
Fashion. Had the *Roman* Tongue continued vulgar in that City
till this Time; it would have been absolutely necessary, from
the mighty Changes that have been made in Law and Religion;
from the many Terms of Art required in Trade and in War;
from the new Inventions that have happened in the World;
from the vast spreading of Navigation and Commerce; with

many other obvious Circumstances, to have made great
Additions to that Language; yet the Antients would still have
been read, and understood with Pleasure and Ease. The *Greek*
Tongue received many Enlargements between the Time of
Homer, and that of *Plutarch*; yet the former Author was
probably as well understood in *Trajan*'s Time, as the latter.
What *Horace* says of *Words going off, and perishing like Leaves,
and new ones coming in their Place*, is a Misfortune he laments,
rather than a Thing he approves: But I cannot see why this
should be absolutely necessary, or if it were, what would have
become of his *Monumentum ære perennius*.

WRITING by Memory only, as I do at present, I would
gladly keep within my Depth; and therefore shall not enter
into further Particulars. Neither do I pretend more than to
shew the Usefulness of this Design, and to make some general
Observations; leaving the rest to that Society, which I hope
will owe its Institution and Patronage to your Lordship.
Besides, I would willingly avoid Repetition; having about a
Year ago, communicated to the Publick, much of what I
had to offer upon this Subject, by the Hands of an ingenious
* Gentleman, who for a long Time did thrice a Week divert
or instruct the Kingdom by his Papers; and is supposed to
pursue the same Design at present, under the Title of *Spectator*.
[In a Conversation some Time ago with the Person to whom
these Productions are ascribed, I happened to mention the
Proposall I have here made to Your Lordship; and in a few
dayes after I observed that Author had taken the Hint and
treated the same matter in one of his Papers, and with much
Judgement, except where he is pleased to put so great a
Compliment upon me, as I can never pretend to Deserve.]
This Author, who hath tried the Force and Compass of our
Language with so much Success, agrees entirely with me in
most of my Sentiments relating to it: So do the greatest Part
of the Men of Wit and Learning, whom I have had the Happiness to converse with: And therefore I imagine, that such a
Society would be pretty unanimous in the main Points.

YOUR Lordship must allow, that such a Work as this,

* *Mr.* ADDISON.

brought to Perfection, would very much contribute to the Glory of Her Majesty's Reign; which ought to be recorded in Words more durable than Brass, and such as our Posterity may read a thousand Years hence, with Pleasure as well as Admiration. I have always disapproved that false Compliment to Princes: That the most lasting Monument they can have, is the Hearts of their Subjects. It is indeed their greatest present Felicity to reign in their Subjects Hearts; but these are too perishable to preserve their Memories, which can only be done by the Pens of able and faithful Historians. And I take it to be your Lordship's Duty, as *prime Minister*, to give Order for inspecting our Language, and rendering it fit to record the History of so great and good a Princess. Besides, my Lord, as disinterested as you appear to the World, I am convinced, that no Man is more in the Power of a prevailing favourite Passion than your self; I mean, that Desire of true and lasting Honour, which you have born along with you through every Stage of your Life. To this you have often sacrificed your Interest, your Ease, and your Health: For preserving and encreasing this, you have exposed your Person to secret Treachery, and open Violence. There is not perhaps an Example in History of any Minister, who in so short a Time hath performed so many great Things, and overcome so many great Difficulties. Now, although I am fully convinced, that you fear God, honour your Queen, and love your Country, as much as any of your Fellow-Subjects; yet I must believe, that the Desire of Fame hath been no inconsiderable Motive to quicken you in the Pursuit of those Actions which will best deserve it. But, at the same Time, I must be so plain as to tell your Lordship, that if you will not take some Care to settle our Language, and put it into a State of Continuance, I cannot promise that your Memory shall be preserved above an Hundred Years, further than by imperfect Tradition.

As barbarous and ignorant as we were in former Centuries; there was more effectual Care taken by our Ancestors, to preserve the Memory of Times and Persons, than we find in this Age of Learning and Politeness, as we are pleased to call it.

The rude *Latin* of the *Monks* is still very intelligible; whereas, had their Records been delivered down only in the vulgar Tongue, so barren and so barbarous, so subject to continual succeeding Changes; they could not now be understood, unless by Antiquaries, who made it their Study to expound them: And we must, at this Day, have been content with such poor Abstracts of our *English* Story, as laborious Men of low Genius would think fit to give us: And even these, in the next Age, would be likewise swallowed up in succeeding Collections. If Things go on at this Rate; all I can promise your Lordship, is, that about two Hundred Years hence, some painful Compiler, who will be at the Trouble of studying old Language, may inform the World, that in the Reign of Queen *Anne*, *Robert* Earl of *Oxford*, a very wise and excellent Man, was made *High-Treasurer*, and saved his Country, which in those Days was almost ruined by a *foreign War*, and a *domestick Faction*. Thus much he may be able to pick out, and willing to transfer into his new History; but the rest of your Character, which I, or any other Writer, may now value our selves by drawing; and the particular Account of the great Things done under your Ministry, for which you are already so celebrated in most Parts of *Europe*, will probably be dropt, on Account of the antiquated Style, and Manner they are delivered in.

How then shall any Man, who hath a Genius for History, equal to the best of the Antients, be able to undertake such a Work with Spirit and Chearfulness, when he considers, that he will be read with Pleasure but a very few Years, and in an Age or two shall hardly be understood without an Interpreter? This is like employing an excellent Statuary to work upon mouldring Stone. Those who apply their Studies to preserve the Memory of others, will always have some Concern for their own. And I believe it is for this Reason, that so few Writers among us, of any Distinction, have turned their Thoughts to such a discouraging Employment: For the best *English* Historian must lie under this Mortification, that when his Style grows antiquated, he will be only considered as a tedious Relater of Facts; and perhaps consulted in his Turn, among other neglected Authors, to furnish Materials for some future Collector.

I DOUBT your Lordship is but ill entertained with a few scattered Thoughts, upon a Subject that deserves to be treated with Ability and Care: However, I must beg Leave to add a few Words more, perhaps not altogether foreign to the same Matter. I know not whether that which I am going to say, may pass for Caution, Advice, or Reproach; any of which will be justly thought very improper from one in my Station, to one in yours. However, I must venture to affirm, that if Genius and Learning be not encouraged under your Lordship's Administration, you are the most inexcuseable Person alive. All your other Virtues, my Lord, will be defective without this: Your Affability, Candour, and good Nature; that perpetual Agreeableness of Conversation, so disengaged in the Midst of such a Weight of Business and Opposition; even your Justice, Prudence, and Magnanimity, will shine less bright without it. Your Lordship is universally allowed to possess a very large Portion in most Parts of Literature; and to this you owe the cultivating those many Virtues, which otherwise would have been less adorned, or in lower Perfection. Neither can you acquit your self of these Obligations, without letting the Arts, in their Turn, share your Influence and Protection. Besides, who knows but some *true Genius* may happen to arise under your Ministry, *exortus ut ætherius* Sol. Every Age might, perhaps, produce one or two of these to adorn it, if they were not sunk under the Censure and Obloquy of plodding, servile, imitating Pedants: I do not mean by a true Genius, any bold Writer, who breaks through the Rules of Decency to distinguish himself by the Singularity of Opinions; but one, who upon a deserving Subject, is able to open new Scenes, and discover a Vein of true and noble Thinking, which never entered into any Imagination before: Every Stroke of whose Pen is worth all the Paper blotted by Hundreds of others in the Compass of their Lives. I know, my Lord, your Friends will offer in your Defence, that in your private Capacity, you never refused your Purse and Credit to the Service and Support

of learned or ingenious Men: And that ever since you have
been in publick Employment, you have constantly bestowed
your Favours to the most deserving Persons. But I desire
your Lordship not to be deceived: We never will admit
of these Excuses; nor will allow your private Liberality, as
great as it is, to attone for your excessive publick Thrift. But
here again, I am afraid most good Subjects will interpose in
your Defence, by alledging the desperate Condition you found
the Nation in, and the Necessity there was for so able and
faithful a Steward to retrieve it, if possible, by the utmost
Frugality. We grant all this, my Lord; but then, it ought
likewise to be considered, that you have already saved several
Millions to the Publick; and that what we ask is too inconsiderable to break into any Rules of the strictest good Husbandry. The *French* King bestows about half a Dozen Pensions
to learned Men in several Parts of *Europe*; and perhaps a Dozen
in his own Kingdom; which, in the whole, do probably not
amount to half the Income of many a private Commoner in
England; yet have more contributed to the Glory of that Prince,
than any Million he hath otherwise employed. For Learning,
like all true Merit, is easily satisfied; whilst the False and
Counterfeit is perpetually craving, and never thinks it hath
enough. The smallest Favour given by a great Prince, as a
Mark of Esteem, to reward the Endowments of the Mind,
never fails to be returned with Praise and Gratitude, and loudly
celebrated to the World. I have known, some Years ago,
several Pensions given to particular Persons, (how deservedly
I shall not enquire) any one of which, if divided into smaller
Parcels, and distributed by the Crown to those who might,
upon Occasion, distinguish themselves by some extraordinary
Production of Wit or Learning; would be amply sufficient to
answer the End. Or, if any such Persons were above Money,
(as every great *Genius* certainly is, with very moderate Con-
veniences of Life) a Medal, or some Mark of Distinction,
would do full as well.

But I forget my Province; and find my self turning Projector
before I am aware; although it be one of the last Characters

under which I should desire to appear before your Lordship;
especially when I have the Ambition of aspiring to that of
being, with the greatest Respect and Truth,

> *My* LORD,
>
> *Your* LORDSHIP'S
>
>> *most Obedient, most Obliged,*
>>
>> *and most Humble Servant,*

> J. SWIFT.

LONDON, Feb.
22, 1711–12.

Mr. Collins's Discourse of Free-Thinking

Mr. *C——ns's*

DISCOURSE

OF

𝕱𝖗𝖊𝖊-𝕿𝖍𝖎𝖓𝖐𝖎𝖓𝖌,

Put into plain *English*, by way of

ABSTRACT,

FOR THE

Use of the Poor.

By a Friend of the AUTHOR.

LONDON

Printed for *John Morphew*, near *Stationers-Hall* 1713.   Price 4 *d.*

E

OUR *Party having failed, by all their Political Arguments, to re-establish their Power; the wise Leaders have determined, that the last and principal Remedy should be made use of, for opening the Eyes of this blinded Nation; and that a short, but perfect, System of their* Divinity, *should be publish'd, to which we are all of us ready to subscribe, and which we lay down as a Model, bearing a close Analogy to our Schemes in Religion. Crafty designing Men, that they might keep the World in Awe, have, in their several Forms of Government, placed a* Supream Power *on* Earth, *to keep human Kind in fear of being* Hanged; *and a* Supream Power *in* Heaven, *for fear of being* Damned. *In order to cure Mens Apprehensions of the former, several of our learned Members have writ many profound Treatises in* Anarchy; *but a brief compleat Body of* Atheology *seemed yet wanting, till this irrefragable Discourse appeared. However it so happens, that our ablest Brethren, in their elaborate Disquisitions upon this Subject, have written with so much Caution, that ignorant* Unbelievers *have edified very little by them. I grant that those daring Spirits, who first adventured to write against the direct Rules of the Gospel, the Current of Antiquity, the Religion of the Magistrate, and the Laws of the Land, had some Measures to keep; and particularly when they railed at Religion, were in the right to use little artful Disguises, by which a Jury could only find them guilty of abusing Heathenism or Popery. But the* Mystery *is now* revealed, *that there is no such Thing as* Mystery *or* Revelation; *and though our Friends are out of Place and Power, yet we may have so much Confidence in the present Ministry to be secure, that those who suffer so many* Free Speeches *against their Sovereign and themselves to pass unpunished, will never resent our expressing the* freest Thoughts *against their Religion; but think with* Tiberius, *That if there be a God, he is able enough to revenge any Injuries done to* **him***-self, without expecting the* Civil Power *to interpose.*

By these Reflections I was brought to think, that the most ingenious Author of the Discourse upon Free Thinking, *in a Letter to* Somebody, *Esq; although he hath used less reserve than any of his Predecessors, might yet have been more free and open. I considered, that several* Well-willers *to* Infidelity *might be discouraged by a shew of Logick, and multiplicity of Quotations, scattered through his*

27

Book, which to Understandings of that Size might carry an appearance of something like Book-learning, *and consequently fright them from reading for their Improvement: I could see no Reason why these great Discoveries should be hid from our Youth of Quality, who frequent* White's *and* Tom's; *why they should not be adapted to the Capacities of the* Kit-Cat *and* Hannover *Clubs, who might* then *be able to read Lectures on them to their several* Toasts: *And it will be allowed on all Hands, that nothing can sooner help to restore our abdicated Cause, than a firm universal Belief of the Principles laid down by this sublime Author.*

For I am sensible that nothing would more contribute to the con-tinuance of the War, *and the Restoration of the late Ministry, than to have the Doctrines delivered in this Treatise well infused into the People. I have therefore compiled them into the following Abstract, wherein I have adhered to the very Words of our Author, only adding some few Explanations of my own, where the Terms happen to be too learned, and consequently a little beyond the Comprehension of those for whom the Work was principally intended, I mean the Nobility and Gentry of our Party. After which I hope it will be impossible for the Malice of a* Jacobite, High-flying, Priest-ridden *Faction, to misrepresent us. The few Additions I have made, are for no other use than to help the Transition, which could not otherwise be kept in an Abstract; but I have not presumed to advance any thing of my own; which besides would be needless to an Author, who hath so fully handled and demonstrated every Particular. I shall only add, that though this Writer, when he speaks of* Priests, *desires chiefly to be understood to mean the* English *Clergy, yet he includes all* Priests *whatsoever, except the antient and modern* Heathens, *the* Turks, Quakers, *and* Socinians.

The LETTER.

SIR,

I Send you this Apology for *Free Thinking*, without the least
hopes of doing good, but purely to comply with your
Request; for those Truths which no Body can deny, will do
no good to those who deny them. The Clergy, who are so
impudent to teach the People the Doctrines of Faith, are all
either cunning Knaves or mad Fools; for none but artificial
designing Men, and crackt-brained Enthusiasts, presume to be
Guides to others in matters of Speculation, which all the
Doctrines of Christianity are; and whoever has a mind to learn
the Christian Religion, naturally chuses such Knaves and
Fools to teach them. Now the *Bible*, which contains the
Precepts of the Priests Religion, is the most difficult Book in
the World to be understood; It requires a thorow Knowledge
in Natural, Civil, Ecclesiastical History, Law, Husbandry,
Sailing, Physick, Pharmacy, Mathematicks, Metaphysicks,
Ethicks, and every thing else that can be named: And every
Body who believes it, ought to understand it, and must do so
by force of his own *Free Thinking*, without any Guide or
Instructor.

How can a Man *think* at all, if he does not think freely?
A Man who does not eat and drink freely, does not eat and
drink at all. Why may not I be deny'd the liberty of *Free-
seeing*, as well as *Free-thinking*? Yet no body pretends that the
first is unlawful, for a Cat may look on a King; though you be
near-sighted, or have weak or soar Eyes, or are blind, you
may be a *Free-seer*; you ought to see for your self, and not trust
to a Guide to chuse the Colour of your Stockings, or save you
from falling into a Ditch.

In like manner there ought to be no restraint at all on
thinking freely upon any Proposition, however impious or

absurd. There is not the least hurt in the wickedest Thoughts, provided they be free; nor in telling those Thoughts to every Body, and endeavouring to convince the World of them; for all this is included in the Doctrine of *Free-thinking*, as I shall plainly shew you in what follows; and therefore you are all along to understand the Word *Free-thinking* in this Sense.

If you are apt to be afraid of the Devil, *think freely* of him, and you destroy him and his Kingdom. *Free-thinking* has done him more Mischief than all the Clergy in the World ever could do; they *believe in the Devil*, they have an *Interest* in him, and therefore are the great Supports of his Kingdom. The Devil was in the *States General* before they began to be *Free-thinkers*. For *England* and *Holland* were formerly the *Christian* Territories of the Devil; I told you how he left *Holland*; and *Free-thinking* and the *Revolution* banish'd him from *England*; I defy all the Clergy to shew me when they ever had such Success against him. My Meaning is, that to think freely of the Devil, is to think there is no Devil at all; and he that thinks so, the Devil's in him if he be afraid of the Devil.

But within these two or three Years the Devil has come into *England* again, and Dr. *Sacheverell* has given him Commission to appear in the shape of a *Cat*, and carry old Women about upon Broomsticks: And the Devil has now so many *Ministers ordained to his Service*, that they have rendred *Free-thinking* odious, and nothing but the Second Coming of *Christ* can restore it.

The Priests tell me I am to believe the *Bible*, but *Free-thinking* tells me otherwise in many Particulars: The *Bible* says, the *Jews* were a Nation favoured by God; but I who am a *Free-thinker* say, that cannot be, because the *Jews* lived in a *Corner* of the Earth, and *Free-thinking* makes it clear, that those who live in *Corners* cannot be Favourites of God. The *New Testament* all along asserts the Truth of Christianity, but *Free-thinking* denies it; because Christianity was communicated but to a few; and whatever is communicated but to a few, cannot be true; for that is like *Whispering*, and the Proverb says, that there is no Whispering without Lying.

Here is a Society in *London* for propagating *Free-thinking* throughout the World, encouraged and supported by the Queen and many others. You say perhaps, it is for propagating the Gospel. Do you think the Missionaries we send, will tell the Heathens that they must not *think freely?* No surely; why then, 'tis manifest those Missionaries must be *Free-thinkers*, and make the Heathens so too. But why should not the King of *Siam*, whose Religion is Heathenism and Idolatry, send over a parcel of his Priests to convert us to *his Church*, as well as we send Missionaries there? Both Projects are exactly of a Piece, and equally reasonable; and if those Heathen Priests were here, it would be our Duty to hearken to them, and *think freely* whether *they* may not be in the right rather than we. I heartily wish a Detachment of such Divines as Dr. *Atterbury*, Dr. *Smalridge*, Dr. *Swift*, Dr. *Sacheverell*, and some others, were sent every Year to the furthest part of the Heathen World, and that we had a Cargo of their Priests in return, who would spread *Free-thinking* among us; then the War would go on, the late Ministry be restored, and Faction cease, which our Priests inflame by haranguing upon Texts, and falsly call that preaching the Gospel.

I have another Project in my Head which ought to be put in execution, in order to make us *Free-thinkers:* It is a great Hardship and Injustice, that our Priests must not be disturbed while they are prating in their Pulpit. For Example: Why should not *William Penn* the Quaker, or any *Anabaptist, Papist, Muggletonian, Jew* or *Sweet Singer*, have liberty to come into St. *Paul's* Church, in the midst of Divine Service, and endeavour to convert first the Aldermen, then the Preacher, and Singing-Men? Or pray, why might not poor Mr. *Whiston*, who denies the Divinity of Christ, be allow'd to come into the Lower House of Convocation, and convert the Clergy? But alas we are over-run with such false Notions, that if *Penn* or *Whiston* should do their Duty, they would be reckoned Fanaticks, and Disturbers of the Holy Synod, although they have as good a Title to it, as St. *Paul* had to go into the Synagogues of the *Jews*; and their Authority is full as Divine as his.

Christ himself commands us to be *Free-thinkers*, for he bids us search the Scriptures, and take heed what and whom we hear; by which he plainly warns us, not to believe our Bishops and Clergy; for *Jesus Christ*, when he consider'd that all the *Jewish* and *Heathen* Priests, whose Religion he came to abolish, were his Enemies, rightly concluded that those appointed by him to preach his own Gospel, would probably be so too; and could not be secure, that any Sett of Priests, of the Faith he deliver'd, would ever be otherwise; therefore it is fully demonstrated that the Clergy of the Church of *England* are mortal Enemies to Christ, and ought not to be believ'd.

But without the Priviledge of *Free-thinking*, how is it possible to know which is the right *Scripture?* Here are perhaps twenty Sorts of *Scriptures* in the several Parts of the World, and every Sett of Priests contends that their *Scripture* is the true One. The *Indian Bramines* have a Book of Scripture call'd the *Shaster*; the *Persees* their *Zundivastaw*; the *Bonzes* in *China* have theirs, written by the Disciples of *Fo-he*, whom they call *God and Saviour of the World, who was born to teach the way of Salvation, and to give satisfaction for all Men's Sins*. Which you see is directly the same with what our *Priests* pretend of *Christ*; And must we not *think freely* to find out which are in the right, whether the *Bishops* or the *Bonzes?* But the *Talapoins* or *Heathen* Clergy of *Siam* approach yet nearer to the System of our Priests; they have a Book of *Scripture* written by *Sommonocodum*, who, the *Siamese* say, was *born of a Virgin*, and was *the God expected by the Universe*; just as our *Priests* tell us, that *Jesus Christ* was born of the *Virgin Mary*, and was the *Messiah* so long expected. The *Turkish* Priests or *Dervises* have their Scripture, which they call the *Alcoran*. The *Jews* have the *Old Testament* for their Scripture, and the *Christians* have both the Old and the New. Now among all these Scriptures there cannot above one be right; and how is it possible to know which is that, without reading them all, and then *thinking freely*, every one of us for our selves, without following the Advice or Instruction of any Guide, before we venture to chuse? The Parliament ought to be at the Charge of finding a sufficient number of these *Scriptures* for every one of Her Majesty's Subjects, for there are Twenty to One against us, that we may be in the wrong: But a great deal of *Free-thinking* will at last set us all right, and every one will adhere to the *Scripture* he likes best; by which means Religion, Peace, and Wealth, will be for ever secured in Her Majesty's Realms.

And it is the more necessary that the good People of *England* should have liberty to chuse some other *Scripture*, because all *Christian* Priests differ so much about the Copies of theirs, and about the various Readings of the several Manuscripts, which quite destroys the Authority of the Bible: For what Authority can a Book pretend to, where there are various Readings? And for this reason, it is manifest that no Man can know the Opinions of *Aristotle* or *Plato*, or believe the Facts related by *Thucidydes* or *Livy*, or be pleased with the Poetry of *Homer* and *Virgil*, all which Books are utterly useless, upon account of their various Readings. Some Books of *Scripture* are said to be lost, and this utterly destroys the Credit of those that are left: Some we reject, which the *Africans* and *Copticks* receive; and why may we not *think freely*, and reject the rest? Some think the Scriptures wholly inspired, some partly; and some not at all. Now this is just the very Case of the *Bramines*, *Persees*, *Bonzes*, *Talapoins*, *Dervizes*, *Rabbi*'s, and all *other Priests* who build their Religion upon Books, as our Priests do upon their Bibles; they all equally differ about the Copies, various Readings and Inspirations, of their several Scriptures, and God knows which are in the right; *Free-thinking* alone can determine it.

It would be endless to shew in how many Particulars the Priests of the *Heathen* and *Christian Churches* differ about the Meaning even of those Scriptures which they universally receive as Sacred. But to avoid Prolixity, I shall confine my self to the different Opinions among the Priests of the Church of *England*, and here only give you a Specimen, because even these are too many to be enumerated.

I have found out a Bishop (though indeed his Opinions are condemn'd by all his Brethren) who allows the Scriptures to be so difficult, that God has left them rather as a Trial of our Industry than a Repository of our Faith, and Furniture of *Creeds* and Articles of *Belief*; with several other admirable

Schemes of *Free-thinking*, which you may consult at your leisure.

The Doctrine of the *Trinity* is the most fundamental Point of the whole *Christian* Religion. Nothing is more easie to a *Free-thinker*, yet what different Notions of it do the *English* Priests pretend to deduce from Scripture, explaining it by *specifick Unities, eternal Modes of Subsistance*, and the like unintelligible Jargon? Nay, 'tis a Question whether this Doctrine be Fundamental or no; for though Dr. *South* and Bishop *Bull* affirm it, yet Bishop *Taylor* and Dr. *Wallis* deny it. And that excellent *Free-thinking* Prelate, Bishop *Taylor*, observes, that *Athanasius*'s Example was followed with too much greediness; by which means it has happened, that the greater number of our Priests are in that Sentiment, and think it necessary to believe the *Trinity*, and Incarnation of *Christ*.

Our Priests likewise dispute several Circumstances about the Resurrection of the Dead, the Nature of our Bodies after the Resurrection, and in what manner they shall be united to our Souls. They also attack one another *very weakly with great Vigour*, about Predestination. And it is certainly true, (for Bishop *Taylor* and Mr. *Whiston* the Socinian say so) that all Churches in Prosperity alter their Doctrines every Age, and are neither satisfy'd with themselves, nor their own Confessions; neither does any Clergymen of Sense believe the Thirty nine Articles.

Our Priests differ about the Eternity of Hell-Torments. The famous Dr. *Henry Moor*, and the most pious and rational of all Priests Doctor *Tillotson*, (both *Free-thinkers*) believe them to be not Eternal. They differ about keeping the Sabbath, the Divine Right of Episcopacy, and the Doctrine of Original Sin; which is the Foundation of the whole Christian Religion; for if Men are not liable to be damned for *Adam*'s Sin, the Christian Religion is an Imposture: Yet this is now disputed among them; so is Lay-Baptism; so was formerly the lawfulness of Usury, but now the Priests are common Stock-jobbers, Attorneys and Scriveners. In short there is no end of disputing among Priests, and therefore I conclude, that there ought to be no such Thing in the World as Priests, Teachers, or Guides, for instructing ignorant People in Religion; but that every Man ought to *think freely* for himself.

I will tell you my meaning in all this; the Priests dispute every Point in the Christian Religion, as well as almost every Text in the Bible; and the force of my Argument lies here, that whatever Point is disputed by one or two Divines, however condemned by the Church, not only that particular Point, but the whole Article to which it relates, may lawfully be received or rejected by any *Free Thinker*. For Instance, suppose *Moor* and *Tillotson* deny the Eternity of Hell Torments, a *Free Thinker* may deny all future Punishments whatsoever. The Priests dispute about explaining the *Trinity*; therefore a *Free Thinker* may reject one or two, or the whole three *Persons*; at least he may reject Christianity, because the *Trinity* is the most fundamental Doctrine of that Religion. So I affirm Original Sin, and that Men are now liable to be damned for *Adam*'s Sin, to be the Foundation of the whole Christian Religion; but this Point was formerly, and is now disputed, therefore a *Free Thinker* may deny the whole. And I cannot help giving you one further Direction, how I insinuate all along, that the wisest *Free Thinking* Priests, whom you may distinguish by the Epithets I bestow them, were those who differed most from the generality of their Brethren.

But besides, the Conduct of our Priests, in many other Points, makes *Free Thinking* unavoidable; for some of them own, that the Doctrines of the Church are contradictory to one another, as well as to Reason: Which I thus prove; Dr. *Sacheverell* says in his Speech at his Tryal, that by abandoning Passive Obedience we must render our selves the most inconsistent Church in the World: Now 'tis plain, that one Inconsistency could not make the most inconsistent Church in the World; *ergo*, there must have been a great many Inconsistencies and contradictory Doctrines in the Church before. Dr. *South* describes the Incarnation of Christ, as an astonishing Mystery, impossible to be conceived by Mans Reason; *ergo*, it is contradictory to it self, and to Reason, and ought to be exploded by all *Free Thinkers*.

Another Instance of the Priests Conduct, which multiplies

Free Thinkers, is their acknowledgments of Abuses, Defects, and false Doctrines in the Church; particularly that of eating *Black Pudding*, which is so plainly forbid in the *Old* and *New Testament*, that I wonder those who pretend to believe a Syllable in either, will presume to taste it. Why should I mention the want of Discipline, and of a Side-board at the Altar, with Complaints of other great Abuses and Defects made by some of the Priests, which no Man can *think* on without *Free Thinking*, and consequently rejecting Christianity?

When I see an honest Free Thinking Bishop endeavour to destroy the Power and Privileges of the Church, and Dr. *Atterbury* angry with him for it, and calling it *dirty Work*, what can I conclude, by vertue of being a *Free Thinker*, but that Christianity is all a Cheat?

Mr. *Whiston* has publish'd several Tracts, wherein he absolutely denies the Divinity of *Christ:* A Bishop tells him, *Sir, in any Matter where you have the Church's Judgment against you, you should be careful not to break the Peace of the Church, by Writing against it, though you are sure you are in the right.* Now my Opinion is directly contrary; and I affirm, that if Ten thousand Free Thinkers thought differently from the received Doctrine, and from each other, they would be all in Duty bound to publish their Thoughts (provided they were all sure of being in the right) though it broke the Peace of the Church and State, Ten thousand times.

And here I must take leave to tell you, although you cannot but have perceived it from what I have already said, and shall be still more amply convinced by what is to follow; That *Free Thinking* signifies nothing, without *Free Speaking* and *Free Writing*. It is the indispensable Duty of a *Free Thinker*, to endeavour *forcing* all the World to think as he does, and by that means make them *Free Thinkers* too. You are also to understand, that I allow no Man to be a *Free Thinker*, any further than as he differs from the received Doctrines of Religion. Where a Man falls in, though by perfect Chance, with what is generally believed, he is in that Point a confined and limited Thinker; and you shall see by and by, that I celebrate those for the noblest *Free Thinkers* in every Age, who differed from the

Religion of their Countries in the most fundamental Points, and especially in those which bear any Analogy to the chief Fundamentals of Religion among us.

Another Trick of the Priests, is to charge all Men with Atheism, who have more Wit than themselves; which therefore I expect will be my Case for Writing this Discourse: This is what makes them so implacable against Mr. *Gildon*, Dr. *Tindal*, Mr. *Toland*, and my self, and when they call us *Wits* Atheists, it provokes us to be *Free Thinkers*.

Again; The Priests cannot agree when their Scripture was wrote. They differ about the number of Canonical Books, and the various Readings. Now those few among us who understand Latin, are careful to tell this to our Disciples, who presently fall a *Free Thinking*, that the Bible is a Book not to be depended upon in any thing at all.

There is another Thing that mightily spreads *Free Thinking*, which I believe you would hardly guess: The Priests have got a way of late of Writing Books against *Free Thinking*; I mean Treatises in Dialogue, where they introduce *Atheists*, *Deists*, *Scepticks* and *Socinians* offering their several Arguments. Now these *Free Thinkers* are too hard for the Priests themselves in their own Books; and how can it be otherwise? For if the Arguments usually offered by *Atheists*, are fairly represented in these Books, they must needs convert every Body that reads them; because *Atheists*, *Deists*, *Scepticks* and *Socinians*, have certainly better Arguments to maintain their Opinions, than any the Priests can produce to maintain the contrary.

Mr. *Creech*, a Priest, translated *Lucretius* into *English*, which is a compleat System of Atheism; and several Young Students, who were afterwards Priests, writ Verses in Praise of this Translation. The Arguments against Providence in that Book are so strong, that they have added mightily to the Number of *Free Thinkers*.

What should I mention the pious Cheats of the Priests, who in the *New Testament* translate the Word *Ecclesia* sometimes the *Church*, and sometimes the *Congregation*; and *Episcopus*, sometimes a *Bishop*, and sometimes an *Overseer*? A Priest translating a Book, left out a whole Passage that reflected on the *King*, by which he was an Enemy to *Political Free Thinking*, a most considerable Branch of our System. Another Priest translating a Book of Travels, left out a lying Miracle, out of meer Malice to conceal an Argument for *Free Thinking*. In short, these Frauds are very common in all Books which are published by *Priests:* But however, I love to excuse them whenever I can: And as to this Accusation, they may plead the Authority of the Ancient Fathers of the Church for Forgery, Corruption, and mangling of Authors, with more Reason than for any of their Articles of Faith. St. *Jerom*, St. *Hilary*, *Eusebius Vercellensis*, *Victorinus*, and several others, were all guilty of arrant Forgery and Corruption: For when they translated the Works of several *Free-thinkers*, whom they called *Hereticks*, they omitted all their Heresies or *Free-thinkings*, and had the Impudence to own it to the World.

From these many notorious Instances of the Priests' Conduct, I conclude they are not to be relied on in any one thing relating to Religion, but that every Man must think freely for himself.

But to this it may be objected, that the Bulk of Mankind is as well qualified for *flying* as *thinking*, and if every Man thought it his Duty to *think freely*, and trouble his Neighbour with his Thoughts (which is an essential Part of *Free-thinking*,) it would make wild work in the World. I answer; whoever cannot *think freely*, may let it alone if he pleases, by virtue of his Right to *think freely*; that is to say, if such a Man *freely thinks* that he cannot *think freely*, of which every Man is a sufficient Judge, why then he need not *think freely*, unless he *thinks* fit.

Besides, if the Bulk of Mankind cannot *think freely* in Matters of Speculation, as the Being of a God, the Immortality of the Soul, *&c.* why then, *Free-thinking* is indeed no Duty: But then the *Priests* must allow, that Men are not concerned to believe whether there is a God or no. But still those who are disposed to *think freely*, may *think freely* if they please.

It is again objected, that *Free-thinking* will produce endless Divisions in Opinion, and by consequence disorder Society. To which I answer,

When every single Man comes to have a different Opinion

every Day from the whole World, and from himself, by Virtue
of *Free-thinking*, and thinks it his Duty to convert every Man
to his own *Free-thinking* (as all we *Free-thinkers* do) how can
that possibly create so great a Diversity of Opinions, as to
have a Sett of Priests agree among themselves to teach the
same Opinions in their several Parishes to all who will come
to hear them? Besides, if all People were of the same Opinion,
the Remedy would be worse than the Disease; I will tell you
the Reason some other time.

Besides, difference in Opinion, especially in Matters of great
Moment, breeds no Confusion at all. Witness *Papist* and
Protestant, *Roundhead* and *Cavalier*, and *Whig* and *Tory* now
among us. I observe, the *Turkish* Empire is more at Peace
within it self than *Christian* Princes are *with one another*. Those
noble *Turkish* Virtues of Charity and Toleration, are what
contribute chiefly to the flourishing State of that happy
Monarchy. There *Christians* and *Jews* are tolerated, and live at
ease, if they can hold their Tongues and *think freely*, provided
they never set foot within the *Moschs*, nor write against
Mahomet: A few Plunderings now and then by their *Janisaries*
are all they have to fear.

It is objected, that by *Free-thinking*, Men will *think* themselves into *Atheism*; and indeed I have allowed all along, that
Atheistical Books convert Men to *Free-thinking*. But suppose
that be true; I can bring you two Divines who affirm Superstition and Enthusiasm to be worse than Atheism, and more
mischievous to Society, and in short it is necessary that the
Bulk of the People should be Atheists or Superstitious.

It is objected, that Priests ought to be relied on by the
People, as Lawyers and Physicians, because it is their Faculty.

I answer, 'Tis true, a Man who is no Lawyer is not suffered
to plead for himself; But every Man may be his own Quack
if he pleases, and he only ventures his Life; but in the other
Case the Priest tells him he must be damned; therefore do not
trust the Priest, but *think freely* for your self, and if you happen
to think there is no Hell, there certainly is none, and consequently you cannot be damned; I answer further, that wherever
there is no *Lawyer*, *Physician*, or *Priest*, that Country is *Paradise*.

Besides, all Priests (except the Orthodox, and those are not ours, nor any that I know) are hired by the Publick to lead Men into Mischief; but *Lawyers* and *Physicians* are not, you hire them your self.

It is objected (by Priests no doubt, but I have forgot their Names) that false Speculations are necessary to be imposed upon Men, in order to assist the Magistrate in keeping the Peace, and that Men ought therefore to be deceived like Children, for their own Good. I answer, that Zeal for imposing Speculations, whether true or false (under which Name of Speculations I include all Opinions of Religion, as the Belief of a God, Providence, Immortality of the Soul, future Rewards and Punishments, &c.) has done more hurt than it is possible for Religion to do good. It puts us to the Charge of maintaining Ten thousand Priests in *England*, which is a Burthen upon Society never felt on any other occasion; and a greater Evil to the Publick than if these Ecclesiasticks were only employed in the most innocent Offices of Life, which I take to be *Eating* and *Drinking*. Now if you offer to impose any thing on Mankind besides what relates to moral Duties, as to pay your Debts, not pick Pockets, nor commit Murder, and the like; that is to say, if besides this, you oblige them to believe in God and Jesus Christ, what you add to their Faith will take just so much off from their Morality. By this Argument it is manifest that a perfect moral Man must be a perfect Atheist, every Inch of Religion he gets, loses him an Inch of Morality: For there is a certain *Quantum* belongs to every Man, of which there is nothing to spare. This is clear from the common Practice of all our Priests, they never once Preach to you to love your Neighbour, to be just in your Dealings, or to be Sober and Temperate: The Streets of *London* are full of Common Whores, publickly tolerated in their Wickedness; yet the Priests make no Complaints against this Enormity, either from the Pulpit or the Press: I can affirm, that neither you nor I Sir, have ever heard one Sermon against Whoring since we were Boys. No, the Priests allow all these Vices, and love us the better for them, provided we will promise not to *harangue upon a Text*, nor to sprinkle a little Water in a Child's Face, which they call Baptizing, and would engross it all to themselves.

Besides, the *Priests* engage all the Rogues, Villains and Fools in their Party, in order to make it as large as they can: By this means they seduced *Constantine the Great* over to their Religion, who was the first Christian Emperor, and so horrible a Villain, that the *Heathen* Priests told him they could not expiate his Crimes in their Church; so he was at a loss to know what to do, till an *Ægyptian* Bishop assured him that there was no Villainy so great, but was to be expiated by the Sacraments of the Christian Religion; upon which he became a Christian, and to him that Religion owes its first Settlement.

It is objected, that *Free-thinkers* themselves are the most infamous, wicked and senseless of all Mankind.

I answer, First, We say the same of *Priests* and other Believers. But the Truth is, Men of all Sects are equally good and bad; for no Religion whatsoever contributes in the least to mend Mens Lives.

I answer, Secondly, That *Free-thinkers* use their Understanding, but those who have Religion, do not, therefore the first have more Understanding than the others; Witness *Toland, Tindal, Gildon, Clendon, Coward,* and my self. For, use Legs and have Legs.

I answer, Thirdly, That *Free-thinkers* are the most virtuous Persons in the World; for every *Free-thinker* must certainly differ from the *Priests,* and from Nine hundred ninety nine of a Thousand of those among whom they live; and are therefore Virtuous of course, because every Body hates them.

I answer, Fourthly, That the most virtuous People in all Ages have been *Free-thinkers*; of which I shall produce several Instances.

Socrates was a *Free-thinker*; for he disbelieved the Gods of his Country, and the common *Creeds* about them, and declared his Dislike when he heard Men attribute *Repentance, Anger, and other Passions to the Gods, and talk of Wars and Battles in Heaven, and of the Gods getting Women with Child,* and such like fabulous and blasphemous Stories. I pick out these Particulars, because they are the very same with what the Priests have in their

F

Bibles, where *Repentance* and *Anger* are attributed to God, where it is said, there was *War in Heaven*; and that the *Virgin* Mary *was with Child by the Holy Ghost*, whom the Priests call God; all fabulous and blasphemous Stories. Now, I affirm *Socrates* to have been a true *Christian*. You will ask perhaps how that can be, since he lived Three or four hundred Years before Christ? I answer with *Justin Martyr*, that *Christ* is nothing else but *Reason*, and I hope you do not think *Socrates* lived before *Reason*. Now, this true Christian *Socrates* never made Notions, Speculations, or Mysteries any Part of his Religion, but demonstrated all Men to be Fools who troubled themselves with Enquiries into heavenly Things. Lastly, 'tis plain that *Socrates* was a *Free-thinker*, because he was calumniated for an *Atheist*, as *Free-thinkers* generally are, only because he was an Enemy to all Speculations and Enquiries into heavenly Things. For I argue thus, that if I never trouble my self to think whether there be a God or no, and forbid others to do it, I am a *Free-thinker*, but not an *Atheist*.

Plato was a *Free-thinker*, and his Notions are so like some in the Gospel, that a Heathen charged Christ with borrowing his Doctrine from *Plato*. But *Origen* defends Christ very well against this Charge, by saying he did not understand *Greek*, and therefore could not borrow his Doctrines from *Plato*. However their two Religions agreed so well, that it was common for Christians to turn *Platonists*, and *Platonists* Christians. When the Christians found out this, one of their zealous Priests (worse than any Atheist) forged several Things under *Plato*'s Name, but conformable to Christianity, by which the Heathens were fraudulently converted.

Epicurus was the greatest of all *Free-thinkers*, and consequently the most virtuous Man in the World. His Opinions in Religion were the most compleat System of Atheism that ever appeared. Christians ought to have the greatest Veneration for him, because he taught a higher Point of Virtue than Christ; I mean the Virtue of *Friendship*, which in the Sense we usually understand it, is not so much as named in the New Testament.

Plutarch was a *Free-thinker*, notwithstanding his being a

Priest; but indeed he was a *Heathen Priest*. His *Free-thinking* appears by shewing the Innocence of Atheism (which at worst is only false Reasoning) and the Mischiefs of Superstition; and explains what Superstition is, by calling it a Conceit of immortal Ills after Death, the Opinion of Hell Torments, dreadful Aspects, doleful Groans, and the like. He is likewise very Satyrical upon the publick Forms of Devotion in his own Country (a *Qualification* absolutely necessary to a *Free-thinker*) yet those Forms which he ridicules, are the very same that now pass for *true Worship* in almost all Countries: I am sure some of them do so in ours; such as abject Looks, Distortions, wry Faces, beggarly Tones, Humiliation, and Contrition.

Varro the most Learned among the *Romans* was a *Free-thinker*; for he said, the Heathen Divinity contained many Fables below the Dignity of Immortal Beings; such for Instance as Gods BEGOTTEN and PROCEEDING from other Gods. These two Words I desire you will particularly remark, because they are the very Terms made use of by our Priests in their Doctrine of the *Trinity:* He says likewise, that there are many Things false in Religion, and so say all *Free-thinkers*; but then he adds; *Which the Vulgar ought not to know, but it is Expedient they should believe.* In this last he indeed discovers the whole Secret of a Statesman and Politician, by denying the Vulgar the Priviledge of *Free-thinking*, and here I differ from him. However it is manifest from hence, that the *Trinity* was an Invention of Statesmen and Politicians.

The Grave and Wise *Cato* the Censor will for ever live in that noble *Free-thinking* Saying; I wonder, said he, how one of your Priests can forbear laughing when he sees another. (For Contempt of Priests is another grand Characteristick of a Free-thinker). This shews that *Cato* understood the whole Mystery of the *Roman* Religion, *as by Law Established.* I beg you Sir, not to overlook these last Words, *Religion as by Law Established.* I translate *Haruspex* into the general Word, *Priest:* Thus I apply the Sentence to our *Priests* in *England*, and when Dr. *Smalridge* sees Dr. *Atterbury*, I wonder how either of them can forbear laughing at the Cheat they put upon the People, by making them believe their *Religion as by Law Established*.

Cicero, that consummate Philosopher, and noble Patriot, though he were a *Priest*, and consequently more likely to be a *Knave*; gave the greatest Proofs of his *Free-thinking*. First, He professed the *Sceptick* Philosophy, which doubts of every thing. Then, he wrote two Treatises; in the first, he shews the Weakness of the *Stoicks* Arguments for the Being of the Gods: In the latter, he has destroyed the whole *reveal'd* Religion of the *Greeks* and *Romans* (for why should not theirs be a *reveal'd* Religion as well as that of Christ?) *Cicero* likewise tells us, as his own Opinion, that they who study Philosophy, do not believe there are any Gods: He denies the Immortality of the Soul, and says, there can be nothing after Death.

And because the Priests have the Impudence to quote *Cicero* in their Pulpits and Pamphlets, against *Free-thinking*; I am resolved to disarm them of his Authority. You must know, his Philosophical Works are generally in Dialogues, where People are brought in disputing against one another: Now the Priests when they see an Argument to prove a God, offered perhaps by a *Stoick*, are such Knaves or Blockheads, to quote it as if it were *Cicero*'s own; whereas *Cicero* was so noble a *Free-thinker*, that he believed nothing at all of the Matter, nor ever shews the least Inclination to favour Superstition, or the Belief of God, and the Immortality of the Soul; unless what he throws out sometimes to save himself from Danger, in his Speeches to the *Roman* Mob; whose Religion was, however, much more Innocent and less Absurd, than that of *Popery* at least: And I could say more,—but you understand me.

Seneca was a great *Free-thinker*, and had a noble Notion of the Worship of the Gods, for which our Priests would call any Man an Atheist: He laughs at Morning-Devotions, or Worshipping upon Sabbath-Days; he says God has no need of *Ministers* and *Servants*, because he himself *serves* Mankind. This religious Man, like his religious Brethren the *Stoicks*, denies the Immortality of the Soul, and says, all that is feign'd to be so terrible in Hell, is but a Fable: Death puts an end to all our Misery, *&c.* Yet the Priests were anciently so fond of

Seneca, that they forged a Correspondence of Letters between him and St. *Paul.*

Solomon himself, whose Writings are called the Word of God, was such a *Free Thinker,* that if he were now alive, nothing but his Building of Churches could have kept our Priests from calling him an Atheist. He affirms the Eternity of the World almost in the same manner with *Manilius* the *Heathen* Philosophical Poet (which Opinion entirely overthrows the History of the Creation by *Moses,* and all the *New Testament*): He denies the Immortality of the Soul, assures us that Men die like Beasts, and that both go to one Place.

The Prophets of the *Old Testament* were generally *Free Thinkers:* You must understand, that their way of learning to Prophesie was by *Musick* and *Drinking.* These Prophets writ against the *Established Religion* of the *Jews,* (which those People looked upon as the Institution of God himself) as if they believed it was all a Cheat: That is to say, with as great liberty against the Priests and Prophets of *Israel,* as Dr. *Tindall* did lately against the Priests and Prophets of our *Israel,* who has clearly shewn them and their Religion to be Cheats. To prove this, you may read several Passages in *Isaiah, Ezekiel, Amos, Jeremiah, &c.* wherein you will find such Instances of *Free Thinking,* that if any *Englishman* had talked so in our Days, their Opinions would have been Registred in Dr. *Sacheverell's* Tryal, and in the Representation of the Lower House of Convocation, and produced as so many Proofs of the Prophaneness, Blasphemy, and Atheism of the Nation; there being nothing more Prophane, Blasphemous, or Atheistical in those Representations, than what these Prophets have spoke, whose Writings are yet called by our Priests the *Word of God.* And therefore these Prophets are as much *Atheists* as my self, or as any of my Free-thinking Brethren, whom I lately named to you.

Josephus was a great *Free-thinker:* I wish he had chosen a better Subject to write on, than those ignorant, barbarous, ridiculous Scoundrels the *Jews,* whom God (if we may believe the Priests) thought fit to chuse for his own People. I will give you some Instances of his *Free-thinking.* He says, *Cain* travelled through several Countries, and kept Company with Rakes and profligate Fellows, he corrupted the Simplicities of former Times, *&c.* which plainly supposes Men before *Adam*, and consequently that the Priests' History of the Creation by *Moses*, is an Imposture. He says, the *Israelites* passing through the Red Sea, was no more than *Alexander*'s passing at the *Pamphilion* Sea; that as for the appearance of God at Mount *Sinai*, the Reader may believe it as he pleases; that *Moses* persuaded the *Jews*, he had God for his Guide, just as the *Greeks* pretended they had their Laws from *Apollo*. These are noble Strains of *Free Thinking*, which the Priests know not how to solve, but by *thinking* as *freely*; for one of them says, that *Josephus* writ this to make his Work acceptable to the *Heathen*, by striking out every thing that was incredible.

Origen, who was the first Christian that had any Learning, has left a noble Testimony of his *Free Thinking*; for a general Council has determined him to be damn'd; which plainly shews he was a *Free Thinker:* And was no *Saint*; for People were only Sainted because of their want of Learning and excess of Zeal; so that all the Fathers, who are called *Saints* by the Priests, were worse than Atheists.

Minutius Fælix seems to be a true, Modern, Latitudinarian, *Free Thinking* Christian, for he is against Altars, Churches, publick Preaching, and publick Assemblies; and likewise against Priests; for he says, there were several great flourishing Empires before there were any Orders of Priests in the World.

Synesius, who had too much Learning and too little Zeal for a *Saint*, was for some time a great *Free Thinker*; he could not believe the Resurrection till he was made a Bishop, and then pretended to be convinced by a Lying Miracle.

To come to our own Country: My Lord *Bacon* was a great *Free Thinker*, when he tells us, that whatever has the least Relation to Religion, is particularly liable to Suspicion, by which he seems to suspect all the Facts whereon most of the Superstitions (that is to say, what the Priests call the Religions) of the World are grounded. He also prefers Atheism before Superstition.

Mr. *Hobbs* was a Person of great Learning, Virtue and *Free Thinking*, except in his *High-Church* Politicks.

But *Arch Bishop Tillotson* is the Person whom all *English Free Thinkers* own as their Head; and his Virtue is indisputable for this manifest Reason, that Dr. *Hicks*, a Priest, calls him an Atheist; says, he caused several to turn Atheists, and to ridicule the Priesthood and Religion. These must be allowed to be noble effects of *Free Thinking*. This great Prelate assures us, that all the Duties of the Christian Religion, with respect to God, are no other but what natural Light prompts Men to, except the two Sacraments, and praying to God in the Name and Mediation of Christ: As a Priest and Prelate he was obliged to say something of Christianity; but pray observe, Sir, how he brings himself off. He justly affirms that even these things are of less Moment than natural Duties; and because Mothers nursing their Children is a natural Duty, it is of more Moment than the two Sacraments, or than praying to God in the Name and by the Mediation of Christ. This *Free Thinking* Archbishop could not allow a Miracle sufficient to give Credit to a Prophet who taught any thing contrary to our natural Notions: By which it is plain, he rejected at once all the Mysteries of Christianity.

I could name one and twenty more great Men, who were all *Free Thinkers*; but that I fear to be tedious. For, 'tis certain that all Men of Sense depart from the Opinions commonly received; and are consequently more or less Men of Sense, according as they depart more or less from the Opinions commonly received; neither can you name an Enemy to *Free Thinking*, however he be dignify'd or distinguish'd, whether *Archbishop*, *Bishop*, *Priest* or *Deacon*, who has not been either a *crack-brain'd Enthusiast*, a *diabolical Villain*, or a most *profound ignorant Brute*.

Thus, Sir, I have endeavour'd to execute your Commands, and you may print this Letter if you please; but I would have you conceal your Name, For my Opinion of Virtue is, that we ought not to venture doing our selves harm, by endeavouring to do good. I am

Yours, *&c.*

I have here given the Publick a brief, but faithful Abstract, of this most excellent Essay; wherein I have all along religiously adhered to our Author's Notions, and generally to his Words, without any other Addition than that of explaining a few necessary Consequences, for the sake of ignorant Readers; For, to those who have the least degree of Learning, I own they will be wholly useless. I hope I have not, in any single Instance, misrepresented the Thoughts of this admirable Writer. If I have happened to mistake through Inadvertency, I entreat he will condescend to inform me, and point out the Place, upon which I will immediately beg Pardon both of him and the World. The Design of his Piece is to recommend Free-thinking, *and one chief Motive is the Example of many Excellent Men who were of that Sect. He produces as the principal Points of their* Free-thinking; *That they denied the Being of a God, the Torments of Hell, the Immortality of the Soul, the Trinity, Incarnation, the History of the Creation by* Moses, *with many other such* fabulous and blasphemous *Stories, as he judiciously calls them: And he asserts, that whoever denies the most of these, is the compleatest* Free-thinker, *and consequently the wisest and most virtuous Man. The Author, sensible of the Prejudices of the Age, does not directly affirm himself an Atheist; he goes no further than to pronounce that Atheism is the most perfect degree of* Free-thinking; *and leaves the Reader to form the Conclusion. However, he seems to allow, that a Man may be a tolerable* Free-thinker, *tho' he does believe a God; provided he utterly rejects* Providence, Revelation, the Old and New Testament, Future Rewards *and* Punishments, *the* Immortality of the Soul, *and other the like impossible Absurdities. Which Mark of superabundant Caution, sacrificing* Truth *to the* Superstition *of* Priests, *may perhaps be* forgiven, *but ought not to be* imitated *by any who would arrive (even in this Author's Judgment) at the true Perfection of* Free-thinking.

FINIS.

SOME THOUGHTS ON FREE-THINKING

Discoursing one day with a prelate of the kingdom of Ireland, who is a person of excellent wit and learning, he offered a notion applicable to the subject, we were then upon, which I took to be altogether new and right. He said, that the difference betwixt a mad-man and one in his wits, in what related to speech, consisted in this: That the former spoke out whatever came into his mind, and just in the confused manner as his imagination presented the ideas. The latter only expressed such thoughts, as his judgment directed him to chuse, leaving the rest to die away in his memory. And that if the wisest man would at any time utter his thoughts, in the crude indigested manner, as they come into his head, he would be looked upon as raving mad. And indeed, when we consider our thoughts, as they are the seeds of words and actions, we cannot but agree, that they ought to be kept under the strictest regulation. And that in the great multiplicity of ideas, which ones mind is apt to form, there is nothing more difficult than to select those, which are most proper for the conduct of life: So that I cannot imagine what is meant by the mighty zeal in some people, for asserting the freedom of thinking: Because, if such thinkers keep their thoughts within their own breasts, they can be of no consequence, further than to themselves. If they publish them to the world, they ought to be answerable for the effects their thoughts produce upon others. There are thousands in this kingdom, who, in their thoughts prefer a republick or absolute power of a prince before a limited monarchy; yet, if any of these should publish their opinions, and go about, by writing or discourse, to persuade the people to innovations in government, they would be liable to the severest punishments the law can inflict, and therefore they are usually so wise as to keep their sentiments to themselves. But with respect to religion, the matter is quite otherwise And the publick, at least here in England, seems to be of opinion with Tiberius, that *Deorum injurias diis curæ*. They leave it to God Almighty to vindicate the injuries done to himself, who is no doubt sufficiently able, by perpetual miracles, to revenge the affronts of impious men. And it should seem, that this is what princes expect from him, though I cannot readily conceive the grounds they go upon: Nor why, since they are God's vice-gerents, they do not think themselves at least equally obliged to preserve their master's honour, as their own. Since this is what they expect from those they depute, and since they never fail to represent the disobedience of their subjects, as offences against God: It is true, the visible reason of this neglect is obvious enough. The consequences of atheistical opinions published to the world, are not so immediate or so sensible, as doctrines of rebellion and sedition, spread in a proper season: However, I cannot but think the same consequences are as natural and probable for the former, though more remote. And whether these have not been in view among our great planters of infidelity in England, I shall hereafter examine.

A Preface to the Right Reverend Dr. Burnet, Bishop of Sarum's Introduction

A
PREFACE
TO THE
B----p of *S--r--m's*
INTRODUCTION

To the Third Volume of the

History of the Reformation

OF THE

Church of *England*.

By *GREGORY MISOSARVM.*

―――*Spargere voces*
In vulgum ambiguas; & quærere conscius arma.

LONDON:
Printed for *John Morphew,* near Stationers
Hall, 1713. Price 6 d.

A

PREFACE

To the RIGHT REVEREND

Dr. *Burnet*, Bishop of *Sarum*'s

INTRODUCTION

To the THIRD VOLUME of the

HISTORY of the REFORMATION,

OF THE

CHURCH of *England*.

———

———— *Spargere voces*
In vulgum ambiguas ; & quærere conscius arma.

———

WRITTEN in the YEAR, 1712.

═══════════

DUBLIN:
Printed by and for GEORGE FAULKNER.
MDCCXXXVII

THE
PREFACE.

Mr. Morphew,

YOUR *Care in putting an Advertisement in the* Examiner *hath been of very great Use to me. I do now send you my Preface to the Bishop of Sarum's* Introduction *to his third Volume, which I desire you to print in such a Form, as in the Bookseller's Phrase, will make a* Sixpenny Touch; *hoping, it will give such a publick Notice of my Design, that it may come into the Hands of those who perhaps look not into the Bishop's* Introduction. *I desire you will prefix to this a Passage out of* Virgil, *which doth so perfectly agree with my present Thoughts of his Lordship, that I cannot express them better, nor more truly than those Words do.*

I am, Sir,

Your humble Servant,

G. Misosarum.

A

PREFACE

Dr. *Burnet*, Bishop of *Sarum*'s

INTRODUCTION.

THIS Way of publishing Introductions to Books that are, God knows when, to come out, is either wholly new, or so long unpracticed, that my small Reading cannot trace it: However, we are to suppose, that a Person of his Lordship's great Age and Experience, would hardly act such a Piece of Singularity, without some extraordinary Motives. I cannot but observe, that his Fellow-Labourer, the Author of the Paper, called, * *The English Man*, seems, in some of his late Performances, to have almost transcribed the Notions of the Bishop: These Notions, I take to have been dictated by the same Masters, leaving to each Writer that peculiar Manner of expressing himself, which the Poverty of our Language forceth me to call their Stile. When the *Guardian* changed his Title, and professed to engage in Faction, I was sure the Word was given, that grand Preparations were making against next Sessions: That, all Advantages would be taken of the little Dissentions reported to be among those in Power; and, that the *Guardian* would soon be seconded by some other Piquerers from the same Camp. But I will confess, my Suspicions did not carry me so far, as to conjecture, that this venerable Champion would be in such mighty Haste to come into the Field, and

* *Mr.* Steele.

serve in the Quality of an *Enfant perdu*, armed only with a *Pocket Pistol*, before his great *Blunderbuss* could be got ready, his old rusty *Breast-Plate* scoured, and his *cracked Head-piece* mended.

I was debating with my self, whether this Hint of producing a small Pamphlet to give Notice of a large Folio, were not borrowed from the Ceremonial in *Spanish* Romances, where a *Dwarf* is sent out upon the Battlements, to signify to all Passengers, what a mighty *Giant* there is in the Castle: Or, whether the Bishop copied this Proceeding from the *Fanfaronnade* of Monsieur *Bouffleurs*, when the Earl of *Portland* and that General had an Interview. Several Men were appointed at certain Periods to ride in great Haste towards the *English* Camp, and cry out, *Monseigneur vient, Monseigneur vient:* Then, small Parties advanced with the same Speed, and the same Cry; and this Foppery held for many Hours, until the *Mareschal* himself arrived. So here, the Bishop (as we find by his Dedication to Mr. *Churchill* the Bookseller) hath for a long Time sent Warning of his Arrival, by Advertisements in *Gazettes*; and now his Introduction advanceth to tell us again, *Monseigneur vient:* In the mean Time, we must gape, and wait, and gaze, the Lord knows how long, and keep our Spirits in some reasonable Agitation, until his Lordship's real self shall think fit to appear in the Habit of a Folio.

I have seen the same Sort of Management at a Puppet Show. Some Puppets of little or no Consequence appeared several Times at the Window, to allure the Boys and the Rabble: The Trumpeter sounded often, and the Door-keeper cried an hundred Times, until he was Hoarse, that they were just going to begin; yet after all, we were forced some Times to wait an Hour before *Punch* himself in Person made his Entry.

But why this Ceremony among old Acquaintance? The World and he have long known one another: Let him appoint his Hour and make his Visit, without troubling us all Day with a Succession of Messages from his Lacqueys and Pages.

With Submission, these little Arts of getting off an Edition, do ill become any Author above the Size of *Marten* the Surgeon.

My Lord tells us, That *many thousands of the two former Parts of his History are in the Kingdom*; and now he perpetually *advertiseth in the Gazette*, that he intends to publish the Third: This is exactly in the Method and Stile of *Marten: The seventh Edition (many thousands of the former Editions having been sold off in a small Time)* of Mr. Marten's *Book concerning secret Diseases, &c.*

DOTH his Lordship intend to publish his great Volume by Subscription, and is this Introduction only by Way of Specimen? I was inclined to think so, because in the prefixed Letter to Mr. *Churchill*, which *introduces* this *Introduction*, there are some dubious Expressions: He says, *The Advertisements he published, were in order to move People to furnish him with* Materials *which might help him to finish his Work* with great *Advantage*. If he means half a Guinea upon the Subscription, and the other Half at the Delivery, why doth he not tell us so in plain Terms?

I AM wondering how it came to pass, that this diminutive Letter to Mr. *Churchill*, should understand the Business of *introducing* better than the *Introduction* it self; or why the Bishop did not take it into his Head to send the former into the World some Months before the latter; which would have been yet a greater Improvement upon the Solemnity of the Procession.

SINCE I writ these last Lines, I have perused the whole Pamphlet (which I had only dipt in before) and found I have been hunting upon a wrong Scent; for the Author hath in several Parts of his Piece, discovered the true Motives, which put him upon sending it abroad at this Juncture; I shall therefore consider them as they come in my Way.

MY Lord begins his *Introduction* with an Account of the Reasons, why he was guilty of so many Mistakes in the first Volume of his History of the Reformation: His Excuses are just, rational, and extremely consistent. He says, *He wrote in Haste*, which he confirms by adding, *That it lay a Year after he wrote it, before it was put into the* Press: At the same Time he mentions a Passage extremely to the Honour of that pious and excellent Prelate, Archbishop *Sancroft*, which demonstrates his Grace to have been a Person of great Sagacity, and almost a Prophet. Doctor *Burnet*, then a private Divine, *desired admittance to the Cotton Library, but was prevented by the Archbishop, who told Sir* John Cotton, *that the said Doctor was no Friend to the Prerogative of the Crown, or to the Constitution of the Kingdom.* This Judgment was the more extraordinary, because the Doctor had not long before published a Book in *Scotland*, with his Name prefixed, which carries the Regal Prerogative higher than any Writer of the Age: However, the good Archbishop lived to see his Opinion become universal in the Kingdom.

THE Bishop goes on for many Pages, with an Account of certain Facts relating to the publishing his two former Volumes of the Reformation; the great Success of that Work, and the Adversaries who appeared against it. These are Matters out of the Way of my Reading; only I observe that poor Mr. *Henry Wharton*, who hath deserved so well of the Commonwealth of Learning, and who gave himself the Trouble of detecting some Hundreds of the Bishop's Mistakes, meets very ill Quarter from his Lordship. Upon which I cannot avoid mentioning a peculiar Method which this Prelate takes to revenge himself upon those who presume to differ from him in Print. The present * Bishop of *Rochester* happened some Years ago to be of this Number. My Lord of *Sarum* in his Reply ventured to tell the World, that the Gentleman who had writ against him, meaning Dr. *Atterbury*, was one upon whom he had conferred great Obligations; which was a very generous Christian Contrivance of charging his Adversary with Ingratitude. But it seems, the Truth happened to be on the other Side, which the Doctor made appear in such a Manner as would have silenced his Lordship for ever, if he had not been Writing-proof. Poor Mr. *Wharton* in his Grave, is charged with the same Accusation, but with Circumstances the most aggravating that Malice and something else could invent; and which I will no more believe, than five hundred Passages in a certain Book of Travels. See the Character he gives of a Divine, and a Scholar, who shortened his Life in the Service of GOD and the Church. *Mr.* Wharton *desired me to intercede with* Tillotson *for a*

* Dr. ATTERBURY.

Prebend of Canterbury. *I did so, but* Wharton *would not believe it*; *said he would be revenged, and so writ against me. Soon after he was convinced I had spoke for him, said he was set on to do what he did, and if I would procure any Thing for him, he would discover every Thing to me.* What a Spirit of Candor, Charity, and good Nature, Generosity, and Truth, shines through this Story, told of a most excellent and pious Divine, twenty Years after his Death, without one single Voucher!

COME we now to the Reasons which moved his Lordship to set about this Work at this Time. *He could delay it no longer, because the Reasons of his engaging in it at first, seemed to return upon him.* He was then frightened with *the Danger of a Popish Successor in View, and the dreadful Apprehensions of the Power of* France. England *hath forgot these Dangers*, and yet is *nearer to them than ever*, and therefore he is resolved to *awaken them* with his third Volume; but in the mean Time, sends this Introduction to let them know they are asleep. He then goes on in describing the Condition of the Kingdom after such a Manner as if Destruction hung over us by a single Hair; as if the *Pope*, the *Devil*, the *Pretender*, and *France*, were just at our Doors.

WHEN the Bishop published his History, there was a *Popish* Plot on Foot: The Duke of *York*, a known *Papist*, was presumptive Heir to the Crown; the House of Commons would not hear of any Expedients for securing their Religion under a *Popish* Prince, nor would the King or Lords consent to a Bill of Exclusion: The *French* King was in the Height of his Grandeur, and the Vigour of his Age. At this Day the Presumptive Heir, with that whole illustrious Family, are *Protestants*; the *Popish Pretender* excluded for ever by several Acts of Parliament; and every Person in the smallest Employment, as well as Member in both Houses, obliged to *abjure* him. The *French* King is at the lowest Ebb of Life; his Armies have been conquered, and his Towns won from him for ten Years together; and his Kingdom is in Danger of being torn by Divisions during a long Minority. Are these Cases Parallel? Or are we now in more Danger of *France* and *Popery* than we were thirty Years ago? What can be the Motive for advancing such false, such detestable Assertions? What Conclusions would his Lordship draw from such Premises as these? If injurious Appellations were of any Advantage to a Cause, (as the Stile of our Adversaries would make us believe) what Appellations would those deserve, who thus endeavour to sow the Seeds of Sedition, and are impatient to see the Fruits? *But,* saith he, *the deaf Adder stops her Ear, let the Charmer charm never so wisely.* True, my Lord, there are indeed too many *Adders* in this Nation's Bosom; *Adders* in all Shapes, and in all Habits, whom neither the *Queen* nor Parliament, can *charm* to Loyalty, Truth, Religion, or Honour.

AMONG other Instances produced by him of the dismal Condition we are in, he offers one which could not easily be guessed. It is this, *That the little factious Pamphlets written about the End of King* Charles II. *Reign, lie dead in Shops, are looked on as waste Paper, and turned to Pasteboard.* How many are there of his Lordship's Writing, which could otherwise never have been of any real Service to the Publick? Hath he indeed so mean an Opinion of our Taste, to send us at this Time of Day into all the Corners of *Holborn, Duck-Lane,* and *Moorfields,* in quest after the factious Trash, published in those Days by *Julian Johnson, Hickeringil,* Dr. *Oates,* and himself?

HIS Lordship taking it for a *Postulatum,* that the QUEEN and Ministry, both Houses of Parliament, and a vast Majority of the Landed Gentlemen throughout *England,* are running headlong into *Popery,* layeth hold on the Occasion to describe *the Cruelties in Queen* MARY's *Reign: An Inquisition setting up, Faggots in* Smithfield, *and Executions all over the Kingdom.* Here *is that,* says he, *which those that look towards a Popish Successor must look for.* And he insinuates, through his whole Pamphlet, that all who are not of his Party, *look towards a Popish Successor.* These he divides into two Parts, the *Tory* Laity, and the *Tory* Clergy. He tells the former, *Although they have no Religion at all, but resolve to change with every Wind and Tide; yet they ought to have Compassion on their Countrymen and Kindred.* Then he applies himself to the *Tory* Clergy, assures them, that *the Fires revived in* Smithfield, *and all over the Nation, will have no amiable View; but least of all to them, who if they have any Principles at all, must be turned out of their Livings, leave their Families, be hunted from Place to Place, into Parts beyond the Seas, and meet with that Contempt, with which they treated Foreigners who took Sanctuary among us.*

THIS requires a Recapitulation, with some Remarks. First, I do affirm, that in every hundred of professed *Atheists, Deists* and *Socinians* in the Kingdom, ninety-nine at least, are stanch thorow-paced *Whigs*, entirely agreeing with his Lordship in Politicks and Discipline; and therefore will venture all the Fires of Hell rather than singe one Hair of their Beards in *Smithfield.* Secondly, I do likewise affirm; That those whom we usually understand by the Appellation of *Tory* or Highchurch Clergy, were the greatest Sticklers against the exorbitant Proceedings of King *James* the Second, the best Writers against Popery, and the most exemplary Sufferers for the Established Religion. Thirdly, I do pronounce it to be a most false and infamous Scandal upon the Nation in General, and on the Clergy in particular, to reproach them for *treating Foreigners with Haughtiness and Contempt:* The *French Hugonots* are many thousand Witnesses to the contrary; and, I wish, they deserved a thousandth Part of the good Treatment they have received.

LASTLY, I observe that the Author of a Paper, called, *The Englishman*, hath run into the same Cant, gravely advising the whole Body of the Clergy, not to bring in *Popery*, because that will put them under a Necessity of parting with their Wives, or losing their Livings.

THE Bulk of the Kingdom, both Clergy and Layety, happen to differ extremely from this Prelate in many Principles, both of Politicks and Religion: Now I ask, Whether if any Man of them had signed their Name to a System of *Atheism* or *Popery*, he could have argued with them otherways than he doth? Or, if I should write a grave Letter to his Lordship with the same Advice, taking it for granted, that he was half an *Atheist* and half a *Papist*, and conjuring him, by all he held dear, to have Compassion upon all those who believed a God, *not to* revive the Fires in Smithfield, *that he must either forfeit his*

Bishoprick, or not marry a fourth Wife; I ask, Whether he would not think I intended him the highest Injury and Affront?

BUT as to the *Tory* Layety, he gives them up in a Lump for abandoned Atheists: They are a Set of Men so *impiously corrupted in the Point of Religion that no Scene of Cruelty can fright them from leaping into it* (Popery) *and perhaps acting such a Part in it, as may be assigned them.* He therefore despairs of influencing them by any Topicks drawn from Religion or Compassion, and advances the Consideration of *Interest*, as the only powerful Argument to persuade them against *Popery.*

WHAT he offers upon this Head is so very amazing from a *Christian,* a *Clergyman,* and a *Prelate* of the *Church of England,* that I must in my own Imagination, strip him of those three Capacities, and put him among the Number of *that Set of Men* he mentions in the Paragraph before; or else it will be impossible to shape out an Answer.

HIS Lordship, in order to dissuade the *Tories* from their Design of bringing in *Popery,* tells them, *How valuable a Part of the whole Soil of* England, *the Abbey Lands, the Estates of the Bishops, of the Cathedrals, and the Tythes are:* How difficult such a *Resumption would be to many Families; yet all these must be thrown up; for, Sacrilege in the Church of* Rome, *is a mortal Sin.* I desire it may be observed, What a Jumble here is made of Ecclesiastical Revenues, as if they were all upon the same Foot, were alienated with equal Justice; and the Clergy had no more Reason to complain of one than the other. Whereas, the four Branches mentioned by him, are of very different Consideration. If I might venture to guess the Opinion of the Clergy upon this Matter, I believe they could wish, that some small Part of the *Abbey Lands* had been applied to the Augmentation of poor Bishopricks; and a very few Acres to serve for Glebes in those Parishes where there are none; after which, I think they would not repine that the Laity should possess the rest. If the Estates of some Bishops and Cathedrals were exorbitant before the Reformation, I believe the present Clergy's Wishes reach no further, than that some reasonable Temper had been used, instead of paring them to the Quick: But, as to the *Tythes,* without examining whether they be of divine Institution, I conceive there is hardly one of that sacred Order in *England*, and very few even among the Layety who love the Church, who will not allow the misapplying those Revenues to secular Persons, to have been at first a most flagrant Act of Injustice and Oppression: Although at the same Time, God forbid they should be restored any other Way, than by gradual Purchase, by the Consent of those who are now the lawful Possessors, or by the Piety and Generosity of such worthy Spirits, as this Nation sometimes produceth. The Bishop knows very well, that the Application of *Tythes* to the Maintenance of Monasteries, was a scandalous Usurpation, even in Popish Times: That the Monks usually sent out some of their Fraternity to supply the Cures; and that, when the Monasteries were granted away by *Henry* VIII. the Parishes were left destitute, or very meanly provided of any Maintenance for a Pastor. So that in many Places the whole Ecclesiastical Dues, even to *Mortuaries*, *Easter-Offerings*, and the like, are in Lay-Hands, and the Incumbent lieth wholly at the Mercy of his Patron for his daily Bread. By these Means there are several hundred Parishes in *England* under 20 l. a Year, and many under Ten. I take his Lordship's Bishoprick to be worth near 2500*l.* annual Income; and I will engage, at half a Year's Warning, to find him above 100 beneficed Clergy-men who have not so much among them all to support themselves and their Families; most of them Orthodox, of good Life and Conversation; as loath to see the Fires kindled in *Smithfield*, as his Lordship; and, at least, as ready to face them under a *Popish* Persecution. But nothing is so hard for those, who abound in Riches, as to conceive how others can be in Want. How can the neighbouring Vicar feel Cold or Hunger, while my Lord is seated by a good Fire in the warmest Room of his Palace, with a dozen Dishes before him? I remember one other Prelate much of the same Stamp, who, when his Clergy would mention their Wishes, that some Act of Parliament might be thought of for the Good of the Church; would say, *Gentlemen*, WE *are very well as* WE *are; if they would let* US *alone,* WE *should ask no more.*

SACRILEGE (says my Lord) *in the Church of* Rome, *is a*

mortal Sin: And is it only so in the *Church* of *Rome?* Or, is it but a venial Sin in the Church of *England?* Our Litany calls *Fornication a deadly Sin;* and, I would appeal to his Lordship for fifty Years past, whether he thought that or *Sacrilege* the *deadliest.* To make light of such a Sin, at the same Moment that he is frighting us from an idolatrous Religion, should seem not very consistent. THOU *that sayest, a Man should not commit Adultery, dost* THOU *commit Adultery?* THOU *that abhorrest Idols, dost thou commit Sacrilege?*

To smooth the Way for the Return of Popery in Queen *Mary's* Time, the Grantees were confirmed by the *Pope* in the Possession of the Abbey-Lands. But the Bishop tells us, that *this Confirmation was fraudulent and invalid.* I shall believe it to be so, although I happen to read it in his Lordship's History: But he adds, *that although the Confirmation had been good, the Priests would have got their Lands again, by these two Methods:* First, *The Statute of Mortmain was repealed for twenty Years, in which time, no doubt they reckoned they would recover the best Part of what they had lost: Beside; that engaging the Clergy to renew no Leases, was a thing entirely in their own Power; and this in forty Years time, would raise their Revenues to be about ten times their present Value.* These two Expedients for encreasing the Revenues of the *Church,* he represents as pernicious Designs, fit only to be practised in Times of *Popery,* and such as the Laity ought never to consent to: From whence, and from what he said before about Tithes, his Lordship hath freely declared his Opinion, that the Clergy are rich enough, and that the least Addition to their Subsistence would be a Step towards *Popery.* Now it happens, that the two only Methods which could ever be thought on, with any Probability of Success, towards some reasonable Augmentation of Ecclesiastical Revenues, are here rejected by a Bishop, as a Means for introducing Popery; and the Nation publickly warned against them. Whereas, the Continuance of the Statute of *Mortmain* in full Force, after the Church had been so terribly stripped, appeared to her Majesty and the Kingdom a very unnecessary Hardship; upon which Account it was at several times *relaxed* by the Legislature. Now, as the Relaxation of that Statute is manifestly one of the

Reasons which gives the Bishop those terrible Apprehensions of Popery coming on us; so I conceive another Ground of his Fears, is the Remission of the First-Fruits and Tenths. But where the Inclination to Popery lay, whether in her Majesty, who proposed this Benefaction, the Parliament which confirmed, or the Clergy who accepted it, his Lordship hath not thought fit to determine.

THE other Popish Expedient for augmenting Church Revenues, is *engaging the Clergy to renew no Leases.* Several of the most eminent Clergymen have assured me, that nothing hath been more wished for by good Men, than a Law to prevent (at least) Bishops from setting Leases for Lives. I could name ten Bishopricks in *England*, whose Revenues, one with another do not amount to 600*l.* a Year for each: And, if his Lordship's, for Instance, would be above ten times the Value, when the Lives are expired, I should think the Overplus would not be ill disposed towards an Augmentation of such as are now shamefully poor. But I do assert, That such an Expedient was not always thought Popish and Dangerous by this Right Reverend Historian. I have had the Honour formerly to converse with him; and he hath told me several Years ago, that he lamented extremely the Power which Bishops had of letting Leases for Lives; whereby, as he said, they were utterly deprived of raising their Revenues, whatever Alterations might happen in the Value of Money by Length of Time: I think the Reproach of betraying private Conversation, will not, upon this Account, be laid to my Charge. Neither do I believe he would have changed his Opinion upon any Score, but to take up another more agreeable to the Maxims of his Party; that *the least Addition of Property to the Church, is one Step towards Popery.*

THE Bishop goes on with much Earnestness and Prolixity to prove, That the *Pope*'s Confirmation of the *Church Lands* to those who held them by King *Henry*'s Donation, was null and fraudulent, which is a Point that I believe no *Protestant* in *England* would give three Pence to have his Choice, whether it should be true or false: It might indeed serve as a Passage in his History, among a thousand other Instances, to detect the Knavery of the Court of *Rome:* But I ask, Where could be the Use of it in this Introduction? Or, why all this Haste in publishing it at this Juncture; and so out of all Method, apart, and before the Work it self? He gives his Reasons in very plain Terms, We are now, it seems, *in more Danger of Popery than towards the End of King* Charles *the Second's Reign. That Set of Men* (the Tories) *is so impiously corrupted in the Point of Religion, that no Scene of Cruelty can fright them from leaping into it, and perhaps from acting such a Part in it as may be assigned them.* He doubts whether the High Church Clergy have any Principles, and therefore will be ready to turn off their Wives, and look on the Fires kindled in *Smithfield* as an *amiable View.* These are the Facts he all along takes for granted, and argues accordingly: Therefore in Despair of dissuading the Nobility and Gentry of the Land, from introducing *Popery* by any Motives of Honour, Religion, Alliance or Mercy, he assures them, *that the Pope hath not duly confirmed their Tythes to the Church Lands in their Possession;* which therefore must be infallibly restored, as soon as that Religion is established among us.

THUS, in his Lordship's Opinion, there is nothing wanting to make the Majority of the Kingdom, both for Number, Quality and Possession, immediately embrace *Popery,* except a *firm Bull from the Pope* to secure the Abbey and other Church Lands and Tythes to the present Proprietors and their Heirs: If this only Difficulty could now be adjusted, the Pretender would be restored next Session, the two Houses reconciled to the Church of *Rome* against *Easter* Term, and the Fires lighted in *Smithfield* by *Midsummer.* Such horrible Calumnies against a Nation are not the less injurious to Decency, Good Nature, Truth, Honour, and Religion, because they may be vented with Safety: And I will appeal to any Reader of common Understanding, whether this be not the most natural and necessary Deduction from the Passages I have cited and referred to.

YET, all this is but friendly Dealing, in Comparison with what he affords the Clergy upon the same Article. He supposes that whole Reverend Body, who differ from him in Principles of *Church* or *State,* so far from disliking *Popery,* upon the above mentioned Motives *of Perjury, quitting their Wives, or burning their Relations:* That, the Hopes of *enjoying the Abbey Lands* would soon bear down all such Considerations, and be an effectual Incitement to their Perversion: And so he goes gravely on, as with the only Argument, which he thinks can have any Force, to assure them; that *the Parochial Priests in Roman Catholick Countries are much poorer than in ours; the several Orders of Regulars, and the Magnificence of their Church, devouring all their Treasure;* and by Consequence, *their Hopes are vain of expecting to be richer after the Introduction of Popery.*

BUT after all, his Lordship despairs, that even this Argument will have any Force with our abominable Clergy, because, to use his own Words, *They are an insensible and degenerate Race, who are thinking of nothing but their present Advantages: And so that they may now support a luxurious and brutal Course of irregular and voluptuous Practices, they are easily hired to betray their Religion, to sell their Country, and to give up that Liberty and those Properties, which are the present Felicities and Glories of this Nation.*

HE seems to reckon all these Evils as Matters fully determined on, and therefore falls into the last usual Forms of Despair, by threatning the Authors of these Miseries with *lasting Infamy, and the Curses of Posterity upon perfidious Betrayers of their Trust.*

LET me turn this Paragraph into vulgar Language *for the Use of the Poor;* and strictly adhere to the Sense of the Words. I believe it may be faithfully translated in the following Manner, *The Bulk of the Clergy, and one Third of the Bishops are stupid Sons of Whores, who think of nothing but getting Money as soon as they can: If they may but procure enough to supply them in Gluttony, Drunkenness, and Whoring, they are ready to turn Traytors to* GOD *and their Country, and make their Fellow Subjects Slaves.* The rest of the Period about threatning Infamy and the Curses of Posterity upon such Dogs and Villains, may stand as it doth in the Bishop's own Phrase; and so make the Paragraph all of a Piece.

I WILL engage on the other Side, to paraphrase all the *Rogues* and *Rascals* in the *Englishman,* so as to bring them up exactly to his Lordship's Stile: But, for my own Part, I much prefer the plain *Billingsgate* Way of calling Names, because it expresseth our Meaning full as well, and would save abundance of Time which is lost by Circumlocution: So, for Instance, *John Dunton*, who is retained on the *same Side* with the Bishop, calls my *Lord Treasurer* and *Lord Bolingbroke*, Traytors, Whoremongers, and Jacobites; which three Words cost our Right Reverend Author thrice as many Lines to define them; and I hope his Lordship doth not think there is any Difference in point of Morality, whether a Man calls me *Traitor* in one Word, or says I am one *hired to betray my Religion, and sell my Country*.

I AM not surprized to see the Bishop mention with Contempt all Convocations of the Clergy; For *Toland, Asgil, Molesworth, Collins, Tindal*, and others of the Fraternity, talk the very same Language. His Lordship confesseth, he *is not* inclined *to expect much from the Assemblies of Clergymen*. There lies the Misfortune: For, if he and some more of his Order would correct their *Inclinations*, a great deal of Good might be expected from such Assemblies; as much as they are now cramped by that Submission, which a corrupt Clergy brought upon their innocent Successors. He *will not deny that his Copiousness in these Matters is, in his own Opinion, one of the meanest Parts of his new Work*. I will agree with him, unless he happens to be more *copious* in any Thing else. However, it is not easy to conceive why he should be so *copious* upon a Subject he so much despiseth, unless it were to gratify his Talent of railing at the *Clergy*, in the Number of whom he disdains to be reckoned, because he is a *Bishop:* For, it is a Stile I observe some Prelates have fallen into of late Years, to talk of Clergymen, as if themselves were not of the Number: You will read in many of their Speeches at Dr. *Sacheverell*'s Tryal, Expressions to this or the like Effect: *My Lords, if Clergymen be suffered, &c.* wherein they seem to have Reason: And I am pretty confident, that a great Majority of the Clergy were heartily inclined to disown any Relation they had to the *Managers in Lawn*. However, it was a confounding Argument against *Presbytery*, to see those Prelates, who are most suspected to lean that Way, treating their inferior Brethren with *Haughtiness, Rigour*, and *Contempt*; although to say the Truth, nothing better could be hoped for;

because, I believe, it may pass for an universal Rule, that in every Diocese governed by Bishops of the Whig Species, the Clergy (especially the poorer Sort) are under double Discipline; and the Layety left to themselves. The Opinion of Sir *Thomas More*, which he produceth to prove the ill Consequences or Insignificancy of Convocations, advanceth no such Thing; but says, *If the Clergy assembled often, and might act as other Assemblies of Clergy in Christendom, much Good might have come:* But the Misfortune lay *in their long Disuse, and that in his own, and a good Part of his Father's Time, they never came together, except at the Command of the Prince.*

I suppose his Lordship thinks, there is some original Impediment in the Study of Divinity, or secret Incapacity in a Gown and Cassock *without Lawn*, which disqualifies all inferior Clergymen from debating upon Subjects of Doctrine or Discipline in the Church. It is a famous Saying of his, *That he looks upon every Layman to be an honest Man, until he is by Experience convinced to the contrary: And on every Clergyman as a Knave, until he finds him to be an honest Man.* What Opinion then must he have of a lower House of Convocation; where, I am confident he will hardly find three Persons that ever convinced him of their Honesty, or will ever be at the Pains to do it? Nay, I am afraid they would think such a Conviction might be no very advantageous Bargain, to gain the Character of an honest Man with his Lordship, and lose it with the rest of the World.

In the famous *Concordate* that was made between *Francis* I. of *France*, and Pope *Leo* X. the Bishop tells us, that *the King and Pope came to a Bargain, by which they divided the Liberties of the* Gallican *Church between them, and indeed quite enslaved it.* He intends, in the third Part of his History which he is going to publish, *to open this whole Matter to the World.* In the mean Time, he mentions some ill Consequences to the *Gallican* Church from that *Concordate*, which are worthy to be observed; *the Church of France became a Slave, and this Change in their Constitution put an End, not only to National, but even to Provincial Synods in that Kingdom. The Assemblies of the Clergy there, meet now only to give Subsidies,* &c. and he says, *our Nation may see by that*

Proceeding, what it is to deliver up the essential Liberties of a free Constitution to a Court.

ALL I can gather from this Matter is, That our King *Henry* made a better Bargain than his Contemporary *Francis*, who divided the Liberties of the Church between himself and the Pope, while the King of *England* seized them all to himself. But, how comes he to number the Want of Synods in the *Gallican* Church, among the Grievances of that *Concordate*, and as a Mark of their Slavery, since he reckons all Convocations of the Clergy in *England* to be useless and dangerous? Or, what Difference in Point of Liberty was there between the *Gallican* Church under *Francis*, and the *English* under *Harry*? For, the latter was as much a Papist as the former, unless in the Point of Obedience to the See of *Rome*; and in every Quality of a good Man, or a good Prince (except personal Courage wherein both were equal) the *French* Monarch had the Advantage by as many Degrees as is possible for one Man to have over another.

HENRY VIII. had no Manner of Intention to change Religion in his Kingdom; he continued to persecute and burn Protestants after he had cast off the *Pope*'s Supremacy: And, I suppose, his Seizure of Ecclesiastical Revenues (which *Francis* never attempted) cannot be reckoned as a Mark of the Church's *Liberty*. By the Quotations the Bishop sets down to shew the Slavery of the *French* Church, he represents it as a Grievance, that *Bishops are not now elected there as formerly, but wholly appointed by the Prince; and that those made by the Court have been ordinarily the chief Advancers of Schisms, Heresies, and Oppressions of the Church.* He cites another Passage from a *Greek* Writer, and plainly insinuates, that it is justly applicable to her Majesty's Reign: *Princes chuse such Men to that Charge* (of a Bishop) *who may be their Slaves, and in all Things obsequious to what they prescribe; and may lie at their Feet, and have not so much as a Thought contrary to their Commands.*

THESE are very singular Passages for his Lordship to set down in order to shew the dismal Consequences of the *French Concordate*, by the Slavery of the *Gallican* Church, compared with the Freedom of ours. I shall not enter into a long

Dispute, whether it were better for Religion, that Bishops should be chosen by the Clergy, or People, or both together: I believe our Author would give his Vote for the second: (which however would not have been of much Advantage to himself and some others that I could name.) But I ask, whether Bishops are any more elected in *England* than in *France?* And the Want of Synods are in his own Opinion, rather a Blessing than a Grievance, unless he will affirm, that more Good can be expected from a Popish Synod, than an *English* Convocation. Did the *French* Clergy ever receive a greater Blow to their Liberties, than the Submission made to *Henry* VIII. or so great a one as the Seizure of their Lands? The Reformation owed nothing to the good Intentions of King *Henry:* He was only an Instrument of it, (as the Logicians speak) by Accident; nor doth he appear throughout his whole Reign, to have had any other Views, than those of gratifying his insatiable Love of Power, Cruelty, Oppression, and other irregular Appetites. But this Kingdom, as well as many other Parts of *Europe*, was at that Time generally weary of the Corruptions and Impositions of the *Roman* Court and Church; and disposed to receive those Doctrines, which *Luther* and his Followers had universally spread. *Cranmer* the Archbishop, *Cromwell*, and others of the Court, did secretly embrace the Reformation; and the King's abrogating the *Pope*'s Supremacy, made the People in general run into the new Doctrines with greater Freedom, because they hoped to be supported in it, by the *Authority and Example* of their *Prince*; who disappointed them so far, that he made no other Step, than rejecting the *Pope*'s Supremacy, as a Clog upon his own Power and Passions; but retained every Corruption beside, and became a cruel Persecutor, as well of those who denied his own Supremacy, as of all others who professed any Protestant Doctrine. Neither hath any Thing disgusted me more in reading the Histories of those Times, than to see one of the worst Princes of any Age or Country, celebrated as an Instrument in that glorious Work of the Reformation.

THE Bishop having gone over all the Matters, that properly fall within his *Introduction*, proceeds to expostulate with several

H

Sorts of People: First, with *Protestants*, who are no *Christians*, such as *Atheists, Deists, Free-thinkers*, and the like Enemies to Christianity: But these he treats with the Tenderness of a Friend, because they are all of them of sound Whig-Principles in Church and State. However, to do him Justice, he lightly toucheth some old Topicks for the Truth of the Gospel; and concludes by *wishing that the* Freethinkers *would consider well, If* (Anglice, whether) *they think it is possible to bring a Nation to be without any Religion at all*; *and what the Consequences of that may prove*; and, in Case they allow the Negative, he gives it clearly for Christianity.

SECONDLY, He applieth himself (if I take his Meaning right) to Christian Papists, *who have a Taste of Liberty*; and desires them to *compare the Absurdities of their own Religion with the Reasonableness of the Reformed:* Against which, as good Luck would have it, I have nothing to object.

THIRDLY, He is somewhat rough against his own Party; *who having tasted the Sweets of Protestant Liberty, can look back so tamely on Popery coming on them*; it looks as if they were bewitched, or that the Devil were in them, to be so negligent. *It is not enough, that they resolve not to turn Papists themselves: They ought to awaken all about them, even the most ignorant and stupid, to apprehend their Danger, and to exert themselves with their utmost Industry to guard against it, and to resist it. If after all their Endeavours to prevent it, the Corruption of the Age, and the Art and Power of our Enemies, prove too hard for us; then, and not until then, we must submit to the Will of* GOD, *and be silent; and prepare ourselves for all the Extremities of Suffering and of Misery*; with a great deal more of the same Strain.

WITH due Submission to the profound Sagacity of this Prelate, who can smell *Popery* at five hundred Miles distance, better than *Fanaticism* just under his Nose; I take Leave to tell him, that this Reproof to his Friends, for want of Zeal and Clamour against Popery, Slavery, and the *Pretender*, is what they have not deserved. Are the Pamphlets and Papers daily published by the sublime Authors of his Party, full of any Thing else? Are not the QUEEN, the Ministers, the Majority of Lords and Commons, loudly taxed in print with this Charge against them at full Length? Is it not the perpetual Eccho of every Whig Coffee-House and Club? Have they not quartered *Popery* and the *Pretender* upon the Peace and Treaty of Commerce; upon the possessing, and quitting, and keeping, and demolishing of *Dunkirk?* Have they not clamoured because the *Pretender* continued in *France*, and because he left it? Have they not reported, that the Town swarmed with many thousand Papists; when upon Search, there were never found so few of that Religion in it before? If a Clergyman preacheth Obedience to the higher Powers, is he not immediately traduced as a Papist? Can mortal Man do more? To deal plainly, my Lord, your Friends are not strong enough *yet* to make an Insurrection, and it is unreasonable to expect one from them, until their Neighbours be ready.

MY Lord, I have a *little* Seriousness at Heart upon this *Point*, where your Lordship *affects* to shew so *much.* When you can prove, that one single Word hath ever dropt from any Minister of State, in *publick* or *private*, in Favour of the *Pretender*, or his Cause; when you can make it appear, that in the Course of this Administration, since the QUEEN thought fit to change her Servants, there hath one Step been made towards weakening the *Hanover* Title, or giving the least Countenance to any other whatsoever; then, and not until then, go dry your *Chaff* and *Stubble*, give Fire to the Zeal of your Faction, and reproach them with Luke-warmness.

FOURTHLY, The Bishop applies himself to the Tories in general; taking it for granted, after his charitable Manner, that they are all ready prepared to introduce Popery: He puts an Excuse into their Mouths, by which they would endeavour to justify their Change of Religion: *Popery is not what it was before the Reformation: Things are now much mended; and further Corrections might be expected, if we would enter into a Treaty with them: In particular, they see the Error of proceeding severely with Hereticks; so that there is no Reason to apprehend the Returns of such Cruelties as were practised an Age and a Half ago.*

THIS he assures us, is a Plea, offered by the *Tories*, in defence of themselves, for going about at this Juncture to establish the Popish Religion among us: What Argument doth he bring to prove the Fact it self? *Quibus indiciis, quo teste probavit? Nil horum: Verbosa & grandis epistola venit.* Nothing but this tedious *Introduction,* wherein he supposeth it all along as a Thing granted. That there might be a perfect Union in the whole Christian Church, is a Blessing which every good Man wisheth, but no reasonable Man can hope. That the more polite Roman Catholicks have in several Places given up some of their superstitious Fopperies, particularly concerning *Legends, Relicks,* and the like, is what no Body denies. But the material Points in difference between us and them, are universally retained and asserted, in all their controversial Writings. And, if his Lordship really thinks that every Man who differs from him under the Name of a Tory in some Church and State Opinions, is ready to believe *Transubstantiation, Purgatory, the Infallibility* of Popes or Councils, to worship Saints and Angels, and the like; I can only pray GOD to enlighten his Understanding, or graft in his Heart the first Principles of Charity; a Virtue which some *People* ought not by any Means wholly to renounce, *because it covereth a Multitude of Sins.*

FIFTHLY, The Bishop applies himself to his own Party in both Houses of Parliament, whom he exhorts to *guard their Religion and Liberty against all Danger at what Distance soever it may appear. If they are absent and remiss on critical Occasions,* That is to say, If they do not attend close next Sessions, to vote upon all Occasions whatsoever, against the Proceedings of the QUEEN and her Ministry: *Or,* if any Views of Advantage to themselves prevail on them. In other Words, If any of them vote for the Bill of Commerce, in hopes of a Place, or a Pension, a Title, or a Garter; GOD *may work a Deliverance for us another Way.* That is to say, by inviting the Dutch: *But they and their Families*; i. e. Those who are negligent or Revolters, *shall perish,* by which is meant; they shall be hanged as well as the present Ministry and their Abettors, as soon as we recover our Power. *Because they let in Idolatry, Superstition, and Tyranny.* Because they stood by and suffered the Peace to be made, the Bill of Commerce to pass, and *Dunkirk* lie undemolished longer than we expected, without raising a Rebellion.

His last Application is to the Tory Clergy, a Parcel of *blind, ignorant, dumb, sleeping, greedy, drunken Dogs.* A pretty artful Episcopal Method is this, of calling his Brethren as many injurious Names as he pleaseth. It is but quoting a Text of Scripture, where the Characters of evil Men are described, and the Thing is done; and at the same Time the Appearances of Piety and Devotion preserved. I would engage, with the Help of a good *Concordance*, and the Liberty of perverting Holy Writ, to find out as many injurious Appellations, as the *Englishman* throws out in any of his politick Papers; and apply them to those Persons, *who call Good, Evil; and Evil, Good*; to those who cry without Cause, *Every Man to his Tents, O* Israel! *And to those who curse the Queen in their Hearts!*

THESE decent Words he tells us, make up *a lively Description of such Pastors, as will not study Controversy, nor know the Depths of Satan.* He means, I suppose, the Controversy between us and the Papists; for as to the *Free-thinkers* and *Dissenters* of every Denomination, they are some of the best Friends to the Cause. Now, I have been told, there is a Body of that Kind of Controversy published by the *London* Divines, which is not to be matched in the World. I believe likewise, there is a good Number of the Clergy at present, thoroughly versed in that Study; after which, I cannot but give my Judgment, that it would be a very idle Thing for Pastors in general to busy themselves much in Disputes against *Popery:* It being a dry heavy Employment of the Mind at best; especially when, GOD be thanked, there is so little Occasion for it in the generality of Parishes throughout the Kingdom, and must be daily less and less by the just Severity of the Laws, and the utter Aversion of our People from that Idolatrous Superstition.

IF I might be so bold to name those, who have the Honour to be of his Lordship's Party, I would venture to tell him, that *Pastors* have much more Occasion to study *Controversies* against the several Classes of *Free-thinkers* and *Dissenters:* The former (I beg his Lordship's Pardon for saying so) being a little worse than Papists, and both of them more dangerous *at present* to our Constitution both in Church and State. Not that I think Presbytery so corrupt a System of Christian

Religion as Popery; I believe it is not above one Third as bad: But I think the Presbyterians, and their Clans of other *Fanaticks* of *Free-thinkers* and *Atheists*, that dangle after them, are as well inclined to pull down the present Establishment of Monarchy and Religion, as any Sett of Papists in Christendom; and therefore that our Danger, as Things now stand, is infinitely greater from our Protestant Enemies; because they are much more able to ruin us, and full as willing. There is no doubt, but Presbytery and a Commonwealth are less formidable Evils than Popery, Slavery, and the Pretender; for, if the Fanaticks were in Power, I should be in more Apprehension of being starved than burned: But there are probably in *England* forty Dissenters of all Kinds, including their *Brethren* the *Free-thinkers*, for one Papist; and allowing one Papist to be as terrible as three Dissenters, it will appear by Arithmetick, that we are thirteen Times and one Third more in Danger of being ruined by the latter than the former.

THE other Qualification necessary for all Pastors, if they will not be *blind, ignorant, greedy, drunken Dogs,* &c. is, *to know the Depths of Satan.* This is harder than the former; that a poor Gentleman ought not to be Parson, Vicar, or Curate of a Parish, except he be cunninger than the Devil. I am afraid it will be difficult to remedy this Defect for one manifest Reason, because whoever had only half the Cunning of the Devil, would never take up with a Vicarage of ten Pounds a Year, *to live on at his Ease*, as my Lord expresseth it; but seek out for some better Livelihood. His Lordship is of a Nation very much distinguished for that Quality of Cunning, (although they have a great many better) and I think he was never accused for wanting his Share. However, upon a Tryal of Skill, I would venture to lay six to four on the *Devil*'s Side, who must be allowed to be at least the older *Practitioner*. *Telling Truth* shames him, and *Resistance* makes him fly: But to attempt out-witting him, is to fight him at his own Weapon, and consequently no Cunning at all. Another Thing I would observe is, that a Man may be *in the Depths of Satan*, without knowing them all; and such a Man may be so far in *Satan's Depths*, as to be out of his own. One of the *Depths of Satan* is to *counterfeit an Angel of Light*. Another, I believe, is to stir up the People against their Governors, by false Suggestions of Danger. A third, is to be a *Prompter to false Brethren*, and to send *Wolves* about in *Sheeps* Cloathing. Sometimes he sends *Jesuits* about *England* in the Habit and Cant of *Fanaticks*; at other Times he hath *Fanatick* Missionaries in the Habits of ——— I shall mention but one more of Satan's Depths; for I confess I know not the Hundredth Part of them; and that is to employ his Emissaries in crying out against remote imaginary Dangers, by which we may be taken off from defending our selves against those, which are really just at our Elbows.

BUT his Lordship draws towards a Conclusion, and bids us *look about, to consider the Danger we are in, before it is too late*; for he assures us, we are already *going into some of the worst Parts of Popery*; like the Man, who was so much in haste for his new Coat, that he put it on the wrong Side out. *Auricular Confession, Priestly Absolution, and the Sacrifice of the Mass*, have made great Progress in *England*, and no Body hath observed it: Several other Popish Points *are carried higher with us, than by the Priests themselves*. And some Body it seems had the *Impudence to propose an Union with the* Gallican *Church*. I have indeed heard that Mr. *Lesly* published a Discourse to that Purpose, which I have never seen; nor do I perceive the Evil in *proposing an Union* between any two Churches in *Christendom*. Without doubt, Mr. *Lesly* is most unhappily misled in his Politicks; but if he be the Author of the late Tract against Popery, he hath given the World such a Proof of his Soundness in Religion, as *many a Bishop* ought to be proud of. I never saw the Gentleman in my Life: I know he is the Son of a great and excellent Prelate, who, upon several Accounts, was one of the most extraordinary Men of his Age. Mr. *Lesly* hath written many useful Discourses upon several Subjects, and hath so well deserved of the Christian Religion, and the Church of *England* in particular, that to accuse him of *Impudence for proposing an Union* in two very different Faiths, is a Stile which I hope few will imitate. I detest Mr. *Lesly*'s Political Principles as much as his Lordship can do for his Heart; but I verily believe he acts from a mistaken Conscience, and therefore I distinguish between the Principles and the Person. However, it is some Mortification to me, when I see an *avowed Nonjuror* contribute more to the confounding of *Popery*, than could ever be done by a hundred thousand such *Introductions* as this.

His Lordship ends with discovering a small Ray of Comfort. *God be thanked there are many among us that stand upon the Watch-Tower, and that give faithful Warning; that stand in the Breach, and make themselves a Wall for their Church and Country; that cry to God Day and Night, and lie in the Dust mourning before him, to avert those Judgments that seem to hasten towards us. They search into the Mystery of Iniquity that is working among us, and acquaint themselves with all that Mass of Corruption that is in Popery.* He prays, *That the Number of these may encrease, and that* he *may be of that Number, ready either to die in Peace, or to seal that Doctrine* he *hath been preaching above fifty Years, with his Blood.* This being his last Paragraph, I have made bold to transcribe the most important Parts of it. His Design is to end after the Manner of Orators, with leaving the strongest Impression possible upon the Minds of his Hearers. A great *Breach* is made; *the Mystery of Popish Iniquity is working among us*; may GOD avert those *Judgments that are hastening towards us:* I am an old Man, *a Preacher above fifty Years,* and I now expect and am ready to die a Martyr for the Doctrines I have preached. What an amiable Idea doth he here leave upon our Minds, of her Majesty, and her Government! He hath been poring so long upon *Fox*'s Book of Martyrs, that he imagines himself living in the Reign of Queen *Mary,* and is resolved to set up for a *Knight-Errant* against Popery. Upon the Supposition of his being in Earnest, (which I am sure he is not) it would require but a very little more Heat of Imagination, to make a History of such a Knight's Adventures. What would he say, to behold the *Fires kindled in* Smithfield, *and all over the Town,* on the seventeenth of *November*; to behold the *Pope* born in Triumph on the Shoulders of the People, with a *Cardinal on the one Side, and the Pretender on the other?* He would never believe it was Queen *Elizabeth*'s Days, but that of her persecuting Sister: In short, how easily might a *Windmill be taken for* the *Whore of* Babylon, and a *Puppet-Show* for a Popish Procession?

BUT *Enthusiasm* is none of his Lordship's Faculty: I am inclined to believe he might be melancholy enough when he writ this *Introduction:* The Despair at his Age of seeing a Faction restored, to which he hath sacrificed so great a Part of his Life: The little Success he can hope for in Case he should resume those High Church Principles, in the Defence of which he first employed his Pen: No visible Expectation of removing to *Farnham* or *Lambeth:* And lastly, the Misfortune of being hated by every one, who either wears the Habit, or values the Profession of a Clergyman: No wonder such a Spirit, in such a Situation, is provoked beyond the Regards of Truth, Decency, Religion, or Self-Conviction. To do him Justice, he seems to have nothing else left, but to cry out *Halters, Gibbets, Faggots, Inquisition, Popery, Slavery,* and the *Pretender.* But in the mean Time, he little considers what a World of Michief he doth to his Cause. It is very convenient, for the present Designs of that Faction, to spread the Opinion of our immediate Danger from *Popery* and the *Pretender.* His Directors therefore ought, in my humble Opinion, to have employed his Lordship in publishing a Book, wherein he should have asserted, by the most solemn Asseverations, that all things were safe and well: For, the World hath contracted so strong a Habit of believing him backwards, that I am confident nine Parts in ten of those who have read or heard of his *Introduction,* have slept in greater Security ever since. It is like the melancholy Tone of a Watchman at Midnight, who thumps with his Pole, as if some Thief were breaking in; but you know by the Noise, that the Door is fast.

HOWEVER, he *thanks God, there are many among us who stand in the Breach:* I believe they may; it is a *Breach* of their own making, and they design to come forward, and storm and plunder, if they be not driven back. *They make themselves a Wall for their Church and Country.* A *South* Wall, I suppose, for all the best Fruit of the *Church and Country* to be nailed on. Let us examine this Metaphor: The *Wall of our Church and Country* is built of those, who love the Constitution in both. Our domestic Enemies undermine some Parts of the *Wall,* and place themselves in the *Breach;* and then they cry, *We are the*

Wall. We do not like such Patch-Work; they build with untempered Mortar; nor can they ever cement with us, till they get better Materials and better Workmen: God keep us from having our *Breaches* made up with such Rubbish. *They stand upon the Watchtower!* They are indeed pragmatical enough to do so; but who assigned them that Post, to give us false Intelligence, to alarm us with false Dangers, and send us to defend one Gate, while their Accomplices are breaking in at another? *They cry to God Day and Night to avert the Judgment of Popery, which seems to hasten towards us.* Then I affirm, they are *Hypocrites by Day, and filthy Dreamers by Night. When they cry unto him, he will not hear them:* For they cry against the plainest Dictates of their own Conscience, Reason, and Belief.

BUT lastly, *They lie in the Dust, mourning before him.* Hang me, if I believe that, unless it be figuratively spoken. But suppose it to be true, Why do *they lie in the Dust?* Because they love to *raise* it; for what do *they mourn?* Why, for Power, Wealth and Places. There let the Enemies of the QUEEN and Monarchy, and the Church *lie* and *mourn,* and *lick* the *Dust* like *Serpents,* till they are truly sensible of their Ingratitude, Falshood, Disobedience, Slander, Blasphemy, Sedition, *and every evil Work.*

I CANNOT find in my Heart to conclude without offering his Lordship a little humble Advice upon some certain Points.

FIRST, I would advise him, if it be not too late in his Life, to endeavour a little at mending his Style, which is mighty defective in the *Circumstances* of Grammar, Propriety, Politeness and Smoothness. I fancied at first, it might be owing to the Prevalence of his Passion, as People sputter out Nonsense for Haste, when they are in a Rage. And indeed, I believe this Piece before me hath received some additional Imperfections from that Occasion. But whoever hath heard his Sermons, or read his other Tracts, will find him very unhappy in the Choice and Disposition of his Words, and, for want of Variety, repeating them, especially the Particles, in a Manner very grating to an *English* Ear. But I confine my self to this *Introduction,* as his last Work, where endeavouring at Rhetorical

Flowers, he gives us only Bunches of THISTLES; of which I could present the Reader with a plentiful Crop; but I refer him to every Page and Line of the Pamphlet itself.

SECONDLY, I would most humbly advise his Lordship to examine a little into the Nature of Truth, and sometimes to hear what *She* says. I shall produce two Instances among an hundred. When he asserts, That we are *now in more Danger of Popery than towards the End of King* Charles *the Second's Reign*; and gives the broadest Hints, that the QUEEN, the Ministry, the Parliament, and the Clergy are just going to introduce it; I desire to know, whether he really thinks *Truth* is of his Side, or whether he be not sure *She* is against him: If the latter, then *Truth* and he would be found in two different Stories; and which are we to believe? Again, when he gravely advises the Tories not to *light the Fires in Smithfield*; and goes on in twenty Places already quoted, as if the Bargain were made for *Popery* and *Slavery* to enter: I ask again, whether he hath rightly considered the Nature of *Truth?* I desire to put a parallel Case. Suppose his Lordship should take it into his Fancy to write and publish a Letter to any Gentleman of no infamous Character for his Religion or Morals; and there advise him with great Earnestness, not to rob or fire Churches, ravish his Daughter, or murder his Father; shew him the Sin and the Danger of these Enormities; That, if he flattered himself he could escape in Disguise, or bribe his Jury, he was grievously mistaken: That he must in all Probability forfeit his Goods and Chattles, die an ignominious Death, and be curst by Posterity: Would not such a Gentleman justly think himself highly injured, although his Lordship did not affirm, that the said Gentleman had Picklocks or Combustibles ready; that he had attempted his Daughter, and drawn his Sword against his Father in order to stab him? Whereas in the other Case, this Writer affirms over and over, that all Attempts for introducing Popery and Slavery are already made, the whole Business concerted, and that little less than a Miracle can prevent our Ruin.

THIRDLY, I could heartily wish his Lordship would not undertake to charge the Opinions of one or two, and those probably Nonjurors, upon the whole Body of the Nation, that differs from him. Mr. *Lesly* writ a *Proposal for an Union with the* Gallican *Church*; somebody else hath *carried the Necessity of Priesthood in the Point of Baptism farther than Popery:* A third hath *asserted the Independency of the Church on the State, and in many things arraigned the Supremacy of the Crown:* Then he speaks in a dubious insinuating Way, as if some other Popish Tenets had been already advanced: And at last concludes in this affected Strain of Despondency, *What will all these Things end in! And on what Design are they driven! Alas, it is too visible.* It is as clear as the Sun, that these Authors are encouraged by the *Ministry* with a Design to bring in Popery; and in Popery all these Things will End.

I NEVER was so uncharitable to believe, That the whole *Party* of which his Lordship professeth himself a Member, had a real formed Design of establishing *Atheism* among us. The Reason why the *Whigs* have taken the *Atheists* or *Free-thinkers* into their Body, is because they wholly agree in their political Schemes, and differ very little in Church Power and Discipline. However, I could turn the Argument against his Lordship with very great Advantage, by quoting Passages from fifty Pamphlets wholly made up of *Whigism and Atheism*, and then conclude: *What will all these things end in? And on what Design are they driven? Alas, it is too visible.*

LASTLY, I would beg his Lordship not to be so exceedingly outrageous upon the Memory of the Dead; because it is highly probable that in a very short time he will be one of the Number. He hath in plain Words given Mr. *Wharton* the Character of a most malicious, revengeful, treacherous, lying, mercenary Villain. To which I shall only say, That the direct Reverse of this amiable Description, is what appears from the Works of that most learned Divine; and from the Accounts given me by those, who knew him much better than the Bishop seems to have done. I meddle not with the moral Part of this Treatment. God Almighty forgive his Lordship this Manner of revenging himself: And then there will be but little Consequence from an Accusation, which the Dead cannot *feel*, and which none of the *Living* will *believe*.

PART II

Hints towards an Essay on Conversation

HINTS

TOWARDS

AN ESSAY

ON

CONVERSATION.

I HAVE observed few obvious Subjects to have been so seldom, or, at least, so slightly handled as this; and, indeed, I know few so difficult, to be treated as it ought, nor yet upon which there seemeth to be so much to be said.

MOST Things, pursued by Men for the Happiness of publick or private Life, our Wit or Folly have so refined, that they seldom subsist but in Idea; a true Friend, a good Marriage, a perfect Form of Government, with some others, require so many Ingredients, so good in their several Kinds, and so much Niceness in mixing them, that for some thousands of Years Men have despaired of reducing their Schemes to Perfection: But in Conversation, it is, or might be otherwise; for here we are only to avoid a Multitude of Errors, which, although a Matter of some Difficulty, may be in every Man's Power, for Want of which it remaineth as meer an Idea as the other. Therefore it seemeth to me, that the truest Way to understand Conversation, is to know the Faults and Errors to which it is subject, and from thence, every Man to form Maxims to himself whereby it may be regulated; because it requireth few Talents to which most Men are not born, or at least may not acquire without any great Genius or Study. For Nature hath

left every Man a Capacity of being agreeable, though not of
shining in Company, and there are an hundred Men sufficiently
qualified for both, who by a very few Faults, that they might
correct in half an Hour, are not so much as tolerable.

I WAS prompted to write my Thoughts upon this Subject
by mere Indignation, to reflect that so useful and innocent a
Pleasure, so fitted for every Period and Condition of Life, and
so much in all Men's Power, should be so much neglected and
abused.

AND in this Discourse it will be necessary to note those
Errors that are obvious, as well as others which are seldomer
observed, since there are few so obvious or acknowledged,
into which most Men, some Time or other, are not apt to run.

FOR Instance: Nothing is more generally exploded than the
Folly of Talking too much, yet I rarely remember to have seen
five People together, where some one among them hath not
been predominant in that Kind, to the great Constraint and
Disgust of all the rest. But among such as deal in Multitudes
of Words, none are comparable to the sober deliberate Talker,
who proceedeth with much Thought and Caution, maketh his
Preface, brancheth out into several Digressions, findeth a Hint
that putteth him in Mind of another Story, which he promiseth
to tell you when this is done; cometh back regularly to his
Subject, cannot readily call to Mind some Person's Name,
holdeth his Head, complaineth of his Memory; the whole
Company all this while in Suspence; at length says, it is no
Matter, and so goes on. And, to crown the Business, it perhaps
proveth at last a Story the Company hath heard fifty Times
before; or, at best, some insipid Adventure of the Relater.

ANOTHER general Fault in Conversation is, That of those
who affect to talk of themselves: Some, without any Ceremony,
will run over the History of their Lives; will relate the Annals
of their Diseases, with the several Symptoms and Circumstances of them; will enumerate the Hardships and Injustice
they have suffered in Court, in Parliament, in Love, or in Law.
Others are more dexterous, and with great Art will lie on the
Watch to hook in their own Praise: They will call a Witness to
remember, they always foretold what would happen in such a

Case, but none would believe them; they advised such a Man from the Beginning, and told him the Consequences just as they happened; but he would have his own Way. Others make a Vanity of telling their Faults; they are the strangest Men in the World; they cannot dissemble, they own it is a Folly; they have lost Abundance of Advantages by it; but, if you would give them the World they cannot help it; there is something in their Nature that abhors Insincerity and Constraint; with many other unsufferable Topicks of the same Altitude.

OF such mighty Importance every Man is to himself, and ready to think he is so to others; without once making this easy and obvious Reflection, that his Affairs can have no more Weight with other Men, than theirs have with him; and how little that is, he is sensible enough.

WHERE Company hath met, I often have observed two Persons discover, by some Accident, that they were bred together at the same School or University; after which the rest are condemned to Silence, and to listen while these two are refreshing each other's Memory with the arch Tricks and Passages of themselves and their Comrades.

I KNOW a Great Officer of the Army, who will sit for some time with a supercilious and impatient Silence, full of Anger and Contempt for those who are talking; at length of a sudden demand Audience, decide the Matter in a short dogmatical Way; then withdraw within himself again, and vouchsafe to talk no more, until his Spirits circulate again to the same Point.

THERE are some Faults in Conversation, which none are so subject to as the Men of Wit, nor ever so much as when they are with each other. If they have opened their Mouths, without endeavouring to say a witty Thing, they think it is so many Words lost; it is a Torment to the Hearers, as much as to themselves, to see them upon the Rack for Invention, and in perpetual Constraint, with so little Success. They must do something extraordinary, in order to acquit themselves, and answer their Character; else the Standers-by may be disappointed, and be apt to think them only like the rest of Mortals. I have known two Men of Wit industriously brought

I

together, in order to entertain the Company, where they have made a very ridiculous Figure, and provided all the Mirth at their own Expence.

I KNOW a Man of Wit, who is never easy but where he can be allowed to dictate and preside; he neither expecteth to be informed or entertained, but to display his own Talents. His Business is to be good Company, and not good Conversation; and, therefore, he chuseth to frequent those who are content to listen, and profess themselves his Admirers. And, indeed, the worst Conversation I ever remember to have heard in my Life, was that at *Will*'s Coffee-house, where the Wits (as they were called) used formerly to assemble; that is to say, five or six Men, who had writ Plays, or at least Prologues, or had Share in a Miscellany, came thither, and entertained one another with their trifling Composures, in so important an Air, as if they had been the noblest Efforts of human Nature, or that the Fate of Kingdoms depended on them; and they were usually attended with an humble Audience of young Students from the Inns of Courts, or the Universities, who, at due Distance, listened to these Oracles, and returned Home with great Contempt for their Law and Philosophy, their Heads filled with Trash, under the Name of Politeness, Criticism and Belles Lettres.

BY these Means the Poets, for many Years past, were all over-run with Pedantry. For, as I take it, the Word is not properly used; because Pedantry is the too frequent or unseasonable obtruding our own Knowledge in common Discourse, and placing too great a Value upon it; by which Definition Men of the Court or the Army may be as guilty of Pedantry as a Philosopher, or a Divine; and, it is the same Vice in Women, when they are over-copious upon the Subject of their Petticoats, or their Fans, or their China: For which Reason, although it be a Piece of Prudence, as well as good Manners, to put Men upon talking on Subjects they are best versed in, yet that is a Liberty a wise Man could hardly take; because, beside the Imputation of Pedantry, it is what he would never improve by.

THIS great Town is usually provided with some Player,

Mimick, or Buffoon, who hath a general Reception at the good Tables; familiar and domestick with Persons of the first Quality, and usually sent for at every Meeting to divert the Company; against which I have no Objection. You go there as to a Farce, or a Puppet-Show; your Business is only to laugh in Season, either out of Inclination or Civility, while this merry Companion is acting his Part. It is a Business he hath undertaken, and we are to suppose he is paid for his Day's Work. I only quarrel, when in select and private Meetings, where Men of Wit and Learning are invited to pass an Evening, this Jester should be admitted to run over his Circle of Tricks, and make the whole Company unfit for any other Conversation, besides the Indignity of confounding Men's Talents at so shameful a Rate.

RAILLERY is the finest Part of Conversation; but, as it is our usual Custom to counterfeit and adulterate whatever is dear to us, so we have done with this, and turned it all into what is generally called Repartee, or being smart; just as when an expensive Fashion cometh up, those who are not able to reach it, content themselves with some paltry Imitation. It now passeth for Raillery to run a Man down in Discourse, to put him out of Countenance, and make him ridiculous, sometimes to expose the Defects of his Person, or Understanding; on all which Occasions he is obliged not to be angry, to avoid the Imputation of not being able to take a Jest. It is admirable to observe one who is dexterous at this Art, singling out a weak Adversary, getting the Laugh on his Side, and then carrying all before him. The *French*, from whom we borrow the Word, have a quite different Idea of the Thing, and so had we in the politer Age of our Fathers. Raillery was to say something that at first appeared a Reproach, or Reflection; but, by some Turn of Wit unexpected and surprising, ended always in a Compliment, and to the Advantage of the Person it was addressed to. And, surely, one of the best Rules in Conversation is, never to say a Thing which any of the Company can reasonably wish we had rather left unsaid; nor can there any Thing be well more contrary to the Ends for which

People meet together, than to part unsatisfied with each other, or themselves.

THERE are two Faults in Conversation, which appear very different, yet arise from the same Root, and are equally blame-able; I mean, an Impatience to interrupt others, and the Uneasiness at being interrupted ourselves. The two chief Ends of Conversation are to entertain and improve those we are among, or to receive those Benefits ourselves; which whoever will consider, cannot easily run into either of those two Errors; because when any Man speaketh in Company, it is to be supposed he doth it for his Hearer's Sake, and not his own; so that common Discretion will teach us not to force their Attention, if they are not willing to lend it; nor on the other Side, to interrupt him who is in Possession, because that is in the grossest Manner to give the Preference to our own good Sense.

THERE are some People, whose good Manners will not suffer them to interrupt you; but what is almost as bad, will discover Abundance of Impatience, and lye upon the Watch until you have done, because they have started something in their own Thoughts which they long to be delivered of. Mean Time, they are so far from regarding what passes, that their Imaginations are wholly turned upon what they have in Reserve, for fear it should slip out of their Memory; and thus they confine their Invention, which might otherwise range over a hundred Things full as good, and that might be much more naturally introduced.

THERE is a Sort of rude Familiarity, which some People, by practising among their Intimates, have introduced into their general Conversation, and would have it pass for innocent Freedom, or Humour, which is a dangerous Experiment in our Northern Climate, where all the little Decorum and Politeness we have are purely forced by Art, and are so ready to lapse into Barbarity. This among the *Romans*, was the Raillery of Slaves, of which we have many Instances in *Plautus*. It seemeth to have been introduced among us by *Cromwell*, who, by pre-ferring the Scum of the People, made it a Court Entertainment, of which I have heard many Particulars; and, considering all

Things were turned upside down, it was reasonable and judicious; although it was a Piece of Policy found out to ridicule a Point of Honour in the other Extream, when the smallest Word misplaced among Gentlemen ended in a Duel.

THERE are some Men excellent at telling a Story, and provided with a plentiful Stock of them, which they can draw out upon Occasion in all Companies; and, considering how low Conversation runs now among us, it is not altogether a contemptible Talent; however, it is subject to two unavoidable Defects; frequent Repetition, and being soon exhausted; so that whoever valueth this Gift in himself, hath need of a good Memory, and ought frequently to shift his Company, that he may not discover the Weakness of his Fund; for those who are thus endowed, have seldom any other Revenue, but live upon the main Stock.

GREAT Speakers in Publick, are seldom agreeable in private Conversation, whether their Faculty be natural, or acquired by Practice and often venturing. Natural Elocution, although it may seem a Paradox, usually springeth from a Barrenness of Invention and of Words, by which Men who have only one Stock of Notions upon every Subject, and one Set of Phrases to express them in, they swim upon the Superficies, and offer themselves on every Occasion; therefore, Men of much Learning, and who know the Compass of a Language, are generally the worst Talkers on a sudden, until much Practice hath inured and emboldened them, because they are confounded with Plenty of Matter, Variety of Notions, and of Words, which they cannot readily chuse, but are perplexed and entangled by too great a Choice; which is no Disadvantage in private Conversation; where, on the other Side, the Talent of Haranguing is, of all others, most insupportable.

NOTHING hath spoiled Men more for Conversation, than the Character of being Wits, to support which, they never fail of encouraging a Number of Followers and Admirers, who list themselves in their Service, wherein they find their Accounts on both Sides, by pleasing their mutual Vanity. This hath given the former such an Air of Superiority, and made the latter so pragmatical, that neither of them are well to be endured. I say nothing here of the Itch of Dispute and Contradiction, telling of Lies, or of those who are troubled with the Disease called the Wandering of the Thoughts, that they are never present in Mind at what passeth in Discourse; for whoever labours under any of these Possessions, is as unfit for Conversation as a Mad-man in Bedlam.

I think I have gone over most of the Errors in Conversation, that have fallen under my Notice or Memory, except some that are merely personal, and others too gross to need exploding; such as lewd or prophane Talk; but I pretend only to treat the Errors of Conversation in general, and not the several Subjects of Discourse, which would be infinite. Thus we see how human Nature is most debased, by the Abuse of that Faculty which is held the great Distinction between Men and Brutes; and how little Advantage we make of that which might be the greatest, the most lasting, and the most innocent, as well as useful Pleasure of Life: In Default of which, we are forced to take up with those poor Amusements of Dress and Visiting, or the more pernicious ones of Play, Drink and Vicious Amours, whereby the Nobility and Gentry of both Sexes are entirely corrupted both in Body and Mind, and have lost all Notions of Love, Honour, Friendship, Generosity; which, under the Name of Fopperies, have been for some Time laughed out of Doors.

This Degeneracy of Conversation, with the pernicious Consequences thereof upon our Humours and Dispositions, hath been owing, among other Causes, to the Custom arisen, for some Years past, of excluding Women from any Share in our Society, further than in Parties at Play, or Dancing, or in the Pursuit of an Amour. I take the highest Period of Politeness in *England* (and it is of the same Date in *France*) to have been the peaceable Part of King *Charles* the First's Reign; and from what we read of those Times, as well as from the Accounts I have formerly met with from some who lived in that Court, the Methods then used for raising and cultivating Conversation, were altogether different from ours: Several Ladies, whom we find celebrated by the Poets of that Age, had Assemblies at their Houses, where Persons of the best Understanding, and of both Sexes, met to pass the Evenings in discoursing upon whatever agreeable Subjects were occasionally started; and, although we are apt to ridicule the sublime Platonic Notions they had, or personated, in Love and Friendship, I conceive their Refinements were grounded upon Reason, and that a little Grain of the Romance is no ill Ingredient to preserve and exalt the Dignity of human Nature, without which it is apt to degenerate into every Thing that is sordid, vicious and low. If there were no other Use in the Conversation of Ladies, it is sufficient that it would lay a Restraint upon those odious Topicks of Immodesty and Indecencies, into which the Rudeness of our Northern Genius is so apt to fall. And, therefore, it is observable in those sprightly Gentlemen about the Town, who are so very dexterous at entertaining a Vizard Mask in the Park or the Playhouse, that, in the Company of Ladies of Virtue and Honour, they are silent and disconcerted, and out of their Element.

THERE are some People who think they sufficiently acquit themselves, and entertain their Company with relating of Facts of no Consequence, nor at all out of the Road of such common Incidents as happen every Day; and this I have observed more frequently among the *Scots* than any other Nation, who are very careful not to omit the minutest Circumstances of Time or Place; which Kind of Discourse, if it were not a little relieved by the uncouth Terms and Phrases, as well as Accent and Gesture peculiar to that Country, would be hardly tolerable. It is not a Fault in Company to talk much; but to continue it long, is certainly one; for, if the Majority of those who are got together be naturally silent or cautious, the Conversation will flag, unless it be often renewed by one among them, who can start new Subjects, provided he doth not dwell upon them, but leaveth Room for Answers and Replies.

A COMPLETE
COLLECTION

Of Genteel and Ingenious

CONVERSATION,

According to the Most

Polite Mode and Method

Now USED

At COURT, and in the BEST COMPANIES of England.

In THREE DIALOGUES.

By *SIMON WAGSTAFF*, Esq;

LONDON:

Printed for B. Motte, and C. Bathurst, at the *Middle Temple-Gate* in *Fleet-street.*

M.DCC.XXXVIII.

A N

INTRODUCTION

To the following

TREATISE.

AS my Life hath been chiefly spent in consulting the Honour and Welfare of my Country, for more than forty Years past; not without answerable Success, if the World, and my Friends, have not flattered me; so, there is no Point wherein I have so much laboured, as that of improving, and polishing all Parts of Conversation between Persons of Quality, whether they meet by Accident or Invitation, at Meals, Tea, or Visits, Mornings, Noons, or Evenings.

I HAVE passed, perhaps, more Time, than any other Man of my Age and Country, in Visits, and Assemblies, where the polite Persons, of both Sexes, distinguish themselves; and could not, without much Grief observe, how frequently both Gentlemen, and Ladies, are at a Loss for Questions, Answers, Replies, and Rejoynders. However, my Concern was much abated, when I found, that these Defects were not occasioned by any Want of Materials, but because these Materials were not in every Hand. For Instance: One Lady can give an Answer better than ask a Question. One Gentleman is happy at a Reply; another excels in a Rejoynder: One can revive a languishing Conversation, by a sudden surprizing Sentence; another is more dextrous in seconding; a third can fill the Gap with laughing or commending what hath been said. Thus, fresh Hints may be started, and the Ball of Discourse kept up.

BUT alas, this is too seldom the Case, even in the most select Companies. How often do we see at Court, at publick visiting Days, or great Men's Levees, and other Places of general Meeting, that the Conversation falls and drops to nothing, like a Fire without supply of Fuel. This is what we all ought to lament; and against this dangerous Evil, I take upon me to affirm, that I have in the following Papers provided an infallible Remedy.

IT was in the Year 1695, and the Sixth of his late Majesty King WILLIAM the Third, of ever glorious and immortal Memory, who rescued three Kingdoms from Popery and Slavery; when being about the Age of six and thirty, my Judgment mature, of good Reputation in the World, and well acquainted with the best Families in Town; I determined to spend five Mornings, to dine four Times, pass three After-noons, and six Evenings every Week, in the Houses of the most polite Families; of which I would confine my self to fifty; only changing as the Masters or Ladies died, or left the Town, or grew out of Vogue, or sunk in their Fortunes, or (which to me was of the higest Moment) became disaffected to the Government: Which Practice I have followed ever since, to this very Day; except, when I happened at any Time to be sick, or in the Spleen upon cloudy Weather; and except, when I entertained four of each Sex in my own Lodgings once a Month, by Way of Retaliation.

I ALWAYS kept a large Table-Book in my Pocket; and as soon as I left the Company, I immediately entred the choicest Expressions that passed during the Visit; which, returning home, I transcribed in a fair Hand, but somewhat enlarged; and had made the greatest Part of my Collection in twelve Years, but not digested into any Method: For, this I found was a Work of infinite Labour, and what required the nicest Judgment, and consequently could not be brought to any Degree of Perfection, in less than sixteen Years more: Herein, I resolved to exceed the Advice of *Horace*, a *Roman* Poet, (which I have read in Mr. *Creech*'s admirable Translation) that an Author should keep his Works nine Years in his Closet, before he ventured to publish them; and finding, that I still received some additional Flowers of Wit and Language, although in a very small Number, I determined to defer the

Publication, to pursue my Design, and exhaust, if possible, the whole Subject, that I might present a compleat System to the World. For, I am convinced by long Experience, that the Criticks will be as severe as their old Envy against me can make them. 1 foresee they will object, that I have inserted many Answers and Replies, which are neither witty, humourous, polite, or authentick; and have omitted others, that would have been highly useful, as well as entertaining. But let them come to Particulars, and I will boldly engage to confute their Malice.

FOR these last six or seven Years, I have not been able to add above nine valuable Sentences to enrich my Collection: From whence I conclude, that what remains, will amount only to a Trifle. However, if after the Publication of this Work, any Lady or Gentleman when they have read it, shall find the least Thing of Importance omitted, I desire they will please to supply my Defects, by communicating to me their Discoveries; and their Letters may be directed to *Simon Wagstaff*, Esq; at his Lodgings next Door to the *Glocester* Head in St. *James*'s Street, (paying the Postage) in return of which Favour, I shall make honourable mention of their Names in a short Preface to the second Edition.

IN the mean Time, I cannot but with some Pride, and much Pleasure, congratulate with my dear Country, which hath outdone all the Nations of *Europe*, in advancing the whole Art of Conversation, to the greatest Height it is capable of reaching. And therefore, being entirely convinced, that the Collection I now offer to the Publick, is full and compleat; I may at the same Time boldly affirm, that the whole Genius, Humour, Politeness, and Eloquence of *England*, are summed up in it. Nor, is the Treasure small, wherein are to be found, at least, a thousand shining Questions, Answers, Repartees, Replies, and Rejoynders, fitted to adorn every Kind of Discourse that an Assembly of *English* Ladies, and Gentlemen, met together for their mutual Entertainment can possibly want: especially when the several Flowers shall be set off and improved by the Speakers with every Circumstance of Preface and Circumlocution in proper Terms; and attended with

Praise, Laughter, or Admiration. There is a natural involuntary Distortion of the Muscles, which is the anatomical Cause of Laughter: But there is another Cause of Laughter which Decency requires, and is the undoubted Mark of a good Taste, as well as of a polite obliging Behaviour; neither is this to be acquired without much Observation, long Practice, and a sound Judgment. I did therefore once intend, for the Ease of the Learner, to set down in all Parts of the following Dialogues, certain Marks, Asterisks, or Nota Bene's, (in *English*, Markwell's) after most Questions, and every Reply or Answer; directing exactly the Moment when one, two, or all the Company are to laugh. But, having duly considered that this Expedient would too much enlarge the Bulk of the Volume, and consequently the Price; and likewise, that something ought to be left for ingenious Readers to find out: I have determined to leave the whole Affair, although of great Importance, to their own Discretion.

THE Reader must learn by all Means to distinguish between Proverbs, and those polite Speeches which beautify Conversation: For, as to the former, I utterly reject them out of all ingenious Discourse. I acknowledge indeed, that there may possibly be found in this Treatise a few Sayings among so great a Number of smart Turns of Wit and Humour as I have produced, which have a proverbial Air. However, I hope it will be considered, that even these were not originally Proverbs, but the genuine Productions of superior Wits, to embellish and support Conversation; from whence, with great Impropriety, as well as Plagiarism, (if you will forgive a hard Word) they have most injuriously been transferred into proverbial Maxims; and therefore, ought in Justice to be resumed out of vulgar Hands, to adorn the Drawing-Rooms of Princes, both Male and Female, the Levees of great Ministers, as well as the Toylet and Tea-Table of the Ladies.

I CAN faithfully assure the Reader, that there is not one single witty Phrase in this whole Collection, which hath not received the Stamp and Approbation of at least one hundred Years; and, how much longer, it is hard to determine; he may therefore be secure to find them all genuine, sterling, and authentick.

BUT, before this elaborate Treatise can become of universal Use and Ornament to my native Country, two Points that will require Time and much Application, are absolutely necessary. For, first, whatever Person would aspire to be compleatly Witty, Smart, Humorous, and Polite; must by hard Labour be able to retain in his Memory every single Sentence contained in this Work; so as never to be once at a Loss in applying the right Answers, Questions, Repartees, and the like immediately, and without Study or Hesitation. And secondly, after a Lady or Gentleman hath so well overcome this Difficulty as to be never at a Loss upon any Emergency; the true Management of every Feature, and almost of every Limb is equally necessary; without which an infinite Number of Absurdities will inevitably ensue. For Instance; there is hardly a polite Sentence in the following Dialogues, which doth not absolutely require some peculiar graceful Motion in the Eyes, or Nose, or Mouth, or Forehead, or Chin; or suitable Toss of the Head, with certain Offices assigned to each Hand; and in Ladies, the whole Exercise of the Fan, fitted to the Energy of every Word they deliver: By no Means omitting the various Turns and Cadencies of the Voice, the Twistings, and Movements, and different Postures of the Body; the several Kinds and Gradations of Laughter, which the Ladies must daily practise by the Looking-Glass, and consult upon them with their Waiting-Maids.

MY Readers will soon observe what a great Compass of real and useful Knowledge this Science includes; wherein, although Nature assisted by a Genius, may be very instrumental, yet a strong Memory and constant Application, together with Example and Precept, will be highly necessary. For these Reasons, I have often wished, that certain Male and Female Instructors, perfectly versed in this Science, would set up Schools for the Instruction of young Ladies and Gentlemen therein. I remember about thirty Years ago, there was a *Bohemian* Woman, of that Species commonly known by the Name of Gypsies, who came over hither from *France*, and generally attended *Isaac* the Dancing-Master, when he was teaching his Art to Misses of Quality; and while the young Ladies were thus employed, the *Bohemian* standing at some Distance, but full in their Sight, acted before them all proper Airs, and Heavings of the Head, and Motions of the Hands, and Twistings of the Body; whereof you may still observe the good Effects in several of our elder Ladies. After the same Manner, it were much to be desired, that some expert Gentlewomen, gone to Decay, would set up publick Schools, wherein young Girls of Quality or great Fortunes, might first be taught to repeat this following System of Conversation, which I have been at so much Pains to compile; and then to adapt every Feature of their Countenances, every Turn of their Hands, every screwing of their Bodies, every Exercise of their Fans, to the Humour of the Sentences they hear or deliver in Conversation. But above all, to instruct them in every Species and Degree of Laughing, in the proper Seasons at their own Wit, or that of the Company. And, if the Sons of the Nobility and Gentry, instead of being sent to common Schools, or put into the Hands of Tutors at Home, to learn nothing but Words, were consigned to able Instructors in the same Art; I cannot find what Use there could be of Books, except in the Hands of those who are to make Learning their Trade; which is below the Dignity of Persons born to Titles or Estates.

I t would be another infinite Advantage, that by cultivating this Science, we should wholly avoid the Vexations and Impertinence of Pedants; who affect to talk in a Language not to be understood; and, whenever a polite Person offers accidentally to use any of their Jargon-Terms, have the Presumption to laugh at *us* for pronouncing those Words in a genteeler Manner: Whereas, I do here affirm, that whenever any fine Gentleman or Lady condescends to let a hard Word pass out of their Mouths, every Syllable is smoothed and polished in the Passage; and, it is a true Mark of Politeness both in Writing and Reading, to vary the Orthography as well as the Sound, because we are infinitely better Judges of what will please a distinguishing Ear, than those who call themselves Scholars, can possibly be; who consequently ought

speaking, were Patrons rather than Inventors of it, but first brought in by the Fanatick Faction, towards the End of their Power; and, after the Restoration, carried to *Whitehall* by the converted Rumpers, with very good Reason; because, they knew, that King *Charles* the Second, from a wrong Education, occasioned by the Troubles of his Father, had Time enough to observe, that Fanatick Enthusiasm directly led to Atheism; which agreed with the dissolute Inclinations of his Youth: And, perhaps these Principles were farther cultivated in him by the *French* Huguenots, who have been often charged for spreading them among us: However, I cannot see where the Necessity lies of introducing new and foreign Topicks for Conversation, while we have so plentiful a Stock of our own Growth.

I HAVE likewise, for some Reasons of equal Weight, been very sparing in Double-entendres, because, they often put Ladies upon affected Constraints, and affected Ignorance. In short, they break, or very much entangle the Thread of Discourse; neither am I Master of any Rules to settle the disconcerted Countenances of the Females in such a Juncture: I can therefore only allow Innuendoes of this Kind to be delivered in Whispers, and only to young Ladies under Twenty, who being in Honour obliged to blush, it may produce a new Subject for Discourse.

PERHAPS the Criticks may accuse me of a Defect in my following System of polite Conversation; that there is one great Ornament of Discourse, whereof I have not produced a single Example; which, indeed, I purposely omitted, for some Reasons, that I shall immediately offer; and, if those Reasons, will not satisfy the Male Part of my gentle Readers; the Defect may be supplied, in some Manner, by an Appendix to the Second Edition: Which Appendix shall be printed by itself, and sold for Six-pence stitched, and with a Marble Cover; that my Readers may have no Occasion to complain of being defrauded: The Defect I mean, is, my not having inserted into the Body of my Book, all the Oaths now most in Fashion for embellishing Discourse; especially, since it could give no Offence to the Clergy, who are seldom, or never admitted to these polite Assemblies. And, it must be allowed, that Oaths well chosen, are not only very useful Expletives to Matter, but great Ornaments of Style.

WHAT I shall here offer in my own Defence, upon this important Article, will, I hope, be some Extenuation of my Fault. First, I reasoned with my self, that a just Collection of Oaths, repeated as often as the Fashion requires, must have enlarged this Volume, at least to double the Bulk; whereby, it would not only double the Charge, but likewise make the Volume less commodious for Pocket Carriage. Secondly, I have been assured by some judicious Friends, that themselves have known certain Ladies to take Offence (whether seriously or no) at too great a Profusion of Cursing and Swearing; even, when that Kind of Ornament was not improperly introduced: Which, I confess, did startle me not a little; having never observed the like, in the Compass of my own Female Acquaintance, at least for twenty Years past. However, I was forced to submit to wiser Judgments than my own. Thirdly, as this most useful Treatise is calculated for all future Times; I considered, in this Maturity of my Age, how great a Variety of Oaths I have heard, since I began to study the World, and to know Men and Manners. And here, I found it to be true, what I have read in an ancient Poet:

'For, nowadays, Men change their Oaths,
'As often as they change their Cloaths.'

IN short, Oaths are the Children of Fashion; they are, in some Sense, almost Annuals, like what I observed before, of Cant-words; and I my self, can remember about forty different Setts. The old Stock-oaths, I am confident, do not amount to above forty five, or fifty at most; but, the Way of mingling and compounding them, is almost as various, as that of the Alphabet. Sir *John Perrot* was the first Man of Quality, whom I find upon Record, to have sworn by G——'s W——s. He lived in the Reign of Queen *Elizabeth*, and was supposed to have been a natural Son of *Harry* VIII. who might also have probably been his Instructor. This Oath, indeed, still continues, and is a Stock-oath to this Day; so do several others, that have kept their primitive natural Simplicity: But, infinitely the greater Number hath been so frequently changed, and dislocated, that if the Inventors were now alive, they could hardly understand them.

Upon these Considerations, I began to apprehend, that if I should insert all the Oaths as now current; my Book would be out of Vogue with the first Change of Fashion, and grow useless as an old Dictionary. Whereas, the Case is quite otherwise with my Collection of polite Discourse; which, as I before observed, hath descended by Tradition, for at least an hundred Years, without any Change in the Phraseology. I therefore determined with my self, to leave out the whole System of Swearing; because, both the Male and Female Oaths are all perfectly well known and distinguished; new Ones are easily learnt, and with a moderate Share of Discretion, may be properly applyed on every fit Occasion. However, I must here upon this Article of Swearing, most earnestly recommend to my Readers, that they would please a little to study Variety. For, it is the Opinion of our most refined Swearers, that the same Oath or Curse, cannot, consistent with true Politeness, be repeated above nine Times, in the same Company, by the same Person, and at one Sitting.

I am far from desiring, or expecting, that all the polite and ingenious Speeches contained in this Work, should in the general Conversation between Ladies and Gentlemen, come in so quick and so close, as I have here delivered them. By no Means: On the contrary, they ought to be husbanded better, and spread much thinner. Nor, do I make the least Question, but that by a discreet, thrifty Management, they may serve for the Entertainment of a whole Year; to any Person who doth not make too long, or too frequent Visits in the same Family. The Flowers of Wit, Fancy, Wisdom, Humour, and Politeness, scattered in this Volume, amount to one thousand, seventy and four. Allowing then to every Gentleman and Lady thirty visiting Families, (not insisting upon Fractions) there will want but little of an hundred polite Questions, Answers, Replies, Rejoinders, Repartees, and Remarks, to be daily delivered, fresh in every Company, for twelve solar Months; and, even this, is a higher Pitch of Delicacy than the World insists on, or, hath reason to expect. But, I am altogether for exalting this Science to its utmost Perfection.

IT may be objected, that the Publication of my Book, may, in a long Course of Time, prostitute this noble Art to mean and vulgar People. But, I answer; that it is not so easily acquired, as a few ignorant Pretenders may imagine. A Footman can swear; but he cannot swear like a Lord. He can swear as often: But, can he swear with equal Delicacy, Propriety, and Judgment? No certainly; unless he be a Lad of superior Parts, of good Memory, a diligent Observer, one who hath a skilful Ear, some Knowledge in Musick, and an exact Taste; which hardly falls to the Share of one in a thousand among that Fraternity, in as high Favour as they now stand with their Ladies; neither, perhaps hath one Footman in six, so fine a Genius, as to relish and apply those exalted Sentences comprised in this Volume, which I offer to the World: It is true, I cannot see that the same ill Consequences would follow from the Waiting-woman, who, if she hath been bred to read Romances, may have some small subaltern or second-hand Politeness; and, if she constantly attends the Tea, and be a good Listner, may, in some Years, make a tolerable Figure; which, will serve perhaps, to draw in the young Chaplain, or the old Steward. But, alas! after all, how can she acquire, those hundreds of Graces and Motions, and Airs, the whole military Management of the Fan, the Contorsions of every muscular Motion in the Face; the risings and fallings; the quickness, and slackness of the Voice, with the several Tones and Cadences; the proper Junctures of smiling and frowning; how often, and how loud to laugh; when to jibe and when to flout; with all the other Branches of Doctrine and Discipline above recited. I am therefore, not under the least Apprehension, that this Art will be ever in Danger of falling into common Hands, which requires so much Time, Study, Practice, and Genius, before it arrives to Perfection: And therefore, I must repeat my Proposal for erecting publick Schools, provided with the best and ablest Masters and Mistresses, at the Charge of the Nation.

I HAVE drawn this Work into the Form of a Dialogue,

after the Pattern of other famous Writers in History, Law, Politicks, and most other Arts and Sciences, and I hope it will have the same Success: For, who can contest it to be of greater Consequence to the Happiness of these Kingdoms, than all human *Knowledge* put together. Dialogue is held the best Method of inculcating any Part of Knowledge: And, as I am confident, that publick Schools will soon be founded for teaching Wit and Politeness, after my Scheme, to young People of Quality and Fortune; so I have determined, next Sessions, to deliver a Petition to the House of Lords, for an Act of Parliament to establish my Book, as the standard Grammar, in all the principal Cities of both Kingdoms, where this Art is to be taught, by able Masters, who are to be approved and recommended by me; which is no more than *Lilly* obtained, only for teaching Words in a Language wholly useless: Neither, shall I be so far wanting to my self, as not to desire a Patent, granted of Course to all useful Projectors; I mean, that I may have the sole Profit of giving a Licence to every such School, to read my Grammar for fourteen Years.

THE Reader cannot but observe, what Pains I have been at in polishing the Style of my Book to the greatest Exactness: Nor, have I been less diligent in refining the Orthography, by spelling the Words in the very same Manner that they are pronounced. Wherein I follow the chief Patterns of Politeness, at Court, at Levees, at Assemblies, at Play-houses, at the prime visiting Places, by young Templers, and by Gentlemen Commoners of both Universities, who have lived, at least, a Twelve-month in Town, and kept the best Company: Of these Spellings, the Publick will meet with many Examples, in the following Book: For Instance, can't, hav'n't, sha'n't, didn't, coodn't, woodn't, isn't, e'n't; with many more. Besides several Words, which Scholars pretend, are derived from *Greek* and *Latin*; but now pared into a polite Sound, by Ladies, Officers of the Army, Courtiers and Templers; such as Jommetry for Geometry, Verdi for Verdict, Lard for Lord, Larnin for Learning; together with some Abbreviations exquisitely refined: As, Pozz for Positively, Mobb for Mobile, Phizz for Physiognomy, Rep for Reputation, Plenipo for

Plenipotentiary, Incog for Incognito, Hipps, or Hippo for Hypocondriacks, Bam for Bamboozle, and Bamboozle for God knows what; whereby much Time is saved, and the high Road to Conversation, cut short by many a Mile.

I HAVE, as it will be apparent, laboured very much, and I hope with Felicity enough, to make every Character in the Dialogue, agreeable with itself; to a Degree, that whenever any judicious Person shall read my Book aloud for the Entertainment and Instruction of a select Company, he need not so much as name the particular Speakers; because, all the Persons throughout the several Subjects of Conversation, strictly observe a different Manner peculiar to their Characters, which are of different Kinds; but, this I leave entirely to the prudent and impartial Reader's Discernment.

PERHAPS, the very Manner of introducing the several Points of Wit and Humour, may not be less entertaining and instructing than the Matter itself: In the latter, I can pretend to little Merit; because, it entirely depends upon Memory, and the Happiness of having kept polite Company. But, the Art of contriving that those Speeches should be introduced naturally, as the most proper Sentiments to be delivered upon so great a Variety of Subjects; I take to be a Talent somewhat uncommon, and a Labour that few People could hope to succeed in; unless, they had a Genius particularly turned that Way, added to a sincere disinterested Love of the Publick.

ALTHOUGH, every curious Question, smart Answer, and witty Reply, be little known to many People; yet, there is not one single Sentence in the whole Collection, for which I cannot bring most authentick Vouchers, whenever I shall be called: And, even for some Expressions, which to a few nicer Ears, may perhaps appear somewhat gross, I can produce the Stamp of Authority from Courts, Chocolate-houses, Theatres, Assemblies, Drawing-rooms, Levees, Card-meetings, Balls, and Masquerades; from Persons of both Sexes, and of the highest Titles next to Royal. However, to say the Truth, I have been very sparing in my Quotations of such Sentiments that seem to be over free; because, when I began my Collection, such kind of Converse was almost in its Infancy, until it was taken into the Protection of my honoured Patronesses at Court; by whose Countenance and Sanction, it hath become a choice Flower, in the Nosegay of Wit and Politeness.

SOME will, perhaps, object, that when I bring my Company to Dinner, I mention too great a Variety of Dishes, not always consistent with the Art of Cookery, or proper for the Season of the Year; and part of the first Course mingled with the Second; besides a Failure in Politeness, by introducing Black-pudding to a Lord's Table, and at a great Entertainment: But, if I had omitted the Black-pudding, I desire to know, what would have become of that exquisite Reason given by Miss *Notable* for not eating it. The World perhaps might have lost it for ever, and I should have been justly answerable for having left it out of my Collection. I therefore cannot but hope, that such Hypercritical Readers, will please to consider, my Business was to make so full and compleat a Body of refined Sayings, as compact as I could; only taking Care, to produce them in the most natural and probable Manner, in order to allure my Readers into the very Substance and Marrow of this most admirable and necessary Art.

I AM heartily sorry, and was much disappointed to find; that so universal and polite an Entertainment as Cards, hath hitherto contributed very little to the Enlargement of my Work. I have sate by many hundred Times with the utmost Vigilance, and my Table-Book ready, without being able in eight Hours, to gather Matter for one single Phrase in my Book. But this, I think, may be easily accounted for, by the Turbulence and Jostling of Passions upon the various and surprizing Turns, Incidents, Revolutions, and Events, of good and evil Fortune, that arrive in the Course of a long Evening at Play; the Mind being wholly taken up, and the Consequences of Non-Attention so fatal. Play is supported upon the two great Pillars of Deliberation and Action. The Terms of Art are few, prescribed by Law and Custom; no Time allowed for Digressions or Tryals of Wit. *Quadrille* in particular, bears some Resemblance to a State of Nature, which we are told, is a State of War, wherein every Woman is against every Woman: The Unions short, inconstant, and soon broke; the League made this Minute, without knowing the Allye; and dissolved in the next. Thus, at the Game of *Quadrille*, Female Brains are always employed in Stratagem, or their Hands in Action.

NEITHER can I find, that our Art hath gained much by the happy Revival of masquerading among us: The whole Dialogue in these Meetings, being summed up in one sprightly (I confess, but) single Question; and as sprightly an Answer. Do you know me? Yes, I do. And, Do you know me? Yes, I do. For this Reason, I did not think it proper, to give my Readers the Trouble of introducing a Masquerade, meerly for the Sake of a single Question, and a single Answer. Especially, when to perform this in a proper Manner, I must have brought in a hundred Persons together of both Sexes, dressed in fantastick Habits for one Minute, and dismissed them the next. Neither is it reasonable to conceive, that our Science can be much improved by Masquerades, where the Wit of both Sexes is altogether taken up in contriving singular and humoursome Disguises; and their Thoughts entirely employed in bringing Intrigues, and Assignations of Gallantry to an happy Conclusion.

THE judicious Reader will readily discover, that I make Miss *Notable*, my Heroin; and Mr. *Thomas Neverout*, my Hero: I have laboured both their Characters with my utmost Ability. It is into their mouths that I have put the Liveliest Questions, Answers, Repartees, and Rejoynders; because, my Design was to propose them both as Patterns for all young Bachelors, and single Ladies to copy after. By which, I hope, very soon, to see polite Conversation flourish between both Sexes, in a more consummate Degree of Perfection than these Kingdoms have yet ever known.

I HAVE drawn some Lines of Sir *John Linger*'s Character, the *Derbyshire* Knight, on Purpose to place it in Counterview, or Contrast, with that of the other Company. Wherein, I can assure the Reader, that I intended not the least Reflection upon *Derby-shire*, the Place of my Nativity. But, my Intention was only to shew the Misfortune of those Persons, who have the Disadvantage to be bred out of the Circle of Politeness, where-of I take the present Limits, to extend no further than *London*, and ten Miles round, although others are pleased to confine it within the Bills of Mortality. If you compare the Discourses of my Gentlemen and Ladies with those of Sir *John*; you will hardly conceive him to have been bred in the same Climate, or under the same Laws, Language, Religion, or Government: And, accordingly I have introduced him speaking in his own rude Dialect, for no other Reason than to teach my Scholars how to avoid it.

THE curious Reader will observe, that where Conversation appears in Danger to flag; which, in some Places, I have artfully contrived; I took Care to invent some sudden Question, or Turn of Wit to revive it. Such as these that follow. What? I think here is a silent Meeting. Come Madam, a Penny for your Thought; with several others of the like Sort.

I HAVE rejected all Provincial, or Country Turns of Wit, and Fancy, because I am acquainted with a very few; but indeed, chiefly, because I found them so very much inferior to those at Court, especially among the Gentlemen Ushers, the Ladies of the Bed-Chamber, and the Maids of Honour. I must also add the hither End of our noble Metropolis.

WHEN this happy Art of polite conversing, shall be thoroughly improved; good Company will be no longer pestered with dull dry tedious Story-tellers, or brangling Disputers. For, a right Scholar of either Sex, in our Science, will perpetually interrupt them with some sudden surpizing Piece of Wit, that shall engage all the Company in a loud Laugh; and, if after a Pause, the grave Companion resumes his Thread, in the following Manner; well; but, to go on with my Story; new Interruptions come from the Left and Right, until he be forced to give over.

I HAVE likewise made some few Essays, towards selling of Bargains, as well for instructing those who delight in that Accomplishment, as in Compliance with my Female Friends at Court. However, I have transgressed a little in this Point, by doing it in a Manner somewhat more reserved, than as it is now practised at St. *James*'s. At the same Time, I can hardly allow this Accomplishment to pass properly for a Branch of that perfect polite Conversation, which makes the constituent

Subject of my Treatise; and, for this, I have already given my Reasons. I have, likewise, for further Caution, left a Blank in the critical Point of each Bargain, which, the sagacious Reader may fill up in his own Mind.

As to my self; I am proud to own, that except some Smattering in the *French*, I am, what the Pedants, and Scholars call, a Man wholly illiterate; that is to say, unlearned. But, as to my own Language, I shall not readily yield to many Persons; I have read most of the Plays, and all the Miscellany Poems that have been published for twenty Years past. I have read Mr. *Thomas Brown*'s Works entire, and had the Honour to be his intimate Friend, who was universally allowed to be the greatest Genius of his Age. Upon what Foot I stand, with the present chief reigning Wits, their Verses recommendatory, which they have commanded me to prefix before my Book, will be more than a thousand Witnesses. I am, and have been likewise, particularly acquainted with Mr. *Charles Gildon*, Mr. *Ward*, Mr. *Dennis*, that admirable Critick, and Poet; and several others. Each of these eminent Persons, (I mean those who are still alive) have done me the Honour to read this Production, five Times over, with the strictest Eye of friendly Severity; and proposed some, although very few Amendments, which, I gratefully accepted; and, do here publickly return my Acknowledgment for so singular a Favour. And, I cannot conceal, without Ingratitude, the great Assistance I have received from those two illustrious Writers Mr. *Ozel*, and Captain *Stevens*. These, and some others, of distinguished Eminency, in whose Company I have passed so many agreeable Hours; as they have been the great Refiners of our Language, so, it hath been my chief Ambition to imitate them. Let the *Popes*, the *Gays*, the *Arbuthnots*, the *Youngs*, and the rest of that snarling Brood, burst with Envy at the Praises we receive from the Court, and Kingdom. But, to return from this Digression.

THE Reader will find, that the following Collection of polite Expressions, will easily incorporate with all Subjects of genteel and fashionable Life. · Those which are proper for Morning Tea, will be equally useful at the same Entertainment in the Afternoon, even in the same Company, only by shifting the several Questions, Answers, and Replies, into different Hands; and, such as are adapted to Meals, will indifferently serve for Dinners, or Suppers, only distinguishing between Day-light and Candle-Light. By this Method, no diligent Person of a tolerable Memory, can ever be at a Loss.

IT hath been my constant Opinion, that every Man who is intrusted by Nature, with any useful Talent of the Mind, is bound by all the Tyes of Honour; and, that Justice which we all owe our Country, to propose to himself some one illustrious Action to be performed in his Life, for the publick Emolument: And, I freely confess, that so grand, so important an Enterprize as I have undertaken, and executed to the best of my Power, well deserved a much abler Hand, as well as a liberal Encouragement from the Crown. However, I am bound so far to acquit my self, as to declare, that I have often, and most earnestly intreated several of my above-named Friends, universally allowed to be of the first Rank in Wit and Politeness, that they would undertake a Work so honourable to themselves, and so beneficial to the Kingdom: But, so great was their Modesty, that they all thought fit to excuse themselves, and impose the Task on me; yet, in so obliging a Manner, and attended with such Compliments, on my poor Qualifications, that I dare not repeat. And, at last, their Intreaties, or rather, their Commands, added to that inviolable Love I bear to the Land of my Nativity, prevailed upon me to engage in so bold an Attempt.

I MAY venture to affirm, without the least Violation of Modesty, that there is no Man now alive, who hath by many Degrees, so just Pretensions as my self, to the highest Encouragement from the Crown, the Parliament, and the Ministry, towards bringing this Work to its due Perfection. I have been assured, that several great Heroes of Antiquity, were worshipped as Gods, upon the Merit of having civilized a fierce and barbarous People. It is manifest, I could have no other Intentions; and, I dare appeal to my very Enemies, if such a Treatise as mine, had been published some Years ago, and

with as much Success, as I am confident this will meet; I mean,
by turning the Thoughts of the whole Nobility, and Gentry,
to the Study and Practice of polite Conversation; whether such
mean, stupid Writers, as the *Craftsman*, and his Abettors,
could have been able to corrupt the Principles of so many
hundred thousand Subjects, as to the Shame and Grief of every
whiggish, loyal, true Protestant Heart, it is too manifest they
have done. For, I desire the honest, judicious Reader, to make
one Remark; that, after I have exhausted the whole * in sickly
Pay-Day (if I may so call it) of Politeness and Refinement, and
faithfully digested it into the following Dialogues, there
cannot be found one Expression relating to Politicks: That
the Ministry is never mentioned, nor the Word *King*, above
twice or thrice; and then, only to the Honour of Majesty.
So very cautious were our wiser Ancestors, in forming Rules
for Conversation, as never to give Offence to crowned Heads,
nor interfere with Party Disputes in the State. And indeed,
although there seem to be a close Resemblance between the
two Words, *Politeness*, and *Politicks*; yet no Ideas are more
inconsistent in their Natures. However, to avoid all Appearance of Disaffection, I have taken Care to enforce Loyalty, by
an invincible Argument, drawn from the Fountain of this
noble Science, in the following short Terms, that ought to be
writ in Gold, MUST, IS FOR THE KING. Which uncontroulable
Maxim, I took particular Care of introducing in the first Page
of my Book; thereby, to instil only the best Protestant loyal
Notions into the Minds of my Readers. Neither is it meerly
my own private Opinion, that Politeness is the firmest Foundation upon which Loyalty can be supported: For, thus happily
sings the never-to-be-too-much-admired †Lord *H*——, in his
truly sublime Poem, called, *Loyalty defined*.

> *Who's not polite, for the Pretender, is;*
> *A Jacobite, I know him by his Phizz,*

* *This Word is spelt by Latinists* Encyclopædia: *But, the judicious Author,
wisely prefers the polite Reading before the Pedantick.*
† *It is erroneously printed in the* London *Edition, Mr.* Stephen Duck.

In the like Manner, the divine Mr. *Tibbalds*, or *Theobalds*, in one of his Birth-day Poems.

> *I am no Scollard, but I am polite,*
> *Therefore be sure, I am no Jacobite.*

HEAR likewise, to the same Purpose, that great Master of the poetick Quire, our most illustrious Laureat, Mr. *Colly Cibber*.

> *Who in his Talk, can't speak a polite Thing,*
> *Will never loyal be, to* George *our King*.

I COULD produce many more shining Passages out of our principal Poets of both Sexes, to confirm this momentous Truth. From whence, I think it may be fairly concluded, that whoever can most contribute towards propagating the Science contained in the following Sheets, through the Kingdoms of *Great Britain* and *Ireland*, may justly demand all the Favour that the wisest Court, and most judicious Senate, are able to confer, on the most deserving Subject. I leave the Application to my Readers.

THIS is the Work, which I have been so hardy to attempt, and without the least mercenary View. Neither, do I doubt of succeeding, to my full Wish, except among the Tories and their Abettors; who being all Jacobites, and consequently Papists in their Hearts, may perhaps, resolve not to read my Book; chusing, from a Want of true Taste, or by strong Affectation, rather to deny themselves the Pleasure and Honour of shining in polite Company, among the principal Genius's of both Sexes throughout the Kingdom, than adorn their Minds with this noble Art; and probably apprehending (as I confess, nothing is more likely to happen) that a true Spirit of Loyalty to the Protestant Succession should steal in along with it.

IF my favourable and gentle Readers could possibly conceive the perpetual Watchings, the numberless Toyls, the frequent Risings in the Night, to set down several ingenious Sentences, that I suddenly, or accidentally recollected; and which, without my utmost Vigilance, had been irrecoverably lost for ever: If they would consider, with what incredible Diligence, I daily, and nightly attended, at those Houses

L

where Persons of both Sexes, and of the most distinguished Merit used to meet, and display their Talents: With what Attention I listned to all their Discourses, the better to retain them in my Memory; and then, at proper Seasons withdrew unobserved, to enter them in my Table-Book, while the Company little suspected what a noble Work I had then in Embrio: I say, if all this were known to the World, I think it would be no great Presumption in me to expect at a proper Juncture, the publick Thanks of both Houses of Parliament, for the Service and Honour I have done to the whole Nation, by my single Pen.

ALTHOUGH I have never been once charged with the least Tincture of Vanity, the Reader will, I hope, give me Leave to put an easy Question. What is become of all the King of *Sweden*'s Victories? Where are the Fruits of them at this Day? Or, of what Benefit will they be to Posterity? Were not many of his greatest Actions owing, at least, in Part, to Fortune? Were not all of them owing to the Valour of his Troops, as much as to his own Conduct? Could he have conquered the *Polish* King, or the *Czar of Muscovy*, with his single Arm. Far be it from me, to envy or lessen the Fame he hath acquired: But, at the same Time, I will venture to say, without Breach of Modesty, that I, who have alone, with this Right Hand, subdued Barbarism, Rudeness, and Rusticity; who have established, and fixed for ever, the whole System of all true Politeness, and Refinement in Conversation; should think my self most inhumanly treated by my Countrymen, and would accordingly resent it as the highest Indignity, to be put upon the Level, in Point of Fame, in after Ages, with *Charles* XII. late King of *Sweden*.

AND yet, so incurable is the Love of Detraction, perhaps, beyond what the charitable Reader will easily believe, that I have been assured by more than one credible Person, how some of my Enemies have industriously whispered about, that one *Isaac Newton*, an Instrument-Maker, formerly living near *Leicester* Fields, and afterwards a Workman in the Mint, at the Tower, might possibly pretend to vye with me for Fame in future Times. The Man, it seems, was knighted for making

Sun-Dyals better than others of his Trade, and was thought to be a Conjurer, because he knew how to draw Lines and Circles upon a Slate, which no Body could understand. But, adieu to all noble Attempts for endless Renown, if the Ghost of an obscure Mechanick, shall be raised up, to enter into Competition with me, only for his Skill in making Pot-hooks and Hangers, with a Pencil; which many thousand accomplished Gentlemen and Ladies can perform as well, with a Pen and Ink, upon a Piece of Paper, and in a Manner as little intelligible as those of Sir *Isaac*.

M Y most ingenious Friend already mentioned, Mr. *Colly Cibber*, who doth so much Honour to the Laurel Crown he deservedly wears (as he hath often done to many Imperial Diadems placed on his Head) was pleased to tell me, that if my Treatise were shaped into a Comedy, the Representation performed to Advantage on our Theatre, might very much contribute to the spreading of Polite Conversation among all Persons of Distinction through the whole Kingdom. I own, the Thought was ingenious, and my Friend's Intention good: But, I cannot agree to his Proposal. For, Mr. *Cibber* himself, allowed, that the Subjects handled in my Work being so numerous, and extensive, it would be absolutely impossible for one, two, or even six Comedies to contain them. From whence it will follow, that many admirable and essential Rules for Polite Conversation must be omitted. And here, let me do Justice to my Friend Mr. *Tibbalds*, who plainly confessed before Mr. *Cibber* himself, that such a Project, as it would be a great Diminution to my Honour, so it would intolerably mangle my Scheme, and thereby destroy the principal End at which I aimed; to form a compleat Body, or System, of this most useful Science in all its Parts. And therefore Mr. *Tibbalds*, whose Judgment was never disputed, chose rather to fall in with my Proposal mentioned before, of erecting publick Schools, and Seminaries, all over the Kingdom, to instruct the young People, of both Sexes, in this Art, according to my Rules, and in the Method that I have laid down.

I SHALL conclude this long, but necessary Introduction, with a Request, or, indeed, rather, a just and reasonable

Demand from all Lords, Ladies, and Gentlemen, that, while they are entertaining and improving each other with those polite Questions, Answers, Repartees, Replies, and Rejoynders, which I have, with infinite Labour, and close Application, during the Space of thirty six Years been collecting for their Service and Improvement, they shall, as an Instance of Gratitude, on every proper Occasion, quote my Name, after this, or the like Manner: *Madam, as our Master* Wagstaff *says.* *My Lord, as our Friend* Wagstaff *hath it.* I do likewise expect, that all my Pupils shall drink my Health every Day at Dinner and Supper, during my Life; and that they, or their Posterity, shall continue the same Ceremony, to my *not inglorious Memory*, after my Decease, for ever.

A Compleat Collection of Genteel and Ingenious Conversation

A COMPLEAT

COLLECTION

Of genteel and

Ingenious Converſation,

ACCORDING

To the moſt polite Mode and Me-
thod, now uſed at Court, and in the beſt Companies of *England*.

In ſeveral Dialogues.

DUBLIN:

Printed by and for GEORGE FAULKNER.

M,DCC,XXXVIII.

The Men.	*The Ladies.*
Lord SPARKISH	
Lord SMART	Lady SMART
Sir JOHN LINGER	Miss NOTABLE
Mr. NEVEROUT	Lady ANSWERALL
Colonel ATWIT	

The ARGUMENT.

Lord Sparkish *and* Colonel Atwit *meet in the Morning upon the* Mall; *Mr.* Neverout *joins them; they all go to Breakfast at* Lady Smart's. *Their Conversation over their Tea: After which they part; but my Lord and the two Gentlemen are invited to Dinner. Sir* John Linger *invited likewise; and, comes a little too late. Their whole Conversation at Dinner: After which, the Ladies retire to their Tea. The Conversation of the Ladies without the Men; who are supposed to stay and drink a Bottle; but in some Time, go to the Ladies and drink Tea with them. The Conversation there. After which a Party at Quadrill until Three in the Morning; but no Conversation set down. They all take leave, and go Home.*

A COMPLEAT

COLLECTION

Of genteel and

Ingenious Converſation, &c.

St. *James*'s-*Park*.

[*Lord* Sparkish *meeting Colonel* Atwit.]

Colonel. WELL met, my Lord.

Lord Sp. Thank ye Colonel; a Parson would have said, I hope we shall meet in Heaven. When did you see *Tom. Neverout?*

Col. He's just coming towards us. Talk of the Devil.——

[Neverout *comes up.*]

Col. How do you do *Tom?*

Nev. Never the better for you.

Col. I hope you're never the worse. But, where's your Manners? Don't you see my Lord *Sparkish?*

Nev. My Lord, I beg your Lordship's Pardon.

Lord Sp. Tom, How is it? what, you can't see the Wood for Trees? What Wind blew you hither?

Nev. Why, my Lord, it is an ill Wind that blows no Body Good; for it gives me the Honour of seeing your Lordship.

Col. Tom, you must go with us to Lady *Smart*'s to Breakfast.

Nev. Must! why Colonel, *Must* is for the King.

[*Colonel offering in jest to draw his Sword.*]

Col. Have you spoke with all your Friends?

Nev. Colonel, as you are stout, be merciful.

Lord Sp. Come, agree, agree, the Law's costly.

[*Colonel taking his Hand from the Hilt.*]

Nev. What, do you think I was born in a Wood to be scar'd by an Owl?

Col. Well *Tom*, you are never the worse Man for being afraid of me. Come along.

Nev. I'll wait on you. I hope Miss *Notable* will be there. I gad she's very handsome, and has Wit at Will.

Col. Why; every one as they like; as the good Woman said, when she kiss'd her Cow.

[*Lord* Smart's *House. They knock at the Door; Porter comes out.*]

Lord Sp. Pray are you the Porter?

Port. Yes, for Want of a better.

Lord Sp. Is your Lady at home?

Port. She was at home just now, but she is not gone out yet.

Nev. I warrant this Rogue's Tongue is well hung.

[*Lady* Smart's *Anti-Chamber.*]

[*Lady* Smart, *and Lady* Answerall, *at the Tea-Table.*]

Lady Sm. My Lord, your Lordship's most humble Servant.

Lord Sp. Madam, you spoke too late, I was your Ladyship's before.

Lady Sm. O! Colonel, are you here?

Col. As sure as you're there Madam.

Lady Sm. Oh, Mr. *Neverout*, what! such a Man alive!

Nev. Ay Madam, alive, and alive like to be, at your Ladyship's Service.

Lady Sm. Well, I'll get a Knife, and nick it down, that Mr. *Neverout* came to our House. And, pray what News Mr. *Neverout*?

Nev. News; why Madam, Queen *Elizabeth*'s dead.

Lady Sm. Well, Mr. *Neverout*, I see you are no Changeling.

[*Miss* Notable *comes in.*]

Nev. Miss, your Slave; I hope your early Rising will do you no Harm: I find you are but just come out of the *Cloth-Market*.

Miss. I always rise at Eleven, whether it be Day or no.

Col. Miss, I hope you're up for all Day.

Miss. Yes, if I don't get a Fall before Night.

Col. Miss, I heard you were out of Order. Pray how are you now?

Miss. Pretty well Colonel, I thank you.

Col. Pretty, and Well, Miss, that's two very good Things.

Miss. I mean, I am better than I was.

Nev. Why, then 'tis well you were sick.

Miss. What, Mr. *Neverout*, you take me up, before I'm down.

Lord Sp. Come, let us leave off Children's Play, and go to Push-Pin.

Miss. [*to Lady* Smart] Pray Madam, give me some more Sugar to my Tea.

Col. Oh, Miss, you must needs be very good humoured, you love sweet Things so well.

Nev. Stir it up with the Spoon Miss, for the deeper the sweeter.

Lady Sm. I assure you, Miss, the Colonel has made you a great Compliment.

Miss. I am sorry for it; for I have heard 'em say, that Complimenting is lying.

Lady Sm. [*to Lord Sparkish.*] My Lord, methinks the Sight of you is good for sore Eyes: If we had known of your coming, we would have strown Rushes for you. How has your Lordship done this long Time?

Col. Faith Madam, he's better in Health than good Condition.

Lord Sp. Well; I see there's no worse Friend than one brings from Home with one; and I'm not the first Man that has carried a Rod to whip himself.

Nev. Here's poor Miss, has not a Word to throw at a Dog. Come, a Penny for your Thought.

Miss. It is not worth a Farthing; I was thinking of you.

[*Colonel rising up.*]

Lady Sm. Colonel, where are you going so soon? What, I hope you did not come to fetch Fire?

Col. Madam, I must needs go home for half an Hour.

Miss. Why, Colonel, they say the Devil's at home.

Lady Answ. Well, but sit while you stay; 'tis as cheap sitting, as standing.

Col. No, Madam, while I'm *standing, I'm going.*

Miss. Nay, let him go, I promise we won't tear his Cloaths to hold him.

Lady Sm. I suppose, Colonel, we keep you from better Company; I mean only, as to my self.

Col. Madam, I'm all Obedience.

[*Colonel sits down.*]

Lady Sm. Lord, Miss, how can you drink your Tea so hot? Sure your Mouth is paved.

Lady Sm. How do you like this Tea Colonel?

Col. Well enough, Madam, but methinks it is a little Morish.

Lady Sm. Oh, Colonel, I understand you, *Betty* bring the Canister. I have but very little of this Tea left; but, I don't love to make two Wants of one, want when I have it, and want when I have it not. He, he, he, he. [*Laughs.*]

Lady Answ. [*To the Maid.*] Why, sure *Betty*, thou ar't bewitcht, this Cream is burnt too.

Betty. Why, Madam, the Bishop has set his Foot in it.

Lady Sm. Go, run Girl, and warm some fresh Cream.

Betty. Indeed, Madam, there's none left, for the Cat has eaten it all.

Lady Sm. I doubt it was a Cat with two Legs.

Miss. Colonel, don't you love Bread and Butter with your Tea?

Col. Yes, in a Morning Miss. For they say Butter is Gold in a Morning, and Silver at Noon, but it is Lead at Night.

Miss. The Weather is so hot, that my Butter melts on my Bread.

Lady Answ. Why, Butter I've heard 'em say, is mad twice a Year.

Lord Sp. [*To the Maid.*] Mrs. *Betty*, how does your Body politick?

Col. Fye, my Lord, you'll make Mrs. *Betty* blush.

Lady Sm. Blush! Ay, blush like a blue Dog.

Never. Pray, Mrs. *Betty*, are not you *Tom Johnson*'s Daughter?

Betty. So my Mother tells me, Sir.

Lord Sp. But, Mrs. *Betty*, I hear you are in Love.

Betty. My Lord, I thank GOD, I hate no Body, I am in Charity with all the World.

Lady Sm. Why, Wench, I think thy Tongue runs upon Wheels this Morning. How came you by that Scratch on your Nose? Have you been fighting with the Cats?

Col. [*to Miss*] Miss, when will you be married?

Miss. One of these odd-come-shortlies, Colonel.

Nev. Yes, they say the Match is half made; the Spark is willing, but Miss is not.

Miss. I suppose the Gentleman has got his own Consent for it.

Lady Answ. Pray my Lord, did you walk through the Park in this Rain?

Lord Sp. Yes, Madam, we were neither Sugar, nor Salt, we were not afraid the Rain would melt us, He, he, he. [*Laughs.*]

Col. It rained, and the Sun shone at the same Time.

Never. Why, then the Devil was beating his Wife behind the Door with a Shoulder of Mutton. [*Here a loud Laugh.*]

Col. A blind Man would be glad to see that.

Lady Sm. Mr. *Neverout*, methinks you stand in your own Light.

Never. Ah, Madam, I have done so all my Life.

Lord Sp. I am sure he sits in mine: Prithee *Tom*, sit a little further, I believe your Father was no Glazier.

Lady Sm. Miss, dear Girl, fill me a Dish of Tea; for I'm very lazy.

[*Miss fills a Dish of Tea, sweetens it, and then tastes it.*]

Lady Sm. What, Miss, will you be my Taster?

Miss. No, Madam, but they say, she's an ill Cook that can't lick her own Fingers.

Never. Pray, Miss, fill me another.

Miss. Will you have it now, or stay till you get it?

Lady Answ. But, Colonel, they say, you went to Court

last Night very drunk: Nay, I am told for certain, you had been among the *Philistians*. No Wonder the Cat winked, when both her Eyes were out.

Col. Indeed, Madam, that's a Lye.

Lady Answ. Well, 'tis better I should lye, than you should lose your Manners. Besides, I don't lye, I sit.

Never. O faith, Colonel, you must own you had a Drop in your Eye; for when I left you, you were half Seas over.

Lord Sp. Well, I fear Lady *Answerall*, can't live long, she has so much Wit.

Never. No, she can't live, that's certain; but she may linger thirty or forty Years.

Miss. Live long! Ay, longer than a Cat, or a Dog, or a better Thing.

Lady Answ. Oh, Miss, you must give your *Vardi* too.

Lord Sp. Miss, shall I fill you another Dish of Tea?

Miss. Indeed, my Lord, I have drank enough.

Lord Sp. Come, it will do you more Good than a Month's fasting. Here, take it.

Miss. No, I thank your Lordship, enough's as good as a Feast.

Lord Sp. Well, but if you always say no, you'll never be married.

Lady Answ. Do, my Lord, give her a Dish, for they say Maids will say no, and take it.

Lord Sp. Well, and I dare say, Miss is a Maid in Thought, Word, and Deed.

Never. I would not take my Oath of that.

Miss. Pray, Sir, speak for your self.

Lady Sm. Fye, Miss: Maids, they say, should be seen, and not heard.

Lady Answ. Good Miss, stir the Fire, that the Tea-Kettle may boyl. You have done it very well, now it burns purely. Well, Miss, you'll have a chearful Husband.

Miss. Indeed, your Ladyship could have stirred it much better.

Lady Answ. I know that very well Hussy, but I won't keep a Dog, and bark my self.

Never. What; you are stuck Miss?

Miss. Not at all, for her Ladyship meant you.

Nev. O, faith Miss, you are in Lob's Pound, get out as you can.

Miss. I won't quarrel with my Bread and Butter, for all that; I know when I'm well.

Lady Answ. Well, but Miss.

Nev. Ah, dear Madam, let the Matter fall; take Pity upon poor Miss; don't throw Water on a drounded Rat.

Miss. Indeed Mr. *Neverout*, you should be cut for the Simples this Morning. Say a Word more, and you had as good eat your Nails.

Lord Sp. Pray Miss, will you please to favour us with a Song?

Miss. Indeed my Lord I can't; I have got a great Cold.

Col. Oh Miss, they say all good Singers have Colds.

Lord Sp. Pray Madam, does not Miss sing very well?

Lady Answ. She sings, as one may say; my Lord.

Miss. I hear Mr. *Neverout* has a very good Voice.

Col. Yes, *Tom* sings well; but his Luck's naught.

Nev. Faith, Colonel, there you hit yourself a devilish Box of the Ear.

Col. Miss, will you take a Pinch of Snuff?

Miss. No, Colonel, you must know, I never take Snuff but when I'm angry.

Lady Answ. Yes, yes, she can take Snuff, but she has never a Box to put it in.

Miss. Pray Colonel let me see that Box?

Col. Madam, there's never a C. upon it.

Miss. May be there is Colonel.

Col. Ay, but *May-bees* don't fly now Miss.

Nev. Colonel, why so hard upon poor Miss? Don't set your Wit against a Child: Miss give me a Blow, and I'll beat him.

Miss. So she pray'd me to tell you.

Lord Sp. Pray, my Lady *Smart*, what Kin are you to Lord *Pozz*?

M

Lady Sm. Why, his Grandmother and mine had four Elbows.

Lady Answ. Well; methinks here's a silent Meeting. Come Miss, hold up your Head Girl, there's Money bid for you. [*Miss starts.*]

Miss. Lord, Madam, you frighten me out of my seven Senses!

Lord Sp. Well, I must be going.

Lady Answ. I have seen hastier People than you stay all Night.

Col. [*to Lady Smart.*] *Tom Neverout* and I, are to leap To-morrow for a Guinea.

Miss. I believe Colonel, Mr. *Neverout* can leap at a Crust better than you.

Nev. Miss, your Tongue runs before your Wit: Nothing can tame you but a Husband.

Miss. Peace, I think I hear the Church Clock.

Nev. Why, you know as the Fool thinks, the Bell chinks.

Lady Sm. Mr. *Neverout*, your Handkerchief's fallen.

Miss. Let him set his Foot upon it, that it mayn't fly in his Face.

Nev. Well Miss.

Miss. Ay, ay, many a One says *Well*, that thinks *Ill*.

Nev. Well Miss, I'll think of this.

Miss. That's Rhyme, if you take it in Time.

Nev. What! I see you are a Poet.

Miss. Yes, if I had but Wit to shew it.

Nev. Miss, will you be so kind to fill me a Dish of Tea?

Miss. Pray let your Betters be served before you; I am just going to fill one for my self: And, you know the Parson always christens his own Child first.

Nev. But, I saw you fill one just now for the Colonel: Well, I find Kissing goes by Favour.

Col. Ods so, I have cut my Thumb with this cursed Knife.

Lady Answ. Ay, that was your Mother's Fault; because she only warned you not to cut your Fingers.

Lady Sm. No, no; 'tis only Fools cut their Fingers, but wise Folks cut their Thumbs.

Miss. I'm sorry for it, but I can't cry. But pray, Mr. *Neverout*, what Lady was that you were talking with in the Side-box last *Tuesday?*

Nev. Miss; can you keep a Secret?

Miss. Yes, I can.

Nev. Well Miss, and so can I.

Col. Don't you think Miss is grown?

Lady Answ. Ay, ay, ill Weeds grow a-pace.

Miss. No, Madam, with Submission, 'tis Weeds of Grace that grow a-pace.

[*A Puff of Smoak comes down the Chimney.*]

Lady Answ. Lord Madam! does your Ladyship's Chimney smoak?

Col. No Madam, but they say Smoak always pursues the Fair, and your Ladyship sat nearest.

Lady Sm. Madam, do you love Bohea Tea?

Lady Answ. Why really Madam, I must confess, I do love it; but it does not love me.

Miss. [*to Lady* Smart.] Indeed Madam, your Ladyship is very sparing of your Tea; I protest, the last Dish I took, was no more than Water bewitcht.

Col. Pray Miss, if I may be so bold, what Lover gave you that fine Etuy?

Miss. Don't you know? then keep Council.

Lady Answ. I'll tell you Colonel who gave it her; it was the best Lover she will ever have while she lives; even her own dear Papa.

Nev. Methinks Miss, I don't much like the Colour of that Ribband.

Miss. Why then, Mr. *Neverout*, if you don't like it, dy'e see, you may look off of it.

Lord Sp. I don't doubt Madam, but your Ladyship has heard that Sir *John Bearish*, has got an Employment at Court.

Lady Sm. Yes, yes, and I warrant he thinks himself no small Fool now.

Nev. Yet, Madam, I have heard some People take him for a wise Man.

Lady Sm. Ay, some are Wise, and some are otherwise.

Lady Answ. Do you know him Mr. *Neverout?*

Nev. Know him; ay Madam as well as a Beggar knows his Dish.

Col. Well, I can only say he has better Luck than honester Folks: But, pray how came he to get this Enployment?

Lord Sp. Why, by Chance, as the Man killed the Devil.

Nev. Why Miss, you are in a brown Study. What's the Matter; methinks you look like Mum chance, that was hang'd for saying nothing.

Miss. I'd have you to know I scorn your Words.

Nev. Well, ay but scornful Dogs, they say, will eat dirty Puddings.

Miss. Well, my Comfort is, your Tongue's no slander. What, you would not have one be always upon the high Grin?

Nev. Cry Mapsticks, Madam, no Offence I hope.

[*Lady* Smart *breaks a Tea-cup.*]

Lady Answ. Lord, Madam, how came you to break your Cup?

Lady Sm. I can't help it, if I would cry my Eyes out.

Miss. Why sell it, Madam, and buy a new one with some of the Money.

Col. Why, if Things do not break or wear out, how should Tradesmen live?

Miss. Well, I'm very sick, if any Body cared for it. [*She spits.*] I believe I shall dye, for I can't spit from me.

Nev. Come then, Miss, e'en make a Die of it; and then we shall have a burying of our own.

Miss. The Devil take you, *Neverout,* besides all small Curses.

Lady Answ. Marry come up: What, plain *Neverout,* methinks you might have an M under your Girdle, Miss.

Lady Sm. Well, well; naught's ne'er in Danger, I warrant, Miss will spit in her Hand and hold fast. Colonel, do you like this Bisket?

Col. I'm like all Fools, I love every Thing that's good.

Lady Sm. Well and isn't it pure good?

Col. 'Tis better than a worse.

[*Footman brings the Colonel a Letter.*]

Lady Answ. I suppose, Colonel, that's a Billet-doux from your Mistress.

Col. I'gad I don't know whence it comes, but whoever writ it, writes a Hand like a Foot.

Miss. Well you may make a Secret of it, but we can spell and put together.

Nev. Miss, what spells B double uzzard?

Miss. Buzzard in your Teeth, Mr. *Neverout.*

Lady Sm. Mr. *Neverout,* now you are up, will you do me the Favour to do me the Kindness to take off the Tea-Kettle.

Lord Sp. I wonder what makes these Bells ring?

Lady Answ. Why my Lord, I suppose because they pull the Ropes. [*Here all laugh.*]

[Neverout *plays with a Tea-cup.*]

Miss. Now a Child would have cryed half an Hour before he could have found out such a pretty Play-Thing.

Lady Sm. Well said, Miss: I vow Mr. *Neverout,* the Girl is too hard for you.

Nev. Ay, Miss will say any Thing but her Prayers, and those she whistles.

Miss. Pray, Colonel, make me a Present of that pretty Knife.

Nev. Ay, Miss, catch him at that, and hang him.

Col. Not for the World, dear Miss, it will cut Love.

Lord Sp. Colonel, you shall be married first, I was just going to say that.

Lady Sm. Well, but for all that, I can tell you who is a great Admirer of Miss: Pray, Miss, how do you like Mr. *Spruce,* I swear I have seen him often cast a Sheep's Eye out of a Calve's Head at you, deny it if you can.

Miss. O Madam, all the World knows, that Mr. *Spruce* is a general Lover.

Col. Come, Miss, it is too true to make a Jest on. [*Miss blushes.*]

Lady Answ. Well, however blushing is some Sign of Grace.

Nev. Miss says nothing, but I warrant she pays it off with thinking.

Miss. Well, Ladies and Gentlemen, I find you are pleased to divert your selves; but as I hope to be saved there is nothing in it.

Lady Sm. Ah, Miss, Love will creep where it can't go: They say, touch a gall'd Horse, and he'll wince.

Miss. I'd hold a hundred Pound Mr. *Neverout* was the Inventor of that Story; and, Colonel, I doubt you had a Finger in the Pye.

Lady Answ. But, Colonel, you forgot to salute Miss when you came in; she said, you had not seen her a long Time.

Miss. Fye, Madam, I vow, Colonel, I said no such Thing; I wonder at your Ladyship.

Col. Miss, I beg your Pardon.

[*Goes to salute her, she struggles a little.*]

Miss. Well, I had rather give a Knave a Kiss for once, than be troubled with him: But, upon my Word, you are more bold than welcome.

Lady Sm. Fye, fye, Miss, for Shame of the World, and Speech of good People.

[*Neverout to Miss, who is cooking her Tea and Bread and Butter.*]

Nev. Come, come, Miss, make much of naught, good Folks are scarce.

Miss. What, and you must come in with your two Eggs a Penny, and three of them rotten.

Col. [*To Lord* Sparkish.] But, my Lord, I forgot to ask you, how you like my new Cloaths?

Lord Sp. Why, very well, Colonel, only to deal plainly with you, methinks the worst Piece is in the Middle.

[*Here a loud Laugh often repeated.*]

Col. My Lord, you are too severe on your Friends.

Miss. Mr. *Neverout*, I'm hot, are you a Sot?

Nev. Miss, I'm cold, are you a Scold? Take you that.

Lady Sm. I confess that was home: I find, Mr. *Neverout*, you won't give your Head for the washing, as they say.

Miss. O, he's a sore Man where the Skin's off: I see Mr. *Neverout* has a Mind to sharpen the Edge of his Wit on the Whetstone of my Ignorance.

Lord Sp. Faith *Tom*, you are struck; I never heard a better Thing.

Nev. Pray, Miss, give me Leave to scratch you for that fine Speech.

Miss. Pox on your Picture, it cost me a Groat the drawing.

Nev. [*To Lady* Smart.] 'Sbuds, Madam, I have burnt my Hand with your plaguy Tea-Kettle.

Lady Sm. Why then, Mr. *Neverout*, you must say, God save the King.

Nev. Did you ever see the like?

Miss. Never but once at a Wedding.

Col. Miss, pray how old are you?

Miss. Why, I am as old as my Tongue, and a little older than my Teeth.

Lora Sp. [*To Lady* Answerall.] Pray, Madam, is Miss *Buxom* marry'd? I hear it is all over the Town.

Lady Answ. My Lord, she's either marry'd, or worse.

Col. If she ben't marry'd, at least she's lustily promised. But is it certain that Sir *John Blunderbuz* is dead at last?

Lord Sp. Yes, or else he's sadly wrong'd; for they have bury'd him.

Miss. Why, if he be dead, he'll eat no more Bread.

Col. But is he really dead?

Lady Answ. Yes, Colonel, as sure as you're alive.

Col. They say he was an honest Man.

Lady Answ. Yes, with good looking to.

[*Miss feels a Pimple on her Face.*]

Miss. Lord, I think my Goodness is coming out: Madam, will your Ladyship please to lend me a Patch?

Nev. Miss, if you are a Maid, put your Hand upon your Spot.

Miss. There, [*covering her whole Face with both her Hands.*]

Lady Sm. Well, thou art a mad Girl. [*Gives her a Tap.*]

Miss. Lord, Madam, is that a Blow to give a Child?

[*Lady* Smart *lets fall her Handkerchief, and the Colonel stoops for it.*]

Lady Sm. Colonel, you shall have a better Office.

Col. Oh, Madam, I can't have a better than to serve your Ladyship.

Col. [*To Lady* Sparkish] Madam, has your Ladyship read the new Play written by a Lord, it is called, *Love in a hollow Tree?*

Lady Sp. No, Colonel.

Col. Why then, your Ladyship has a new Pleasure to come.

[*Miss sighs.*]

Nev. Pray, Miss, why do you sigh?

Miss. To make a Fool ask, and you are the first.

Nev. Why, Miss, I find there is nothing but a Word and a Blow with you.

Lady Answ. Why, you must know, Miss is in Love.

Miss. I wish my Head may never ake till that Day.

Lord Sp. Come, Miss, never sigh but send for him.

[*Lady* Smart, *and Lady* Answerall, *speaking together.*]

If he be hang'd, he'll come hopping, and if he be drown'd, he'll come dropping.

Miss. Well, I'll swear you'd make one dye with laughing.

[*Miss plays with a Tea-cup, and* Neverout *plays with another.*]

Nev. Well, I see one Fool makes many.

Miss. And you're the greatest Fool of any.

Nev. Pray, Miss, will you be so kind to tye this String for me, with your fair Hands? It will go all in your Day's work.

Miss. Marry come up indeed; tye it your self, you have as many Hands as I, your Man's Man will have a fine Office truly. Come, pray stand out of my spitting Place.

Nev. Well, but Miss, don't be angry.

Miss. No, I was never angry in my Life, but once, and then no Body cared for it; so, I resolved never to be angry again.

Nev. Well; but if you'll tye it, you shall never know what I'll do for you.

Miss. So I suppose truly.

Nev. Well, but I'll make you a fine Present one of these Days.

Miss. Ay, when the Devil is blind, and his Eyes are not sore yet.

Nev. No, Miss, I'll send it you To-morrow.

Miss. Well, well, To-morrow's a new Day: But I suppose, you mean To-morrow come never.

Nev. O, tis the prettiest Thing; I assure you there came but two of them over in three Ships.

Miss. Would I could see it, quoth blind *Hugh:* But, why did not you bring me a Present of Snuff this Morning?

Nev. Because, Miss, you never askt me; and 'tis an ill Dog that is not worth whistling for.

Lord Sp. [*to Lady* Answerall.] Pray, Madam, how came your Ladyship last *Thursday* to go to that odious Puppet-Show?

Col. Why, to be sure her Ladyship went to see, and to be seen.

Lady Ans. You have made a fine Speech, Colonel; pray, what will you take for your Mouthpiece?

Lord Sp. Take that, Colonel. But, pray Madam, was my Lady *Dimple* there? They say she is extreamly handsome.

Lady Sm. They must not see with my Eyes that think so.

Nev. She may pass Muster, and that's all.

Lady Ans. Pray how old do you take her to be?

Col. Why, about five or six and twenty.

Miss. I swear she's no Chicken, she's on the wrong Side of thirty, if she be a Day.

Lady Ans. Depend upon't, she'll never see five and thirty, and a Bit to spare.

Col. Why they say, she's one of the chief Toasts in Town,

Lady Sm. Ay, when all the rest are out of it.

Miss. Well; I would not be as sick, as she's proud, for all the World.

Lady Ans. She looks as if Butter would not melt in her Mouth; but I warrant Cheese won't choak her.

Nev. I hear, my Lord what d'ye call 'um is courting her.

Lord Sp. What Lord d'ye neam, *Tom?*

Miss. Why, my Lord, I suppose, Mr. *Neverout* means the Lord of the Lord knows what.

Col. They say she dances very fine.

Lady Ans. She did; but I doubt her dancing Days are over.

Col. I can't pardon her for her rudeness to me.

Lady Sm. Well, but you must forget and forgive.

[*Footman comes in.*]

Lady Sm. Did you call *Betty?*

Footman. She's coming, Madam.

Lady Sm. Coming? Ay so is *Christmas.*

[Betty *comes in.*]

Lady Sm. Come, get ready my Things, where has the Wench been these three Hours?

Betty. Madam, I can't go faster than my Legs will carry me.

Lady Sm. Ay, thou hast a Head, and so has a Pin.——But, my Lord, all the Town has it, that Miss *Caper* is to be married to Sir *Peter Gibeall.* One Thing is certain, that she has promised to have him.

Lord Sp. Why, Madam, you know Promises are either broken or kept.

Lady Ans. I beg your Pardon, my Lord, Promises and Pye-Crusts, they say, are made to be broken.

Lady Sm. Nay, I had it from my Lady *Carrilye's* own Mouth; I tell my Tale, and my Tale's Author; if it be a Lye, you had it as cheap as I.

Lady Ans. She and I had some Words last *Sunday* at Church; but, I think I gave her her own.

Lady Sm. Her Tongue runs like the Clapper of a Mill; she talks enough for her self and all the Company.

Nev. And yet she simpers like a Furmity Kettle.

Miss. [*Looking in a Glass.*] Lord, how my Head is drest to Day!

Col. O Madam, a good Face needs no Band.

Miss. No, and a bad one deserves none.

Col. Pray, Miss, where is your old Acquaintance Mrs. *Wayward?*

Miss. Why where should she be? If you must needs know; she's in her Skin.

Col. I can answer that: What if you were as far out, as she's in?

Miss. Well, I promised to go this Evening to *Hide-Park* on the * Water; but, I protest, I'm half afraid.

* *A Cant Phrase for taking Pleasure on the River* Thames *in a Boat.*

Nev. Miss, Never fear: You have the old Proverb on your Side; naught's never in Danger.

Col. Why, Miss, let *Tom Neverout* wait on you, and then I warrant you will be as safe as a Thief in a Mill; for you know, he that is born to be hang'd, will never be drown'd.

Nev. Thank ye, Colonel, for your good Word; but faith, if ever I hang, it shall be about a fair Lady's Neck.

Lady Sm. Who's there? Bid the Children be quiet, and not laugh so loud.

Lady Ans. O, Madam, let 'em laugh; they'll ne'er laugh younger.

Nev. Miss, I'll tell you a Secret, if you'll promise never to tell it again.

Miss. No, to be sure, I'll tell it to no Body but Friends and Strangers.

Nev. Why then, here's some Dirt in my Tea-Cup.

Miss. Come, come; the more there's in't, the more there's on't.

Lady Ans. Poh, you must eat a Peck of Dirt before you dye.

Col. Ay, ay, it all goes one Way.

Nev. Pray Miss, what's o' Clock?

Miss. Why, you must know 'tis a Thing like a Bell; and you're a Fool that can't tell.

Nev. [*to Lady* Answ.] Pray Madam do you tell me, for I let my Watch run down.

Lady Answ. Why, 'tis half an Hour past Hanging Time.

Col. Well; I am like the Butcher, that was looking for his Knife, and had it in his Mouth: I have been searching my Pockets for my Snuff-Box, and, I gad, here it is in my Hand.

Miss. If it had been a Bear, 'twould have bit you, Colonel: Well, I wish I had such a Snuff-Box.

Nev. You'll be long enough before you wish your Skin full of Eyelet-Holes.

Col. Wish in one Hand——

Miss. Out upon you; Lord, what can the Man mean?

Lord Sp. This Tea's very hot?

Lady Answ. Why, it came from a hot Place my Lord.
          [*Colonel spils his Tea.*]

Lady Sm. That's as well done, as if I had done it my self.

Col. Madam, I find you live by ill Neighbours, when you are forced to praise your self.

Nev. Well; I won't drink a Drop more: If I do, 'twill go down like chopt Hay.

Miss. Pray don't you say no 'till you are ask'd.

Nev. Well; what you please, and the rest again.

Miss. [*stooping for a Pin.*] I have heard 'em say, a Pin a-Day, is a Groat a Year. Well, as I hope to be marryed (forgive me for Swearing) I vow it is a Needle.

Col. O the wonderful Works of Nature! that a black Hen should have a white Egg.

Nev. What; you have found a Mare's Nest and laugh at the Eggs.

Miss. Pray keep your Breath to cool your Porridge.

Nev. Miss there was a very pleasant Accident last Night in St. *James*'s-*Park*.

Miss. [*to Lady* Smart.] What was it your Ladyship was going to say just now?

Nev. Well Miss; tell a Mare a Tale——

Miss. I find you love to hear yourself talk.

Nev. Why, if you won't hear my Tale, kiss my, &c.

Miss. Out upon you for a filthy Creater.

Nev. What, Miss; must I tell you a Story and find you Ears?

Lord Sp. [*to Lady* Smart.] Pray Madam, don't you think Mrs. *Spendal* very genteel?

Lady Sm. Why, my Lord, I think she was cut out for a Gentlewoman, but she was spoiled in the making. She wears her Cloaths as if they were thrown on with a Pitch-Fork; and, for the Fashion, I believe they were made in the Days of Queen *Bess*.

Nev. Well, that's neither here nor there; for, you know the more careless, the more modish.

Col. Well, I'd hold a Wager there will be a Match between

her and *Dick Dolt*; and I believe I can see as far into a Millstone as another Man.

Miss. Colonel, I must beg your Pardon a thousand Times, but they say, an old Ape has an old Eye.

Nev. Miss, what do you mean? you'll spoil the Colonel's Marriage if you call him old.

Col. Not so old nor yet so cold——You know the rest Miss.

Miss. Manners is a fine Thing truly.

Col. Faith Miss, depend upon it, I'll give you as good as you bring. What? if you give a Jest, you must take a Jest.

Lady Sm. Well, Mr. *Neverout*, you'll never have done 'till you break that Knife, and then the Man won't take it again.

Miss. Why Madam, Fools will be meddling; I wish he may cut his Fingers: I hope, you can see your own Blood without fainting?

Nev. Why, Miss you shine this Morning like a sh—— Barn-Door; you'll never hold out at this Rate; pray save a little Wit for To-morrow.

Miss. Well, you have said your Say: If People will be rude, I have done. My Comfort is, it will be all one a thousand Years hence.

Nev. Miss, and you have shot your Bolt: I find you must have the last Word: Well, I'll go to the Opera to Night.—— No, I can't neither, for I have some Business——and yet I think I must; for I promised to squire the Countess to her Box.

Miss. The Countess of *Puddledock* I suppose.

Nev. Peace or War, Miss?

Lady Sm. Well, Mr. *Neverout* you'll never be mad, you are of so many Minds.

[*As Miss rises, the Chair falls behind her.*]

Miss. Well, I shan't be Lady Mayoress this Year.

Nev. No, Miss, 'tis worse than that, you won't be married this Year.

Miss. Lord! you make me laugh though I a'n't well.

[Neverout *as Miss is standing pulls her suddenly on his Lap.*]

Nev. Colonel, come sit down on my Lap; more Sacks on the Mill.

Miss. Let me go: An't you sorry for my Heaviness?

Nev. No Miss; you are very light, but I don't say, You are a light Hussy. Pray take up the Chair for your Pains.

Miss. 'Tis but one Body's Labour, you may do it your self. I wish you would be quiet, you have more Tricks than a dancing Bear.

[Neverout *rises to take up the Chair, and Miss sits in his.*]

Nev. You would not be so soon in my Grave, Madam.

Miss. Lord, I have torn my Pettycoat with your odious romping; my Rents are coming in; I'm afraid I shall fall into the Ragman's Hands.

Nev. I'll mend it, Miss.

Miss. You mend it! Go teach your Grannum to suck Eggs.

Nev. Why, Miss, you are so cross, I could find in my Heart to hate you.

Miss. With all my Heart; I can assure you, there will be no Love lost between us.

Nev. But, pray my Lady *Smart*, does not Miss look as if she could eat me without Salt?

Miss. I'll make you one Day sup Sorrow for this.

Nev. Well, follow your own Way, you'll live the longer.

Miss. See, Madam, how well I have mended it.

Lady Sm. 'Tis indifferent, as *Doll* danc'd.

Nev. 'Twill last as many Nights as Days.

Miss. Well, I knew I should never have your good Word.

Lady Sm. My Lord; Lady *Answerall* and I, were walking in the Park last Night till near Eleven; 'twas a very fine Night.

Nev. I'gad so was I, and I'll tell you a comical Accident. I'gad I lost my Understanding.

Miss. I'm glad you had any to lose.

Lady Sm. Well, but what do you mean?

Nev. I'gad I kickt my Feet against a Stone, and tore off the Heel of my Shoe, and was forced to limp to a Cobler in the *Pellmell*, to have it put on. He, he, he. [*All laugh.*]

Col. O, 'twas a delicate Night to run away with another Man's Wife.

[Neverout *sneezes*.]

Miss. God bless you, if you have not taken Snuff.

Nev. Why, what if I have, Miss?

Miss. Why then the Duce take you.

Nev. Miss, I want that Diamond Ring of Yours.

Miss. Why then, Want's like to be your Master.

[Neverout *looking at the Ring*.]

Nev. Ay marry, this is not only, but also; pray, where did you get it?

Miss. Why, where it was to be had; where the Devil got the Fryar.

Nev. Well, if I had such a fine Diamond Ring, I would not stay a Day in *England*. But you know, far fetch'd and dear bought, is fit for Ladies. I warrant this cost your Father two Pence half Penny.

[*Miss sitting between* Neverout *and the Colonel*.]

Miss. Well, here's a Rose between two Nettles.

Nev. No, Madam, with Submission, there's a Nettle between two Roses.

[*Colonel stretching himself*.]

Lady Sm. Why, Colonel, you break the King's Laws, you stretch without a Halter.

Lady Answ. Colonel, some Ladies of your Acquaintance have promised to Breakfast with you, and I am to wait on them; what will you give us?

Col. Why, Faith Madam, Batchelor's Fare, Bread and Cheese, and Kisses.

Lady Answ. Poh, what have you Batchelors to do with your Money, but to treat the Ladies? You have nothing to keep but your own four Quarters.

Lady Answ. My Lord; has Captain *Strut* the Honour to be related to your Lordship?

Lord Sp. Very nearly, Madam; he's my Cousin German quite removed.

Lady Answ. Pray is not he rich?

Lord Sp. Ay, a rich Rogue, two Shirts and a Rag.

Col. Well; however they say he has a great Estate, but only the right Owner keeps him out of it.

Lady Sm. What Religion is he of?

Lord Sp. Why; he is an Anythingarian.

Lady Answ. I believe, he has his Religion to chuse, my Lord.

[*Neverout scratches his Neck.*]

Miss. Fye, Mr. *Neverout*, an't you ashamed? I beg Pardon for the Expression; but I'm afraid your Bosom Friends are become your Backbiters.

Nev. Well, Miss, I saw a Flea once on your Pinner; and a Louse is a Man's Companion, but a Flea is a Dog's Companion. However, I wish you would scratch my Neck with your pretty white Hand.

Miss. And who would be Fool then? I would not touch a Man's Flesh for the Universe: You have the wrong Sow by the Ear; I assure you that's Meat for your Master.

Col. Well, I must be plain, here's a very bad Smell.

Miss. Perhaps, Colonel, the Fox is the finder.

Nev. No, Colonel, 'tis only your Teeth against Rain. But,

Miss. Colonel, I find, you would make a very good poor Man's Sow. But,

Nev. Miss *Notable*; all Quarrels laid aside, pray step hither for a Moment.

Miss. I'll wash my Hands and wait on you, Sir; but pray come you hither, and try to open this Lock.

Nev. We'll try what we can do.

Miss. We! what, have you Pigs in your Belly?

Nev. I assure you, Miss, I am very handy at all Things.

Miss. Marry hang them, that can't give themselves a good Word, I believe you may have an even Hand to throw a Louse into the Fire.

[*Colonel coughing.*]

Col. I have got a sad Cold.

Lady Answ. Ay, 'tis well if one can get any Thing these hard Times.

Miss. [*To Colonel.*] Choak Chicken, there's another a Hatching.

Lady Sm. Pray, Colonel, how did you get that Cold?

Lord Sp. Why, Madam, I suppose the Colonel got it by lying a-Bed barefoot.

Lady Answ. Why, then Colonel, you must take it for better for worse, as a Man takes his Wife.

Col. Well, Ladies, I apprehend you without a Constable.

Miss. Mr. *Neverout*, Mr. *Neverout*, come hither this Moment.

Lady Sm. [*imitating her.*] Mr. *Neverout*, Mr. *Neverout*, I wish he were ty'd to your Girdle.

Nev. What's the Matter? Whose Mare's dead now?

Miss. Take your Labour for your Pains, you may go back again like a Fool as you came.

Nev. Well, Miss, if you deceive me a second Time, it's my Fault.

Lady Sm. Colonel, methinks your Coat is too short.

Col. It will be long enough, before I get another, Madam.

Miss. Come, come, the Coat's a good Coat, and come of good Friends.

Nev. Ladies, you are mistaken in the Stuff: 'tis half Silk.

Col. Tom Neverout, you're a Fool, and that's your Fault.

[*A great Noise below.*]

Lady Sm. Hey, what a clattering is there; one would think Hell was broke loose.

Miss. Indeed, Madam, I must take my Leave, for I an't well.

Lady Sm. What, you are sick of the Mulligrubs with eating chopt Hay.

Miss. No indeed, Madam, to say the Truth of it, I'm sick and hungry, more need of a Cook than a Doctor.

Lady Ans. Poor Miss, she's sick as a Cushion, she wants nothing but stuffing.

Col. If you are sick, you shall have a Caudle of Calves Eggs.

Nev. I can't find my Gloves.

Miss. I saw the Dog running away with some dirty Thing a while ago.

Col. Miss, you have got my Handkerchief; pray let me have it.

N

Lady Sm. No, keep it Miss, for they say Possession is eleven Points of the Law.

Miss. Madam, he shall never have it again; it is in Hucksters Hands.

Lady Answ. What; I see 'tis raining again.

Lord Sp. Why then, Madam, we must do as they do in *Spain.*

Lady Sm. Pray, my Lord, how is that?

Lord Sp. Why, Madam, we must let it rain.

[*Miss whispers Lady* Smart.]

Nev. Miss, there's no whispering but there's lying.

Miss. Lord! Mr. *Neverout,* you are grown as pert as a Pearmonger this Morning.

Nev. Indeed, Miss, you are very handsome.

Miss. Poh, I know that already, tell me News.

[*Some Body knocks at the Door.*]

[*Footman comes in.*]

Footman. [*to Col.*] An please your Honour, there's a Man below wants to speak to you.

Col. Ladies, your Pardon for a Minute.

[*Colonel goes out.*]

Lady Sm. Miss, I sent Yesterday to know how you did, but you were gone abroad early.

Miss. Why, Madam, I was huncht up in a Hackney Coach with three Country Acquaintance, who called upon me to take the Air as far as *Highgate.*

Lady Sm. And had you a pleasant Airing?

Miss. No, Madam, it rain'd all the Time: I was jolted to Death, and the Road was so bad, that I screamed every Moment, and call'd to the Coachman, pray Friend don't spill us.

Nev. So, Miss, you were afraid that Pride should have a Fall.

Miss. Mr. *Neverout,* when I want a Fool, I'll send for you.

Lord Sp. Miss, did not your left Ear burn last Night?

Miss. Pray why, my Lord?

Lord Sp. Because I was then in some Company, where you were extolled to the Skies, I assure you.

Miss. My Lord, that was more their Goodness, than my Desert.

Lord Sp. They said you were a compleat Beauty.

Miss. My Lord, I am as God made me.

Lady Sm. The Girl's well enough if she had but another Nose.

Miss. O, Madam, I know I shall always have your good Word; you love to help a lame Dog over the Style.

[*One knocks.*]

Lady Sm. Who's there? You're on the wrong Side of the Door; come in if you be fat.

[*Colonel comes in again.*]

Lord Sp. Why, Colonel, you are a Man of great Business.

Col. Ay, my Lord; I'm like my Lord Mayor's Fool; full of Business, and nothing to do.

Lady Sm. My Lord, don't you think the Colonel's mightily fallen away of late?

Lord Sp. Ay, fallen from a Horse Load to a Cart-Load.

Col. Why, my Lord, I'gad I am like a Rabbit, fat and lean in four and twenty Hours.

Lady Sm. I assure you, the Colonel walks as strait as a Pin.

Miss. Yes, he's a handsome bodied Man in the Face.

Nev. A handsome Foot and Leg, God-a-Mercy Shoe and Stocking.

Col. What? three upon one, that's foul play. This would make a Parson swear.

Nev. Why Miss; what's the Matter? You look as if you had neither won nor lost.

Col. Why, you must know, Miss lives upon Love.

Miss. Yes, upon Love and Lumps of the Cupboard.

Lady Ans. Ay, they say Love and Pease-porridge are two dangerous Things; one breaks the Heart, and t'other the Belly.

[*Miss imitating Lady* Answerall's *Tone.*]

Miss. Very pretty, one breaks the Heart, and t'other the Belly.

Lady Ans. Have a Care, Miss, they say mocking is catching.

Miss. I never heard that.

Nev. Why then, Miss, you have one wrinkle —— more than ever you had before.

Miss. Well; live and learn.

Nev. Ay, and be hang'd, and forget all.

Miss. Well, Mr. *Neverout*, take it as you please; but I swear, you're a sawcy Jack for using such Expressions.

Nev. Why then, Miss, if you go to that, I must tell you, that there's never a Jack, but there's a Jill.

Miss. O, Mr. *Neverout*, every one knows that you are the Pink of Courtesy.

Nev. And, Miss, all the World allows that you are the Flower of Civility.

Lady Sm. Miss, I hear there was a great deal of Company where you visited last Night: Pray who were they?

Miss. Why, there was Lady *Forward*, Miss *Toandagain*, Sir *John Ogle*, my Lady *Clapper*; and I, quoth the Dog.

Col. Was your Visit long, Miss?

Miss. Why truly, they went all to the Opera, and so poor Pillgarlick came home alone.

Nev. Alack a Day, poor Miss, methinks it grieves me to pity you.

Miss. What, you think you said a fine Thing now; well, if I had a Dog with no more Wit, I would hang him.

Lady Sm. Miss, if it be Manners, may I ask which is oldest, you, or Lady *Scuttle?*

Miss. Why, my Lord, when I dye for Age, she may quake for Fear.

Lady Sm. She's a very great Gadder abroad.

Lady Sm. Lord! she made me follow her last Week through all the Shops like a Tantiny Pig.

Lady Sm. I remember you told me, you had been with her from *Dan* to *Bersheba*.

Miss. O, Mr. *Neverout*, my little *Countess* has just littered; speak me fair, and I'll set you down for a Puppy.

Nev. Why Miss, if I speak you fair, perhaps I mayn't tell Truth.

Lord Sp. Ay, but *Tom*, smoak that, she calls you Puppy by Craft.

Nev. Well, Miss, you ride the fore horse To-Day.

Miss. Ay, many a one says well, that thinks ill.

Nev. Fye, Miss, you said that once before; and you know, too much of one Thing is good for nothing.

Miss. Why sure, one can't say a good Thing too often.

Lord Sp. Well; so much for that, and Butter for Fish. Let us call another Cause. Pray, Madam, does your Ladyship know Mrs. *Nice?*

Lady Sm. Perfectly well, my Lord; she is nice by Name, and nice by Nature.

Lord Sp. Is it possible that she could take that Booby *Tom Blunder* for Love?

Miss. She had good Skill in Horse Flesh, that could chuse a Goose to ride on.

Lady Answ. Why, my Lord, it was her Fate; they say Marriage and hanging go by Destiny.

Col. I believe, she'll never be burnt for a Witch.

Lord Sp. They say Marriages are made in Heaven; but I doubt when she was marry'd she had no Friends there.

Nev. Well, she's got out of God's Blessing into the warm Sun.

Col. The Fellow's well enough, if he had any Guts in his Brains.

Lady Sm. They say, thereby hangs a Tale.

Lord Sp. Why, he's a meer Hobbledehoy, neither Man nor Boy.

Miss. Well, if I were to chuse a Husband, I would never be marry'd to a little Man.

Nev. Pray why so, Miss? For they say of all Evils we ought to chuse the least.

Miss. Because Folks would say, when they saw us together; there goes the Woman and her Husband.

Col. [*To Lady* Smart.] Will your Ladyship be on the *Mall* To-morrow Night?

Lady Sm. No, that won't be proper; you know To-morrow is *Sunday*.

Lord Sp. What then, Madam, they say, the better Day the better Deed.

Lady Ans. Pray, Mr. *Neverout*, how do you like my Lady *Fruzz?*

Nev. Pox on her, she's as old as *Pole's*.

Miss. So will you be, if you ben't hang'd when you're young.

Nev. Come, Miss, let us be Friends; will you go to the Park this Evening?

Miss. With all my Heart, and a Piece of my Liver; but not with you.

Lady Sm. I'll tell you one Thing, and that's not two: I'm afraid I shall get a Fit of the Head-ach To-day.

Col. O, Madam, don't be afraid, it comes with a Fright.

Miss. [*To Lady* Answerall.] Madam, one of your Ladyship's Lappets is longer than t'other.

Lady Ans. Well, no Matter; they that ride on a trotting Horse will ne'er perceive it.

Nev. Indeed, Miss, your Lappets hang worse.

Miss. Well, I love a Lyar in my Heart, and you fit me to a Hair.

[*Miss rises up.*]

Nev. Duce take you, Miss, you trod on my Foot, I hope you don't intend to come to my Bed-Side.

Miss. In troth, you are afraid of your Friends, and none of them near you.

Lord Sp. Well said, Girl, [*giving her a Chuck.*] take that, they say a Chuck under the Chin is worth two Kisses.

Lady Answ. But, Mr. *Neverout*, I wonder why such a handsome strait young Gentleman as you, does not get some rich Widow.

Lord Sp. Strait! ay, strait as my Leg, and that's crooked at Knee.

Nev. Faith, Madam, if it rain'd rich Widows, none of them would fall upon me. I'gad I was born under a three Penny Planet, never to be worth a Groat.

Lady Answ. No, Mr. *Neverout*, I believe you were born with a Cawl on your Head; you are such a Favourite among the Ladies. But, what think you of Widow *Prim?* She's immensely rich.

Nev. Hang her, they say her Father was a Baker.

Lady Sm. Ay, but it is not what is she, but what has she now a-days.

Col. *Tom*, Faith put on a bold Face for once, and have at the Widow. I'll speak a good Word for you to her.

Lady Ans. Ay, I warrant you'll speak one Word for him, and two for your self.

Miss. Well, I had that just at my Tongue's End.

Lady Answ. Why, Miss, they say good Wits jump.

Nev. Faith, Madam, I had rather marry a Woman I loved, in her Smock, than Widow *Prim*, if she had her Weight in Gold.

Lady Sm. Come, come, Mr. *Neverout*, Marriage is honourable; but, Housekeeping is a Shrew.

Lady Answ. Consider, Mr. *Neverout*, four bare Legs in a Bed; and you are a younger Brother.

Col. Well, Madam, the younger Brother is the better Gentleman. However, *Tom*, I would advise you to look before you leap.

Lord Sp. The Colonel says true: Besides, you can't expect to wive and thrive in the same Year.

Miss. [*Shuddering.*] Lord, there's some Body walking over my Grave.

Col. Pray, Lady *Answerall*, where was you last Wednesday, when I did my self the Honour to wait on you? I think your Ladyship is one of the Tribe of Gad.

Lady Answ. Why, Colonel; I was at Church.

Col. Nay, then I will be hang'd, and my Horse too.

Nev. I believe her Ladyship was at a Church, with a Chimney in it.

Miss. Lord! my Pettycoat, how it hangs by Jommetry.

Nev. Perhaps, the Fault may be in your Shape.

Miss. [*Looking gravely.*] Come, Mr. *Neverout*, there's no Jest like a true Jest: But, I suppose, you think my Back's broad enough to bear every Thing.

Nev. Madam; I humbly beg your Pardon.

Miss. Well, Sir, your Pardon's granted.

Nev. Well, all Things have an End, and a Pudden has two, up up on, my my Word. [*Stutters*.]

Miss. What; Mr. *Neverout*, can't you speak without a Spoon?

Lady Sp. [*To Lady* Smart.] Has your Ladyship seen the Dutchess since your Falling-out?

Lady Sm. Never, my Lord, but once at a Visit; and she look'd at me, as the Devil look'd over *Lincoln*.

Nev. Pray Miss, take a Pinch of my Snuff.

Miss. What; you break my Head, and give me a Plaister; well, with all my Heart; once and not use it.

Nev. Well, Miss, if you wanted me and your Victuals, you'd want your two best Friends.

Col. [*To* Neverout.] *Tom*, Miss and you must kiss and be Friends.

[Neverout *salutes Miss*.]

Miss. Any Thing for a quiet Life. My Nose itch'd, and I knew I should drink Wine, or kiss a Fool.

Col. Well, *Tom*, if that ben't fair, hang fair.

Nev. I never said a rude Thing to a Lady in my Life.

Miss. Here's a Pin for that Lye. I'm sure Lyars had need of good Memories. Pray, Colonel, was not he very uncivil to me but just now?

Lady Answ. Mr. *Neverout*, if Miss will be angry for nothing, take my Council, and bid her turn the Buckle of her Girdle behind her.

Nev. Come, Lady *Answerall*, I know better Things, Miss and I are good Friends: Don't put Tricks upon Travellers.

Col. *Tom*, not a Word of the Pudden, I beg you.

Lady Sm. Ah, Colonel, you'll never be good, nor then neither.

Lord Sp. Which of the Goods d'ye mean? Good for something, or good for nothing.

Miss. I have a Blister on my Tongue; yet I don't remember I told a Lye.

Lady Ans. I thought you did just now.

Lord Sp. Pray, Madam, what did thought do?

Lady Answ. Well, for my Life I cannot conceive what your Lordship means.

Lord Sp. Indeed, Madam, I mean no Harm.

Lady Sm. No to be sure, my Lord, you are as innocent as a Devil of two Year old.

Nev. Madam, they say, ill Doers, are ill Deemers; but I don't apply it to your Ladyship.

[*Miss mending a Hole in her Lace.*]

Miss. Well, you see I'm mending; I hope, I shall be good in Time. Look, Lady *Answerall*, is it not well mended?

Lady Ans. Ay, this is something like a Tanzy.

Lady Sm. Pray Colonel, are you not very much tann'd?

Col. Yes, Madam, but a Cup of Christmas Ale, will soon wash it off.

Lord Sp. Lady *Smart*, does not your Ladyship think Mrs. *Fade*, is mightily altered since her Marriage?

Lady Answ. Why, my Lord, she was handsome in her Time; but, she can't eat her Cake and have her Cake. I hear she's grown a mere Otomy.

Lady Answ. Poor Creature, the black Ox has set his Foot upon her already.

Miss. Ay, she has quite lost the Blue on the Plum.

Lady Sm. And yet, they say he is very fond of her still.

Lady Answ. O Madam! if she would eat Gold, he would give it her.

* *Nev.* [*To Lady* Smart.] Madam, have you heard that Lady *Queasy*, was lately at the Play-House in Cog?

Lady Sm. What Lady *Queasy*, of all Women in the World! Do you say it upon Rep?

Nev. Pozz; I saw her with my own Eyes; she sat among the Mobb in the Gallery, her own ugly Fizz. And she saw me look at her.

Col. Her Ladyship was plaguily bamb'd; I warrant it put her into the Hipps.

Nev. I smoakt her huge Nose; and I'gad, she put me in Mind of the Woodcock, that strives to hide his long Bill, and then thinks no Body fees him.

* *Here the Author, for Variety, runs into some Cant Words.*

Col. *Tom*, I advise you to hold your Tongue; for you'll never say so good a Thing again.

Lady Sm. Miss, what are you looking for?

Miss. O! Madam, I have lost the finest Needle.

Lady Answ. Why, seek 'till you find it, and you won't lose your Labour.

Nev. The Loop of my Hat is broke. How shall I mend it? [*He fastens it with a Pin.*] well, hang them, say I, that have no Shift.

Miss. Ay, and hang them that has one too many.

Miss. Well, but I don't like such Jesting.

Nev. Oh Miss! I have heard a sad Story of you.

Miss. I defy you, Mr. *Neverout*; no Body can say, black's my Eye.

Nev. I believe you would wish they could.

Miss. Well, but who was your Author? Come, tell Truth for once, and shame the Devil.

Nev. Come, then Miss; guess who it was that told me; come, put on your considering Cap.

Miss. Well, who was it?

Nev. Why, one that lives within a Mile of an Oak.

Miss. Well; go hang yourself in your own Garter; for I'm sure the Gallows groans for you.

Nev. Bite! Miss, I was but in Jest.

Miss. Well, but don't let that stick in your Gizzard.

Col. [*To Lord* Smart.] My Lord, does your Lordship know Mrs. *Talkall?*

Lord Sm. Only by Sight: But, I hear she has a great deal of Wit; and I'gad, as the Saying is, Mettle to the Back-Bone.

Lady Sm. So I hear.

Col. Why; *Dick Lubber*, said to her t'other Day; Madam, you can't cry Bo to a Goose: Yes, but I can said she; and I'gad cry'd Bo full in his Face. We all thought we should break our Hearts with laughing.

Lord Sp. That was cutting with a Vengeance. And, prithee how did the Fool look?

Col. Look: I'gad, he look'd for all the World, like an Owl in an Ivy Bush.

[Child comes in screaming.]

Miss. Well, if that Child was mine, I'd whip it 'till the Blood came. Peace you little Vixen; if I were near you, I wou'd not be far from you.

Lady Sm. Ay, ay, Batchelor's Wives, and Maid's Children, are finely tutor'd.

Lady Answ. Come to me Master, and I'll give you a Sugar-Plum: Why Miss, you forget that ever you was a Child yourself.

[She gives the Child a Lump of Sugar.]

I have heard 'em say Boys will long.

Col. My Lord, I suppose you know, that Mr. *Buzzard* has married again.

Lady Sm. This is his fourth Wife; then he has been shod round.

Col. Why, you must know, she had a Month's Mind to *Dick Frontless*, and thought to run away with him; but, her Parents forced her to take the old Fellow, for a good Settlement.

Lord Sp. So the Man got his Mare again.

Lady Sm. I'm told he said a very good Thing to *Dick*; said he, you *think* us old Fellows are Fools. But we old Fellows *know* young Fellows are Fools.

Col. I know nothing of that; but I know, he's devilish Old, and she's very Young.

Lady Answ. Why, they call that a Match of the World's making.

Miss. What, if he had been Young, and she Old?

Nev. Why, Miss, that would have been a Match of the Devil's making: But, when both are Young, that's a Match of God's making.

[Miss searching her Pocket for a Thimble, brings out a Nutmeg.]

Nev. O Miss! have a Care; for if you carry a Nutmeg in your Pocket, you'll certainly be married to an old Man.

Miss. Well, and if ever I be married, it shall be to an old Man; they always make the best Husbands: And it is better to be an old Man's Darling, than a young Man's Warling.

Nev. Faith, Miss, if you speak, as you think, I'll give you my Mother for a Maid.

[*Lady* Smart *rings the Bell.*]
[*Footman comes in.*]

Lady Sm. Harkee, you Fellow, run to my Lady *Match*; and desire she will remember to be here at Six to play at *Quadrille*, d'ye hear, if you fall by the Way, don't stay to get up again.

Footman. Madam, I don't know the House.

Lady Sm. Well, that's not for Want of Ignorance, follow your Nose. Go enquire among the Servants.

[*Footman goes out, and leaves the Door open.*]

Lady Sm. Here, come back you Fellow, why did you leave the Door open: Remember, that a good Servant must always come, when he's call'd, do what he's bid, and shut the Door after him.

[*The Footman goes out again, and falls down Stairs.*]

Lady Answ. Neck, or nothing. Come down, or I'll fetch you down: Well, but I hope the poor Fellow has not saved the Hangman a Labour.

Nev. Pray, Madam, smoak Miss yonder biting her Lips, and playing with her Fan.

Miss. Who's that takes my Name in vain?

[*She runs up to them, and falls down.*]

Lady Sm. What, more falling? Do you intend the Frolick should go round?

Lady Ans. Why, Miss, I wish you may not have broke her Ladyship's Floor.

Nev. Miss, come to me, and I'll take you up.

Lord Sp. Well, but without a Jest, I hope, Miss, you are not hurt.

Col. Nay, she must be hurt for certain; for you see her Head is all of a Lump.

Miss. Well; remember this, Colonel, when I have Money, and you have none.

Lady Sm. But, Colonel, when do you design to get a House, and a Wife, and a Fire to put her in?

Miss. Lord! who would be marryed to a Soldier, and carry his Knap-Sack.

Nev. O, Madam, *Mars* and *Venus*, you know.

Col. I'gad, Madam, I'd marry To-morrow, if I thought I could bury my Wife just when the Honey Moon is over; but they say, a Woman has as many Lives as a Cat.

Lady Answ. I find, the Colonel thinks a dead Wife under the Table, is the best Goods in a Man's House.

Lady Sm. O, but Colonel, if you had a good Wife, it would break your Heart to part with her.

Col. Yes, Madam, for they say, he that has lost his Wife and Sixpence, has lost a Tester.

Lady Sm. But, Colonel, they say, that every marryed Man should believe there is but one good Wife in the World, and that's his own.

Col. For all that, I doubt, a good Wife must be bespoke; for there is none ready made.

Miss. I suppose, the Gentleman's a Woman Hater; but, Sir, I think you ought to remember that once you had a Mother. And, pray, if it had not been for a Woman, where would you have been, Colonel?

Col. Nay, Miss, you cry'd Whore first, when you talk'd of the Knap-Sack.

Lady Answ. But, I hope, you won't blame the whole Sex, because some are bad.

Nev. And, they say, he that hates Women, suck'd a Sow.

Col. O, Madam, there's no general Rule without an Exception.

Lady Sm. Then, why don't you marry and settle.

Col. I'gad, Madam, there's nothing will settle me but a Bullet.

Miss. I suppose, the Colonel was cross'd in his first Love; which makes him so severe on all the Sex.

Lady Ans. Yes, and I'll hold an hundred to one, that the Colonel has been over Head and Ears in Love with some Lady that has made his Heart ach.

Col. O, Madam, we Soldiers are Admirers of all the fair Sex.

Miss. I wish I could see the Colonel in love, 'till he was ready to dye.

Lady Sm. Ay, but I doubt, few People dye for Love in these Days.

Nev. Well, I confess, I differ from the Colonel, for I hope to have a rich, and a handsome Wife yet, before I dye.

Col. Ay, *Tom*, live Horse, and thou shalt have Grass.

Miss. Well, Colonel, but whatever you say against Women, they are better Creatures than Men; for Men were made of Clay, but Woman was made of Man.

Col. Miss, you may say what you please; but faith, you'll never lead Apes in Hell.

Nev. No, no, I'll be sworn, Miss has not an Inch of Nun's Flesh about her.

Miss. I understumble you, Gentlemen.

Nev. Madam, your humblecumdumble.

Lord Sp. Pray, Miss, when did you see your old Acquaintance Mrs. *Cloudy?* You and she are two, I hear.

Miss. See her: Marry I don't Care whether I ever see her again, God bless my Eye-Sight.

Lady Ans. Lord; why she and you were as great as two Inkle-Weavers. I am sure, I have seen her hug you, as the Devil hugg'd the Witch.

Miss. That's true; but I'm told for certain, she's no better than she should be.

Lady Sm. Well; God mend us all; but you must allow, the World is very censorious. I never heard that she was naughty.

Col. [*To* Neverout.] Come, Sir *Thomas*, when the King pleases, when do you intend to march?

Lord Sp. Have Patience; *Tom*, is your Friend *Ned Rattle* marryed?

Nev. Yes, Faith, my Lord; he has tyed a Knot with his Tongue, that he can never untye with his Teeth.

Lady Sm. Ay, marry in haste, and repent at leisure.

Lady Answ. Has he got a good Fortune with his Lady? For, they say, something has some savour, but nothing has no flavour.

Nev. Faith, Madam, all he gets by her, he may put into his Eye, and see never the worse.

Miss. Then, I believe, he heartily wishes her in *Abraham's* Bosom.

Col. Pray, my Lord, how does *Charles Limber*, and his fine Wife agree?

Lord Sp. Why, they say, he's the greatest Cuckold in Town.

Nev. O but, my Lord, you should always except my Lord Mayor.

Miss. Mr. *Neverout.*

Nev. Hay, Madam, did you call me?

Miss. Hay! Why; Hay is for Horses.

Nev. Why, Miss, than you may——

Col. Pray, my Lord, what's a Clock by your Oracle?

Lord Sp. Faith, I can't tell; I think my Watch runs upon Wheels.

Nev. Miss, pray be so kind to call a Servant to bring me a Glass of Small-Beer. I know you are at Home here.

Miss. Every Fool can do as they're bid. Make a Page of your own Age, and do it yourself.

Nev. Chuse proud Fool; I did but ask you.

[*Miss puts her Hand to her Knee.*]

What, Miss, are you thinking of your Sweetheart? Is your Garter slipping down?

Miss. Pray, Mr. *Neverout*, keep your Breath to cool your Porridge. You measure my Corn by your Bushel.

Nev. Indeed, Miss, you Lye——

Miss. Did you ever hear any Thing so rude.

Nev. I mean, you lye——under a Mistake.

Miss. If a thousand Lyes could choak you, you would have been choaked many a Day ago.

[*Miss tries to snatch Mr.* Neverout's *Snuff-Box.*]

Nev. Madam, you miss'd that, as you miss'd your Mother's Blessing.

[*She tries again, and misses.*]

Nev. Snap short makes you look so lean, Miss.

Miss. Poh; you are so robustious: You had like to put out my Eye: I assure you, if you blind me, you must lead me.

Lady Sm. Dear Miss, be quiet; and bring me a Pin-Cushion out of that Closet.

[*Miss opens the Door, and squals.*]

Lady Sm. Lord bless the Girl, what's the Matter now?

Miss. I vow, Madam, I saw something in black, I thought it was a Spirit.

Col. Why, Miss, did you ever see a Spirit?

Miss. No, Sir, I thank God, I never saw any Thing worse than my self.

Nev. Well, I did a very foolish Thing Yesterday, and was a great Puppy for my Pains.

Miss. Very likely; for they say, many a true Word spoken in Jest.

[*Footman returns.*]

Lady Sm. Well, did you deliver your Message? You are fit to be sent for Sorrow, you stay so long by the Way.

Footman. Madam, my Lady was not at home; so, I did not leave the Message.

Lady Sm. This it is to send a Fool of an Errand.

[*Lord Sparkish looking at his Watch.*]

Lord Sp. 'Tis past twelve a Clock.

Lady Sm. Well, what is that among us all?

Lord Sp. Madam, I must take my Leave.

Lady Sm. Well, but your Lordship, and the Colonel, will dine with us To-Day; and Mr. *Neverout*, I hope, we shall have your good Company. There will be no Soul else, besides my own Lord, and these Ladies. For every Body knows, I hate a Crowd: I would rather want Vittels, than Elbow Room. We dine punctually at three.

Lord Sp. Madam, we'll be sure to attend your Ladyship.

Col. Madam, my Stomach serves me instead of a Clock.

[*Another Footman comes back.*]

Lady Sm. O, you are the other Fellow I sent: Well, have you been with my Lady *Club*. You are good to send of a dead Man's Errand.

Footman. Madam, my Lady *Club* begs your Ladyship's Pardon; but she is engaged To-Night.

Miss. Well, Mr. *Neverout*; here's the Back of my Hand to you.

Nev. Miss, I find you will have the last Word. Ladies, I am more yours than my own.

Second CONVERSATION.

[*Lord* Smart, *and the former Company at three a Clock, coming to dine.*]

[*After Salutations.*]

Lord Sm. I'M sorry I was not at home this Morning, when you all did us the Honour to call here. But I went to the Levee To-Day.

Lord Sp. O, my Lord; I'm sure the Loss was ours.

Lady Sm. Gentlemen, and Ladies, you are come into a sad dirty House, I am sorry for it, but we have had our Hands in Mortar.

Lord Sp. O, Madam, your Ladyship is pleased to say so, but I never saw any Thing so clean and so fine. I profess it is a perfect Paradise.

Lady Sm. My Lord, your Lordship is always very obliging.

Lord Sp. Pray, Madam, whose Picture is that?

Lady Sm. Why, my Lord, it was drawn for me.

Lord Sp. I'll swear, the Painter did not flatter your Ladyship.

Col. My Lord, the Day is finely cleared up.

Lord Sm. Ay, Colonel, 'tis a Pity that fair Weather should ever do any harm. [*to* Neverout.] Why, *Tom*, you are high in the Mode.

Nev. My Lord, it is better to be out of the World, than out of the Fashion.

Lord Sm. But, *Tom*, I hear, you and Miss are always quarelling: I fear, it is your Fault, for I can assure you, she is very good humoured.

Nev. Ay, my Lord, so is the Devil when he's pleas'd.

Lord Sm. Miss, what do you think of my Friend *Tom?*

Miss. My Lord, I think he is not the wisest Man in the World; and truly, he's sometimes very rude.

Lord Sp. That may be true; but yet, he that hangs *Tom* for a Fool, may find a Knave in the Halter.

O

Miss. Well, however, I wish he were hang'd, if it were only to try.

Nev. Well, Miss, if I must be hanged, I won't go far to chuse my Gallows: It shall be about your fair Neck.

Miss. I'll see your Nose Cheese first, and the Dogs eating it. But, my Lord, Mr. *Neverout*'s Wit begins to run low, for I vow he said this before. Pray, Colonel, give him a Pinch, and I'll do as much for you.

Lord Sp. My Lady *Smart*, your Ladyship has a very fine Scarf.

Lady Sm. Yes, my Lord, it will make a flaming Figure in a Country Church.

[*Footman comes in.*]

Footman. Madam, Dinner's upon the Table.

Col. Faith, I'm glad of it; my Belly began to cry Cupboard.

Nev. I wish I may never hear worse News.

Miss. What; Mr. *Neverout*, you are in great haste; I believe your Belly thinks your Throat's cut.

Nev. No, faith Miss, three Meals a Day, and a good Supper at night, will serve my Turn.

Miss. To say the Truth, I'm hungry.

Nev. And I'm angry, so let us both go fight.

[*They go in to Dinner, and after the usual Compliments, take their Seats.*]

Lord Sm. Ladies and Gentlemen, will you eat any Oysters before Dinner.

Col. With all my Heart. [*Takes an Oyster.*] He was a bold Man that first eat an Oyster.

Lady Sm. They say, Oysters are a cruel Meat; because we eat them alive: Then, they are an uncharitable Meat; for we leave nothing to the Poor. And, they are an ungodly Meat, because we never say Grace to them.

Nev. Faith, that's as well said, as if I had said it my self.

Lady Sm. Well, we are all well set, if we be but as well serv'd. Come, Colonel, handle your Arms: Shall I help you to some Beef?

Col. If your Ladyship pleases; and pray don't cut like a

Mother-in-law, but send me a large Slice; for I love to lay a good Foundation: I vow 'tis a noble Sirloyn.

Nev. Ay, here's Cut and come again.

Miss. But pray, why is it called a Sirloyn?

Lord Sp. Why, you must know, that our King *James* I. who loved good Eating, being invited to Dinner by one of his Nobles, and seeing a large Loyn of Beef at his Table; he drew out his Sword, and in a Frolick Knighted it. Few People know the Secret of this.

Lady Sm. Beef is Man's Meat, my Lord.

Lord Sm. But, my Lord, I say, Beef is the King of Meat.

Miss. Pray, what have I done, that I must not have a Plate?

Lady Sm. [*To* Lady *Answerall.*] What will your Ladyship please to eat?

Lady Answ. Pray, Madam, help your self.

Col. They say Eating and Scratching wants but a Beginning. If you will give me Leave, I'll help my self to a Slice of this Shoulder of Veal.

Lady Sm. Colonel, you can't do a kinder Thing. Well, you are all heartily welcome, as I may say.

Col. They say there are thirty and two good Bits in a Shoulder of Veal.

Lady Sm. Ay, Colonel; thirty bad Bits, and two good ones; you see I understand you; but, I hope you have got one of the two good ones?

Nev. Colonel, I'll be of your Mess.

Col. Then, pray *Tom*, carve for your self: They say, two Hands in a Dish, and one in a Purse. Hah, said I well, *Tom*?

Nev. Colonel, you spoke like an Oracle.

[*Miss to Lady* Answerall.]

Miss. Madam, will your Ladyship help me to some Fish?

Lord Sm. [*To* Neverout.] *Tom*, they say Fish should swim thrice.

Nev. How is that, my Lord?

Lord Sm. Why, *Tom*, first it should swim in the Sea; (do you mind me?) then it should swim in Butter; and at last

Sirrah, it should swim in good Claret. I think I have made it out.

[*Footman to Lord* Smart.]

Footman. My Lord, Sir *John Linger* is coming up.

Lord Sm. God so! I invited him to Dinner with me to-Day, and forgot it. Well, desire him to walk in.

[*Sir* John Linger *comes in.*]

Sir John. What, are you at it? Why, then I'll be gone.

Lady Sm. Sir *John*, I beg you will set down; come, the more, the merrier.

Sir John. Ay; but the fewer the better Cheer.

Lady Sm. Well, I am the worst in the World at making Apologies. It was my Lord's Fault. I doubt you must kiss the Hare's Foot.

Sir John. I see you are fast by the Teeth.

Col. Faith, Sir *John*, we are killing that would kill us.

Lord Sp. You see, Sir *John*, we are upon a Business of Life and Death. Come, will you do as we do. You are come in Pudden Time.

Sir John. Ay, this you would be doing if I were dead. What, you keep Court Hours I see. I'll be going, and get a Bit of Meat at my Inn.

Lady Sm. Why, we won't eat you, Sir *John*.

Sir John. It is my own Fault; but, I was kept by a Fellow, who bought some *Derbyshire* Oxen from me.

Nev. You see, Sir *John*, we stayed for you, as one Horse does for another.

Lady Sm. My Lord, will you help Sir *John* to some Beef. Lady *Answerall*, pray eat, you see your Dinner. I am sure, if we had known we should have such good Company, we should have been better provided; but, you must take the Will for the Deed. I'm afraid you are invited to your Loss.

Col. And, pray, Sir *John*, how do you like the Town? You have been absent a long Time.

Sir John. Why, I find little *London* stands just where it did when I left it last.

Nev. What do you think of *Hanover-Square*, why, Sir *John*, *London* is gone out of Town since you saw it.

Lady Sm. Sir *John*, I can only say, you are heartily welcome; and I wish I had something better for you.

Col. Here's no Salt; Cuckolds will run away with the Meat.

Lord Sm. Pray edge a little, to make more Room for Sir *John*. Sir *John* fall to, you know half an Hour is soon lost at Dinner.

Sir John. I protest, I can't eat a Bit; for I took Share of a Beef-Stake, and two Mugs of Ale with my Chapman, besides a Tankard of *March* Beer as soon as I got out of Bed.

Lady Answ. Not fresh and fasting, I hope.

Sir John. Yes faith, Madam, I always wash my Kettle before I put the Meat in it.

Lady Sm. Poh! Sir *John*, you have seen nine Houses since you eat last: Come, you have kept a Corner of your Stomach for a Bit of Venison-Pasty.

Sir John. Well, I'll try what I can do when it comes up.

Lady Answ. Come, Sir *John*, you may go further, and fare worse.

Miss. [*To* Neverout.] Pray, Mr. *Neverout*, will you please to send me a Piece of Tongue?

Nev. By no Means, Madam; one Tongue's enough for a Woman.

Col. Miss, here's a Tongue that never told a Lye.

Miss. That was because it could not speak. Why, Colonel, I never told a Lye in my Life.

Nev. I appeal to all the Company, whether that be not the greatest Lye that ever was told.

Col. [*To* Neverout.] Prethee, *Tom*, send me the two Legs, and Rump, and Liver, of that Pigeon; for you must know, I love what no Body else loves.

Nev. But what if any of the Ladies should long. Well, here take it, and the Devil do you good with it.

Lady Answ. Well; this eating and drinking takes away a Body's Stomach.

Nev. I'm sure I have lost mine.

Miss. What! the Bottom of it, I suppose.

Nev. No really, Miss, I have quite lost it.

Miss. I should be sorry a poor Body had found it.

Lady Sm. But, Sir *John*, we hear you are married since we saw you last. What; you have stolen a Wedding, it seems.

Sir John. Well, one can't do a foolish Thing once in one's Life, but one must hear of it a hundred Times.

Col. And pray, Sir *John*, how does your Lady unknown?

Sir John. My Wife's well, Colonel; and at your Service in a civil Way. Ha, ha. [*He laughs.*]

Miss. Pray, Sir *John*, is your Lady tall, or short?

Sir John. Why, Miss, I thank God, she's a little Evil.

Lord Sp. Come, give me a Glass of Claret.
           [*Footman fills him a Bumper.*]
Why do you fill so much?

Nev. My Lord, he fills as he loves you.

Lady Sm. Miss, shall I send you some Cucumber?

Miss. Madam, I dare not touch it; for they say, Cucumbers are cold in the third Degree.

Lady Sm. Mr. *Neverout*, do you love Pudden?

Nev. Madam, I'm like all Fools; I love every Thing that is good: But the Proof of the Pudden, is in the eating.

Col. Sir *John*, I hear you are a great Walker, when you are at home.

Sir John. No, Faith, Colonel, I always love to walk with a Horse in my Hand. But I have had devilish bad Luck in Horse-Flesh, of late.

Lady Sm. Why then, Sir *John*, you must kiss a Parson's Wife.

Lady Sm. They say, Sir *John*, that your Lady has a great deal of Wit.

Sir John. Madam, she can make a Pudden; and has just Wit enough to know her Husband's Breeches from another Man's.

Lady Sm. My Lord *Sparkish*, I have some excellent Cyder, will you please to taste it.

Lord Sp. My Lord, I should like it well enough, if it were not so treacherous.

Lord Sm. Pray, my Lord, how is it treacherous?

Lord Sp. Because it smiles in my Face, and cuts my Throat. [*Here a loud Laugh.*]

Miss. Odd so, Madam, your Knives are very sharp, for I have cut my Finger.

Lady Sm. I'm sorry for it, pray which Finger?

Miss. Why, this Finger, (God bless the Mark) no, 'tis this: I vow, I can't find which it is.

Nev. Ay, the Fox had a Wound, and he could not tell where, &c. Bring some Water to throw in her Face.

Miss. Pray, Mr. *Neverout*, did you ever draw a Sword in Anger? I warrant, you would faint at the Sight of your own Blood.

Lady Sm. Mr. *Neverout*, shall I send you some Veal?

Nev. No, Madam, I don't love it.

Miss. Then, pray for them that do. I desire your Ladyship will send me a Bit.

Lord Sm. *Tom*, my Service to you.

Nev. My Lord; this Moment, I did my self the Honour to drink to your Lordship.

Lord Sm. Why then, that's *Hartfordshire* Kindness.

Lord Sp. Why then, Colonel, my humble Service to you.

Nev. Pray, my Lord, don't make a Bridge of my Nose.

Lord Sp. Well, a Glass of this Wine is as comfortable, as Matrimony to an old Maid.

Col. Sir *John*, I design one of these Days, to come and beat up your Quarters in *Derbyshire*.

Sir John. Faith, Colonel, come and welcome; and stay away, and heartily welcome. But you were born within the Sound of *Bow* Bell, and don't Care to stir so far from *London*.

Miss. Pray, Colonel, send me some Fritters.

[*Colonel takes them out with his Hand.*]

Col. Here, Miss, they say, Fingers were made before Forks, and Hands before Knives.

Lady Sm. Methinks, this Pudden is too much boyl'd.

Lady Answ. O, Madam, they say a Pudden is Poison, when it's too much boyl'd.

Nev. Miss, shall I help you to a Pigeon? Here's a Pigeon so finely roasted, it cries, Come eat me.

Miss. No, Sir, I thank you.

Nev. Why then, you may chuse.

Miss. I have chosen already.

Nev. Well; you may be worse offered, before you are twice married.

[*The Colonel fills a large Plate of Soupe.*]

Lord Sm. Why, Colonel, you don't mean to eat all that Soupe?

Col. O, my Lord, this is my sick Dish; when I am well, I have a Bigger.

Miss. [*To Colonel.*] Sup *Simon*; good Broth.

Nev. This seems to be a good Pullet.

Miss. I warrant, Mr. *Neverout*, knows what's good for himself.

Lord Sp. *Tom*, I shan't take your Word for it, help me to a Wing.

[*Neverout tries to cut off a Wing.*]

Nev. I'gad, I can't hit the Joynt.

Lord Sp. Why then, think of a Cuckold.

Nev. O, now I have nickt it.

[*Gives it Lord Sparkish.*]

Lord Sp. Why, a Man may eat this, though his Wife lay a Dying.

Col. Pray, Friend, give me a Glass of Small-Beer, if it be good.

Lord Sm. Why, Colonel, they say, there is no such Thing as good Small-Beer, good brown Bread, or a good old Woman.

Lady Sm. [*To Lady Answerall.*] Madam, I beg your Ladyship's Pardon, I did not see you when I was cutting that Bit.

Lady Answ. O, Madam, after you is good Manners.

Lady Sm. Lord, here's a Hair in the Sawce.

Lord Sp. Then, Madam, set the Hounds after it.

Nev. Pray, Colonel, help me, however, to some of that same Sawce.

Col. Come, I think you are more Sawce than Pig.

Lord Sm. Sir *John*, chear up, my Service to you: Well, what do you think of the World to come?

Sir John. Truly, my Lord, I think of it as little as I can.

Lady Sm. [*Putting a Skewer on a Plate.*] Here, take this Skewer, and carry it down to the Cook, to dress it for her own Dinner.

Nev. I beg your Ladyship's Pardon; but this Small-Beer is dead.

Lady Sm. Why then, let it be bury'd.

Col. This is admirable black Pudding; Miss, shall I carve you some? I am the worst Carver in the World; I should never make a good Chaplain. I can just carve Pudding, and that's all.

Miss. No, thank ye, Colonel; for they say, those that eat black Pudding, will dream of the Devil.

Lord Sm. O, here comes the Venison Pasty: Here, take the Soupe away.

[*He cuts it up, and tastes the Venison.*]
S'buds, this Venison is musty.

[Neverout *eats a Piece, and burns his Mouth.*]
Lord Sm. What's the Matter, *Tom?* You have Tears in your Eyes, I think. What dost cry for, Man?

Nev. My Lord, I was just thinking of my poor Grandmother; she dyed just this very Day seven Years.

[*Miss takes a Bit, and burns her Mouth.*]
Nev. And pray, Miss, why do you cry too?

Miss. Because you were not hanged the Day your Grandmother dyed.

Lord Sm. I'd have given forty Pounds, Miss, to have said that.

Col. I'gad, I think, the more I eat, the hungryer I am.

Lord Sp. Why, Colonel, they say, one Shoulder of Mutton drives down another.

Nov. I'gad, if I were to fast for my Life, I would take a good Breakfast in the Morning, a good Dinner at Noon, and a good Supper at Night.

Lord Sp. My Lord, this Venison is plaguily pepper'd. Your Cook has a heavy Hand.

Lord Sm. My Lord, I hope you are Pepper Proof. Come, here's a Health to the Founders.

Lady Sm. Ay, and to the Confounders too.

Lord Sm. Lady *Answerall*, does not your Ladyship love Venison?

Lady Answ. No, my Lord, I can't endure it in my Sight; therefore please to send me a good Piece of Meat and Crust.

Lord Sp. [*Drinks to* Neverout.] Come, *Tom*, not always to my Friends, but once to you.

Nev. [*Drinks to Lady* Smart.] Come, Madam, here's a Health to our Friends, and hang the rest of our Kin.

Lady Sm. [*To Lady* Answerall.] Madam, will your Ladyship have any of this Hare?

Lady Answ. No, Madam; they say 'tis melancholy Meat.

Lady Sm. Then, Madam, shall I send you the Brains: I beg your Ladyship's Pardon, for they say, 'tis not good Manners to offer Brains.

Lady Answ. No, Madam, for perhaps it will make me Hare-brain'd.

Nev. Miss, I must tell you one Thing.

Miss. [*With a Glass in her Hand.*] Hold your Tongue, Mr. *Neverout*; don't speak in my Tip.

Col. Well, he was an ingenious Man that first found out eating and drinking.

Lord Sp. Of all Vittels, Drink digests the quickest. Give me a Glass of Wine.

Nev. My Lord, your Wine is too strong.

Lord Sm. Ay, *Tom*, as much as you are too good.

Miss. This Almond Pudden was pure good; but it is grown quite cold.

Nev. So much the better Miss; cold Pudden will settle your Love.

Miss. Pray, Mr. *Neverout*, are you going to take a Voyage?

Nev. Why, do you ask, Miss?

Miss. Because, you have laid in so much Beef.

Sir John. You two have eat up the whole Pudden betwixt you.

Miss. Sir *John*, here's a little Bit left, will you please to have it?

Sir John. No, thankee, I don't love to make a Fool of my Mouth.

Col. [*Calling to the Butler.*] *John*, is your Small-Beer good?

Butler. An please your Honour, my Lord and Lady like it; I think it is good.

Col. Why then, *John*, d'ye see, if you are sure your Small-

Beer is good, d'ye mark? Then give me a Glass of Wine. [*All laugh.*]

Lady Sm. Sir *John*, how does your Neighbour *Gatherall* of the Park? I hear he has lately made a Purchase.

Sir John. Oh; *Dick Gatherall* knows how to butter his Bread, as well as any Man in *Derbyshire.*

Lady Sm. Why he used to go very fine, when he was here in Town.

Sir John. Ay, and it became him, as a Saddle becomes a Sow.

Col. I knew his Lady; and, I think, she's a very good Woman.

Sir John. Faith, she has more Goodness in her little Finger, than he has in his whole Body.

[*Colonel tasting the Wine.*]

Lord Sm. Well, Colonel, how do you like that Wine?

Col. This Wine should be eaten; 'tis too good to be drank.

Lord Sm. I'm very glad you like it; and, pray don't spare it.

Col. No, my Lord; I'll never starve in a Cook's Shop.

Lady Sm. And, pray Sir *John*, what do you say to my Wine?

Sir John. I'll take another Glass first: Second Thoughts are best.

Lord Sp. Pray, Lady *Smart*, you sit near that Ham, will you please to send me a Bit?

Lady Sm. With all my Heart. [*She sends him a Piece.*] Pray, my Lord, how do you like it?

Lord Sp. I think it is a Limb of *Lot*'s Wife. [*He eats it with Mustard.*] I'gad, my Lord, your Mustard is very uncivil.

Lady Sm. Why uncivil, my Lord?

Lord Sp. Because, it takes me by the Nose, I'gad.

Lady Sm. Mr. *Neverout*, I find you are a very good Carver.

Col. Oh Madam, that's no Wonder; for you must know, *Tom Neverout* carves a-Sundays.

[*Mr.* Neverout *overturns the Saltcellar.*]

Lady Sm. Mr. *Neverout*, you have overturn'd the Salt; and that's a Sign of Anger. I'm afraid Miss and you will fall out.

Lady Answ. No, no; throw a little of it into the Fire, and all will be well.

Nev. O Madam, the falling *out* of Lovers, you know——

Miss. Lovers! very fine! fall *out* with him! I wonder when we were *in*.

Sir John. For my Part, I believe the young Gentlewoman is his Sweet-Heart; there's such fooling and fidling betwixt them. I am sure, they say in our Country, that shiddle come sh——'s the Beginning of Love.

Miss. Nay, I love Mr. *Neverout*, as the Devil loves holy Water. I love him like Pye, I'd rather the Devil wou'd have him than I.

Nev. Miss, I'll tell you one thing.

Miss. Come, here's t'ye to stop your Mouth.

Nev. I'd rather you would stop it with a Kiss.

Miss. A Kiss; marry come up my dirty Couzin: Are you no sicker? Lord! I wonder what Fool it was, that first invented kissing?

Nev. Well, I'm very dry.

Miss. Then you are the better to burn, and the worse to fry.

Lady Answ. God bless you, Colonel, you have a good Stroak with you.

Col. O Madam, formerly I could eat all, but now I leave nothing; I eat but one Meal a-Day.

Miss. What? I suppose, Colonel, that's from Morning till Night.

Nev. Faith, Miss, and well was his Want.

Lord Sm. Pray, Lady *Answerall*, taste this Bit of Venison.

Lady Answ. I hope, your Lordship, will set me a good Example.

Lord Sm. Here's a Glass of Cyder fill'd. Miss, you must drink it.

Miss. Indeed, my Lord, I can't.

Nev. Come Miss; better Belly burst than good Liquor be lost.

Miss. Pish, well, in Life there was never any Thing so

teazing; I had rather shed it in my Shoes: I wish it were in your Guts, for my Share.

Lord Sm. Mr. *Neverout*, you ha'n't tasted my Cyder yet.

Nev. No, my Lord, I have been just eating Soupe; and they say, if one drinks in one's Porridge, one will cough in one's Grave.

Lord Sm. Come, take Miss's Glass, she wish't it was in your Guts; let her have her Wish for once; Ladies can't abide to have their Inclinations cross't.

Lady Sm. [*To Sir* John.] I think, Sir *John*, you have not tasted the Venison yet.

Sir John. I seldom eat it, Madam: However, please to send me a little of the Crust.

Lord Sp. Why, Sir *John*, you had as good eat the Devil, as the Broth he's boyl'd in.

Nev. I have dined as well as my Lord-Mayor.

Miss. I thought I could have eaten this Wing of a Chicken; but, I find, my Eye's bigger than my Belly.

Lord Sm. Indeed, Lady *Answerall*, you have eaten nothing.

Lady Answ. Pray, my Lord, see all the Bones on my Plate. They say, a Carpenter's known by his Chips.

Nev. Miss, will you reach me that Glass of Jelly?

Miss. [*Giving it to him.*] You see, 'tis but ask and have.

Nev. Miss, I would have a bigger Glass.

Miss. What, you don't know your own Mind; you are neither well full nor fasting. I think that is enough.

Nev. Ay, one of the enough's: I am sure it is little enough.

Miss. Yes, but you know sweet Things are bad for the Teeth.

Nev. [*To Lady* Answerall.] Madam, I don't like this Part of the Veal you sent me.

Lady Answ. Well, Mr. *Neverout*, I find you are a true *English*-Man, you never know when you are well.

Col. Well, I have made my whole Dinner of Beef.

Lady Ans. Why, Colonel, a Belly full is a Belly full, if it be but of Wheat-Straw.

Col. Well, after all, Kitchen Physick is the best Physick.

Lord Sm. And the best Doctors in the World, are Doctor *Diet*, Doctor *Quiet*, and Doctor *Merryman*.

Lord Sp. What do you think of a little House well filled?

Sir John. And a little Land well till'd?

Col. Ay, and a little Wife well will'd?

Nev. My Lady *Smart*, pray help me to some of the Breast of that Goose.

Lord Sm. Tom, I have heard, that Goose upon Goose is false Heraldry.

Miss. What! will you never have done stuffing?

Lord Sm. This Goose is quite raw. Well; God sends Meat, but the Devil sends Cooks.

Nev. Miss, can you tell which is the white Goose, or the grey Goose the Gander?

Miss. They say, a Fool will ask more Questions, than twenty wise Men can answer.

Col. Indeed, Miss, *Tom Neverout* has posed you.

Miss. Why, Colonel, every Dog has his Day. But, I believe, I shall never see a Goose again, without thinking on Mr. *Neverout*.

Lord Sm. Well said Miss; I'faith Girl, thou hast brought thy self off cleverly. *Tom*, what say you to that?

Col. Faith, *Tom* is nonplust; he looks plaguily down in the Mouth.

Miss. Why, my Lord, you see he's the provokingest Creature in Life: I believe, there is not such another in the varsal World.

Lady Answ. Oh Miss, the World's a wide Place.

Nev. Well, Miss, I'll give you Leave to call me any Thing, so you don't call me Spade.

Lord Sm. Well, but after all, *Tom*, can you tell me what's *Latin* for a Goose?

Nev. O my Lord, I know that; Why, Brandy is *Latin* for a Goose; and *Tace* is *Latin* for a Caudle.

Miss. Is that Manners, to shew your Learning before Ladies? Methinks you are grown very brisk of a sudden. I think, the Man's glad he's alive.

Sir John. The Devil take your Wit, if this be Wit: for it

spoils Company. Pray, Mr. Butler, bring me a Dram after my Goose; 'tis very good for the Wholesoms.

Lord Sm. Come, bring me the Loaf; I sometimes love to cut my own Bread.

Miss. I suppose, my Lord, you lay longest a Bed to-Day.

Lord Sm. Miss, if I had said so, I should have told a Fib: I warrant you lay a Bed 'till the Cows came home. But, Miss, shall I cut you a little Crust, now my Hand is in?

Miss. If you please, my Lord; a Bit of under Crust.

Nev. [*Whispering Miss.*] I find you love to lie under.

Miss. [*Aloud; pushing him from her.*] What does the Man mean? Sir, I don't understand you at all.

Nev. Come, all Quarrels laid aside: Here, Miss, may you live a thousand Years. [*He drinks to her.*]

Miss. Pray Sir, don't stint me.

Lord Sm. Sir *John*, will you taste my *October?* I think it is very good; but, I believe, not equal to yours in *Derbyshire.*

Sir John. My Lord, I beg your Pardon; but, they say, the Devil made Askers.

Lord Sm. [*To the Butler.*] Here, bring up the great Tankard full of *October*, for Sir *John.*

Col. [*Drinking to Miss.*] Miss, your Health; may you live all the Days of your Life.

Lady Ans. Well, Miss, you'll certainly be soon marryed: Here's two Bachelors drinking to you at once.

Lady Sm. Indeed, Miss, I believe you were wrapt in your Mother's Smock, you are so well beloved.

Miss. Where's my Knife, sure I han't eaten it? O, here it is.

Sir John. No, Miss, but your Maidenhead hangs in your Light.

Miss. Pray, Sir *John*, is that a *Derbyshire* Compliment? Here, Mr. *Neverout*, will you take this Piece of Rabbit, that you bid me carve for you?

Nev. I don't know.

Miss. Why, why, take it, or let it alone.

Nev. I will.

Miss. What will you?

Nev. Why, take it, or let it alone.

Miss. Well, you're a provoking Creature.

Sir John. [*Talking with a Glass of Wine in his Hand.*] I remember a Farmer in our Country——

Lord Sm. [*Interrupting him.*] Pray, Sir *John*, did you ever hear of Parson *Palmer?*

Sir John. No, my Lord, what of him?

Lord Sm. Why, he used to preach over his Liquor.

Sir John. I beg your Pardon. Here's your Lordship's Health; I'd drink it up, if it were a Mile to the Bottom.

Lady Sm. Mr. *Neverout*, have you been at the new Play?

Nev. Yes, Madam, I went the first Night.

Lady Sm. Well, and how did it take?

Nev. Why, Madam, the Poet is *damn'd.*

Sir John. God forgive you; that's very uncharitable; you ought not to judge so rashly of any Christian.

Nev. [*Whispers Lady* Smart.] Was ever such a Dunce? How well he knows the Town! see how he stares like a stuck Pig! Well, but Sir *John*, are you acquainted with any of our fine Ladies yet? Any of our famous Toasts?

Sir John. No, damn your Fireships; I have a Wife of my own.

Lady Sm. Pray, my Lady *Answerall*, how do you like these preserved Oranges?

Lady Ans. Indeed, Madam, the only Fault I find, is, that they are too good.

Lady Sm. O, Madam, I have heard 'em say, that too good, is stark nought.

[*Miss drinking Part of a Glass of Wine.*]

Nev. Pray, let me drink your Snuff.

Miss. No, indeed, you shan't drink after me; for you'll know my Thoughts.

Nev. I know them already; you are thinking of a good Husband. Besides, I can tell your Meaning, by your Mumping.

Lady Sm. Pray, my Lord, did not you order the Butler to bring up a Tankard of our *October* to Sir *John?* I believe, they stay to brew it.

[*The Butler brings the Tankard to Sir* John.]

Sir John. Won't your Lordship please to drink first?

Lord Sm. No, Sir *John*, 'tis in a very good Hand: I'll pledge you.

Col. [*To Lord* Smart.] My Lord, I love *October* as well as Sir *John*; and I hope, you won't make Fish of one, and Flesh of another.

Lord Sm. Colonel, you're heartily welcome: Come, Sir *John*, take it by Word of Mouth, and then give it the Colonel.
[*Sir* John *drinks.*]

Lord Sm. Well, Sir *John*, how do you like it?

Sir John. Not as well as my own in *Derbyshire.* 'Tis plaguy small.

Lady Sm. I never taste Malt Liquor; but they say, 'tis well Hopp'd.

Sir John. Hopp'd! Why, if it had hopp'd a little further, it would have hopp'd into the River. O, my Lord; my Ale is Meat, Drink, and Cloth. It will make a Cat speak, and a wise Man dumb..

Lady Sm. I was told, ours was very strong.

Sir John. Ay, Madam, strong of the Water: I believe, the Brewer forgot the Malt, or the River was too near him. Faith, it is meer Whip-belly-vengeance: He that drinks most, has the worst Share.

Col. I believe, Sir *John*, Ale is as plenty as Water, at your House.

Sir John. Why, Faith, at *Christmas* we have many Comers and Goers; and they must not be sent away without a Cup of good *Christmas* Ale, for fear they should p—ss behind the Door.

Lady Sm. I hear, Sir *John* has the nicest Garden in *England*; they say, 'tis kept so clean, that you can't find a Place where to spit.

Sir John. O, Madam, you are pleased to say so.

Lady Sm. But, Sir *John*, your Ale is terrible strong and heady in *Derbyshire*; and will soon make one drunk and sick, what do you then?

Sir John. Why, indeed, it is apt to Fox one; but our Way is, to take a Hair of the same Dog next Morning. I take a

P

new laid Egg for Breakfast; and Faith, one should drink as much after an Egg, as after an Ox.

Lord Sm. *Tom Neverout*, will you taste a Glass of the *October?*

Nev. No, Faith, my Lord, I like your Wine; and I won't put a Churl upon a Gentleman: Your Honour's Claret is good enough for me.

Lady Sm. What? is this Pigeon left for Manners? Colonel, shall I send you the Legs and Rump?

Col. Madam, I could not eat a Bit more, if the House was full.

Lord Sm. [*Carving a Partridge.*] Well, one may ride to *Rumford* upon this Knife, it is so blunt.

Lady Answ. My Lord, I beg your Pardon; but they say, an ill Workman never had good Tools.

Lord Sm. Will your Lordship have a Wing of it?

Lord Sp. No, my Lord, I love the Wing of an Ox a great deal better.

Lord Sm. I'm always cold after eating.

Col. My Lord, they say, that's a Sign of long Life.

Lord Sm. Ay, I believe I shall live 'till all my Friends are weary of me.

Col. Pray, does any Body here hate Cheese? I would be glad of a Bit.

Lord Sm. An odd kind of Fellow dined with me t'other Day; and when the Cheese came upon the Table, he pretended to faint. So, some Body said, pray take away the Cheese: No, said I, pray take away the Fool: Said I well? [*Here a long and loud Laugh.*]

Col. Faith, my Lord, you served the Coxcomb right enough: And therefore, I wish we had a Bit of your Lordship's *Oxford-shire* Cheese.

Lord Sm. Come, hang saving, being us a halfporth of Cheese.

Lady Answ. They say, Cheese digests every Thing but it-self.

[*Footman brings in a great whole Cheese.*]

Lord Sp. Ay, this would look handsome if any Body should come in.

Sir John. Well, I'm weily brosten, as they sayn in *Lancashire.*

Lady Sm. Oh, Sir *John*, I wou'd I had something to brost you withal.

Lord Sm. Come, they say, 'tis merry in Hall, when Beards wag all.

Lady Sm. Miss, shall I help you to some Cheese? Or, will you carve for your self?

Nev. I'll hold fifty Pound, Miss won't cut the Cheese.

Miss. Pray, why so, Mr. *Neverout?*

Nev. O, there is a Reason, and you know it well enough.

Miss. I can't, for my Life, understand what the Gentleman means.

Lord Sm. Pray, *Tom*, change the Discourse, in troth you are too bad.

[*Colonel whispers* Neverout.]

Col. Smoak Miss, you have made her fret like Gum taffety.

Lady Sm. Well; but Miss, (hold your Tongue, Mr. *Neverout*) shall I cut you a Bit of Cheese?

Miss. No really, Madam, I have dined this half Hour.

Lady Sm. What? quick at Meat, quick at work, they say.

[*Sir* John *nods.*]

Lord Sm. What, you are sleepy Sir *John*. Do you sleep after Dinner?

Sir John. Yes, Faith, I sometimes take a Nap after my Pipe; for when the Belly's full, the Bones will be at rest.

Lord Sm. Come, Colonel, help your self, and your Friends will love you the better.

[*To Lady* Answerall.]

Madam, your Ladyship eats nothing.

Lady Answ. Lord, Madam, I have fed like a Farmer; I shall grow as fat as a Porpoise: I swear, my Jaws are weary with chawing.

Col. I have a Mind to eat a Piece of that Sturgeon, but I fear it will make me sick.

Nev. A rare Soldier indeed; let it alone, and I warrant, it won't hurt you.

Col. Well, but it would vex a Dog to see a Pudden creep.

[*Sir* John *rises.*]

Lord Sm. Sir *John*, what are you doing?

Sir John. Swolks, I must be going, by'r Lady; I have earnest Business; I must do, as the Beggars do, go away when I have got enough.

Lord Sm. Well, but stay 'till this Bottle's out: You know, the Man was hanged that left his Liquor behind him; besides, a Cup in the Pate, is a Mile in the Gate; and, a Spur in the Head, is worth two in the Heel.

Sir John. Come then, one Brimmer to all your Healths.

[The Footman gives him a Glass half full.]

Pray, Friend, what was the rest of this Glass made for? An Inch at the Top, Friend, is worth two at the Bottom.

[He gets a Brimmer, and drinks it off.]

Well; there's no Deceit in a Brimmer; and there's no false Latin in this, your Wine is excellent good, so I thank you for the next; for, I am sure of this. Madam, has your Ladyship any Commands in *Derbyshire?* I must go fifteen Miles To-Night.

Lady Sm. None, Sir *John*, but to take Care of yourself; and my most humble Service to your Lady unknown.

Sir John. Well, Madam, I can but love and thank you.

Lady Sm. Here, bring Water to wash; though really you have all eaten so little, that you have no Need to wash your Mouths.

Lord Sm. But prithee, Sir *John*, stay a while longer.

Sir John. No, my Lord, I am to smoak a Pipe with a Friend, before I leave the Town.

Col. Why, Sir *John*, had not you better set out To-morrow?

Sir John. Colonel, you forget, To-morrow is *Sunday.*

Col. Now, I always love to begin a Journey on Sundays, because I shall have the Prayers of the Church; to preserve all that Travel by Land or by Water.

Sir John. Well, Colonel, thou art a mad Fellow to make a Priest of.

Nev. Fye, Sir *John*, do you take Tobacco? How can you make a Chimney of your Mouth?

Sir John. [*To* Neverout.] What? you don't smoak, I

warrant you, but you smock. (Ladies, I beg your Pardon.)
Colonel, do you never smoke?

Col. No, Sir *John*, but I take a Pipe sometimes.

Sir John. I'Faith, one of your finical *London* Blades dined
with me last Year in *Derbyshire:* So, after Dinner, I took a
Pipe: So, my Gentleman turn'd away his Head: So, said I,
what Sir, do you never smoak? So, he answered as you do,
Colonel, no; but I sometimes take a Pipe: So, he took a Pipe
in his Hand, and fiddled with it, 'till be broke it: So, said I,
pray, Sir, can you make a Pipe? So, he said, no: So, said I,
why then, Sir, if you can't make a Pipe, you should not break
a Pipe. So, we all laught.

Lord Sm. Well, but Sir *John*, they say, that the Corruption
of Pipes, is the Generation of Stoppers.

Sir John. Colonel, I hear you go sometimes to *Derbyshire*,
I wish you would come and foul a Plate with me.

Col. I hope, you'll give me a Soldier's Bottle.

Sir John. Come, and try.

Sir John. Mr. *Neverout*, you are a Town-Wit, can you tell me
what Kind of Herb is Tobacco?

Nev. Why, an *Indian* Herb, Sir *John*.

Sir John. No, 'tis a Pot-Herb; and so here's t'ye in a Pot of
my Lord's *October*.

Lady Sm. I hear, Sir *John*, since you are married, you have
forsworn the Town.

Sir John. No, Madam, I never forswore any Thing but
building of Churches.

Lady Sm. Well, but Sir *John*, when may we hope to see you
again in *London?*

Sir John. Why, Madam, not 'till the Ducks have eat up
the Dirt, as the Children say.

Nev. Come, Sir *John*, I foresee it will rain terribly.

Lord Sm. Come, Sir *John*, do nothing rashly, let us drink
first.

Lord Sp. Nay, I know Sir *John* will go, though he was sure
it would rain Cats and Dogs. But, pray stay, Sir *John*, you'll
be Time enough to go to Bed by Candle-light.

Lord Sm. Why, Sir *John*, if you must needs go, while you

stay, make good Use of your Time. Here's my Service to you.
A Health to our Friends in *Derbyshire*.

Sir John. Not a Drop more.

Col. Why, Sir *John*, you used to love a Glass of good Wine
in former Times.

Sir John. Why, so I do still, Colonel; but a Man may love
his House very well, without riding on the Ridge; besides,
I must be with my Wife on *Tuesday*, or there will be the Devil
and all to pay.

Col. Well, if you go To-Day, I wish you may be wet to the
Skin.

Sir John. Ay, but they say, the Prayers of the Wicked won't
prevail.

[*Sir* John *takes his Leave, and goes away*.]

Lord Sm. Well, Miss, how do you like Sir *John?*

Miss. Why, I think, he's a little upon the Silly, or so;
I believe he has not all the Wit in the World; but I don't
pretend to be a Judge.

Nev. Faith, I believe he was bred at *Hogsnorton*, where the
Pigs play upon the Organs.

Lord Sp. Why, *Tom*, I thought you and he had been Hand
and Glove.

Nev. Faith, he shall have a clean Threshold for me, I never
darkned his Door in my Life, neither in Town, nor Country;
but, he's a queer old Duke, by my Conscience; and yet, after
all, I take him to be more Knave than Fool.

Lord Sm. Well, come, a Man's a Man, if he has but a Hose
on his Head.

Col. I was once with him, and some other Company, over
a Bottle; and I'gad, he fell asleep, and snored so loud, that we
thought he was driving his Hogs to Market.

Nev. Why, what? You can have no more of a Cat, than her
Skin. You can't make a Silk Purse out of a Sow's Ear.

Lord Sp. Well, since he's gone, the Devil go with him,
and Sixpence; and there's Money and Company too.

Nev. Pray, Miss, let me ask you a Question?

Miss. Well, but don't ask Questions with a dirty Face.
I warrant, what you have to say, will keep cold.

Col. Come, my Lord, against you are disposed. Here's to all that love and honour you.

Lord Sp. Ay, that was always *Dick Nimble's* Health, I'm sure you know, he is dead.

Col. Dead! Well, my Lord, you love to be a Messenger of ill News, I'm heartily sorry; but, my Lord, we must all dye.

Nev. I knew him very well; but pray, how came he to dye?

Miss. There's a Question! You talk like a Poticary. Why, he dyed, because he could live no longer.

Nev. Well; rest his Soul; we must live by the Living, and not by the Dead.

Lord Sp. You know his House was burnt down to the Ground.

Col. Yes, it was in the News. Why; Fire and Water are good Servants, but they are very bad Masters.

Lord Sm. Here, take away, and set down a Bottle of Burgundy. Ladies, you'll stay and drink a Glass of Wine before you go to your Tea.

[*All's taken away, and the Wine set down.*]
[*Miss gives* Neverout *a smart Pinch.*]

Nev. Lord, Miss, what d'ye mean? D'ye think I have no feeling?

Miss. I'm forced to pinch, for the Times are hard.

Nev. [*Giving Miss a Pinch.*] Take that, Miss: What's Sawce for a Goose, is Sawce for a Gander.

Miss. [*screaming.*] Well, Mr. *Neverout*, if I live, that shall neither go to Heaven nor Hell with you.

Nev. [*takes Miss's Hand.*] Come, Miss, let us lay all Quarrels aside, and be Friends.

Miss. Don't be mauming and gauming a Body so. Can't you keep your filthy Hands to your self?

Nev. Pray, Miss, where did you get that Pick-Tooth Case?

Miss. I came honestly by it.

Nev. I'm sure it was mine, for I lost just such a one. Nay, I don't tell you a Lye.

Miss. No, if you Lye, 'tis much.

Nev. Well, I'm sure 'tis mine.

Miss. What, you think every Thing is yours; but a little the King has.

Nev. Colonel, you have seen my fine Pick-Tooth Case: Don't you think this is the very same?

Col. Indeed, Miss, it is very like it.

Miss. Ay, what he says, you'll swear.

Nev. Well; but I'll prove it to be mine.

Miss. Ay, do if you can.

Nev. Why; what's yours is mine, and what's mine is my own.

Miss. Well, run on 'till you're weary, no Body holds you.
[Neverout *gapes.*]

Col. What, Mr. *Neverout*, do you gape for Preferment?

Nev. Faith, I may gape long enough before it falls into my Mouth.

Lady Sm. Mr. *Neverout*, I hear you live high.

Nev. Yes, Faith, Madam, live high, and lodge in a Garret.

Col. But, Miss, I forgot to tell you, that Mr. *Neverout* got the devilishest Fall in the Park To-Day.

Miss. I hope he did not hurt the Ground. But, how was it Mr. *Neverout?* I wish I had been there to laugh.

Nev. Why, Madam, it was a Place where a Cuckold had been bury'd, and one of his Horns sticking out, I happened to stumble against it. That was all.

Lady Sm. Ladies, let us leave the Gentlemen to themselves; I think it is Time to go to our Tea.

Lady Answ. and *Miss.* My Lords, and Gentlemen, your most humble Servant.

Lord Sm. Well, Ladies, we'll wait on you an Hour hence.
[*The Gentlemen alone.*]

Lord Sm. Come, *John*, bring us a fresh Bottle.

Col. Ay, my Lord; and pray let him carry off the dead Men, (as we say in the Army.) [*Meaning the empty Bottles.*]

Lord Sp. Mr. *Neverout*, pray is not that Bottle full?

Nev. Yes, my Lord, full of Emptiness.

Lord Sm. And, d'ye hear, *John*, bring clean Glasses.

Col. I'll keep mine, for I think the Wine is the best Liquor to wash Glasses in.

Third CONVERSATION.

[The Ladies at their Tea.]

Lady Smart. WELL, Ladies, now let us have a Cup of Discourse to our selves.

Lady Answ. What do you think of your Friend, Sir *John Spendall?*

Lady Sm. Why, Madam, 'tis happy for him that his Father was born before him.

Miss. They say, he makes a very ill Husband to my Lady.

Lady Ans. Well, but he must be allowed to be the fondest Father in the World.

Lady Sm. Ay, Madam, that's true; for they say, the Devil is kind to his own.

Miss. I am told, my Lady manages him to Admiration.

Lady Sm. That I believe, for she's as cunning as a dead Pig; but not half so honest.

Lady Answ. They say, she's quite a Stranger to all his Gallantries.

Lady Sm. Not at all; but you know, there's none so blind, as they that won't see.

Miss. Oh, Madam, I am told, she watches him as a Cat would watch a Mouse.

Lady Answ. Well, if she ben't foully bely'd; she pays him in his own Coyn.

Lady Sm. Madam, I fancy I know your Thoughts, as well, as if I were within you.

Lady Answ. Madam, I was t'other Day in Company with Mrs. *Clatter*; I find she gives her self Airs of being acquainted with your Ladyship.

Miss. O, the hideous Creature! Did you observe her Nails. They were long enough to scratch her Granum out of her Grave.

Lady Sm. Well, she and *Tom Gosling* were banging Compliments backwards and forwards. It look'd like two Asses scrubbing one another.

Miss. Ay, claw me, and I'll claw thee: But, pray Madam, who were the Company?

Lady Sm. Why; there was all the World, and his Wife. There was Mrs. *Clatter*, Lady *Singular*, the Countess of *Talkham*, (I should have named her first) *Tom Goslin*, and some others, whom I have forgot.

Lady Answ. I think the Countess is very sickly.

Lady Sm. Yes, Madam, she'll never scratch a grey Head, I promise her.

Miss. And pray, what was your Conversation?

Lady Sm. Why, Mrs. *Clatter* had all the Talk to her self, and was perpetually complaining of her Misfortunes.

Lady Answ. She brought her Husband ten thousand Pounds; she has a Town-House, and Country-House; would the Woman have her —— hung with Points?

Lady Sm. She would fain be at the Top of the House, before the Stairs are built.

Miss. Well, Comparisons are odious; but she's as like her Husband, as if she were spit out of his Mouth; as like as one Egg is to another. Pray, how was she drest?

Lady Sm. Why, she was as fine as Five-pence; but truly, I thought there was more Cost than Worship.

Lady Ans. I don't know her Husband; pray, what is he?

Lady Sm. Why, he's a Concealer of the Law; you must know, he came to us as drunk as *David*'s Sow.

Miss. What kind of Creature is he?

Lady Sm. You must know the Man and his Wife are coupled like Rabits; a Fat and a Lean. He's as fat as a Porpoise, and she's one of *Pharaoh*'s lean Kine. The Ladies, and *Tom Goslin*, were proposing a Party at *Quadrille*, but he refused to make one; damn your Cards, said he, they are the Devil's Books.

Lady Ans. A dull, unmannerly Brute! Well, God send him more Wit, and me more Money.

Miss. Lord, Madam, I would not keep such Company for the World.

Lady Sm. O, Miss, 'tis nothing when you are used to it. Besides, you know; for Want of Company, welcome Trumpery.

Miss. Did your Ladyship play?

Lady Sm. Yes, and won; so I came off with Fidler's Fare, Meat, Drink, and Money.

Lady Ans. Ay, what says Pluck?

Miss. Well, my Elbow itches, I shall change my Bed-fellow.

Lady Sm. And my Left-Hand itches, I shall receive Money.

Lady Ans. And my Right-Eye itches, I shall cry.

Nev. Miss, I hear your Friend, Mrs. *Giddy*, has discarded *Dick Shuttle*; pray, has she got another Lover?

Miss. I hear of none.

Nev. Why, the Fellow's rich, and I think she was a Fool, to throw out her dirty Water, before she got clean.

Lady Sm. Miss, that's a very handsome Gown of yours, and finely made, very genteel.

Miss. I'm glad your Ladyship likes it.

Lady Ans. Your Lover will be in Raptures, it becomes you admirably.

Miss. Ay, I assure you, I won't take it as I have done, if this won't fetch him, the Devil fetch him, say I.

Lady Sm. [*To Lady* Answerall.] Pray, Madam, when did you see Sir *Peter Muckworm?*

Lady Ans. Not this Fortnight: I hear, he's laid up with the Gout.

Lady Sm. What does he do for it?

Lady Ans. Why, I hear he's weary of doctoring it, and now makes Use of nothing but Patience, and Flannel.

Miss. Pray, how does he and my Lady agree?

Lady Ans. You know he loves her.——

Miss. They say, she plays deep with Sharpers, that cheat her of her Money.

Lady Ans. Upon my Word, they must rise early that would cheat her of her Money. Sharp's the Word with her: Diamonds cut Diamonds.

Miss. Well, but I was assured from a good Hand, that she lost at one Sitting, to the Tune of a hundred Guineas, make Money of that.

Lady Sm. Well, but do you hear, that Mrs. *Plump* is brought to Bed at last?

Miss. And pray, what has God sent her?

Lady Sm. Why, guess if you can.

Miss. A Boy, I suppose.

Lady Sm. No, you are out, guess again.

Miss. A Girl then.

Lady Sm. You have hit it; I believe you are a Witch.

Miss. O, Madam, the Gentlemen say, all fine Ladies are Witches; but I pretend to no such Thing.

Lady Ans. Well, she had good Luck to draw *Tom Plump* into Wedlock; she rises with her —— upwards.

Miss. Fye, Madam, what do you mean?

Lady Sm. O, Miss, 'tis nothing what we say among ourselves.

Miss. Ay, Madam, but they say, Hedges have Eyes, and Walls have Ears.

Lady Ans. Well, Miss, I can't help it; you know I am old Tell-truth, I love to call a Spade, a Spade.

[*Lady* Smart *mistakes the Tea-Tongs for a Spoon.*]

Lady Sm. What, I think my Wits are a Wooll-gathering To-Day.

Miss. Why, Madam, there was but a Right, and a Wrong.

Lady Sm. Miss, I hear that you and Lady *Couplers*, are as great as Cup, and Can.

Lady Ans. Ay, as great as the Devil, and the Earl of *Kent*.

Lady Sm. Nay, I am told you meet together with as much Love, as there is between the old Cow and the Hay-Stack.

Miss. I own, I love her very well; but there's Difference betwixt staring and stark mad.

Lady Sm. They say, she begins to grow fat.

Miss. Fat, ay, fat as a Hen in the Forehead.

Lady Sm. Indeed, Lady *Answerall*, (pray forgive me) I think your Ladyship looks a little thinner, than when I saw you last.

Miss. Indeed, Madam, I think not; but your Ladyship is one of *Job*'s Comforters.

Lady Ans. Well, no Matter how I look; I am bought and

sold. But really, Miss, you are so very obliging, that I wish I were a handsome young Lord for your Sake.

Miss. O, Madam, your Love's a Million.

Lady Sm. [*To Lady* Answerall.] Madam, will your Ladyship let me wait on you to the Play To-morrow.

Lady Ans. Madam, it becomes me to wait on your Ladyship.

Miss. What, then I'm turn'd out for a Wrangler.

[*The Gentlemen come in to the Ladies, to drink Tea.*]

Miss. Mr. *Neverout*, we wanted you sadly; you are always out of the Way, when you should be hang'd.

Nev. You wanted me? Pray, Miss, how do you look, when you lye?

Miss. Better than you when you cry, Manners indeed. I find, you mend like sower Ale in Summer.

Nev. I beg your Pardon, Miss; I only meant, when you lye alone.

Miss. That's well turn'd; one Turn more would have turn'd you down Stairs.

Nev. Miss, come be kind for once, and order me a Dish of Coffee.

Miss. Pray, go your self; let us wear out the oldest first. Besides, I can't go, for I have a Bone in my Leg.

Col. They say, a Woman need but once look on her Apron Strings to find an Excuse.

Nev. Why, Miss, you are grown so peevish, a Dog would not live with you.

Miss. Mr. *Neverout*, no Offence I hope; but, truly, I think, in a little Time, you intend to make the Colonel as bad as your self; and that's as bad as bad can be.

Nev. My Lord; don't you think Miss improves wonderfully of late? Why, Miss, if I spoil the Colonel, I hope you will use him as you do me; for you know, love me, love my Dog.

Col. How's that, *Tom?* say that again. Why, if I am a Dog, shake Hands Brother.

[*Here a great, loud and long Laugh.*]

Lord Sm. But, pray Gentlemen, why always so severe upon poor Miss. On my Conscience, Colonel, and *Tom Neverout*, one of you two are both Knaves.

Col. My Lady *Answerall*, I intend to do my self the Honour of dining with your Ladyship To-morrow.

Lady Ans. Ay, Colonel, do if you can.

Miss. I'm sure you'll be glad to be welcome.

Col. Miss, I thank you; and to reward you, I'll come and drink Tea with you in the Morning.

Miss. Colonel, there's two Words to that Bargain.

Col. [*To Lady* Smart.] Your Ladyship has a very fine Watch; well may you wear it.

Lady Sm. It is none of mine, Colonel.

Col. Pray, whose is it then?

Lady Sm. Why, 'tis my Lord's; for, they say, a marry'd Woman has nothing of her own, but her Wedding-Ring, and her Hair-Lace. But if Women had been the Law-Makers, it would have been better.

Col. This Watch seems to be quite new.

Lady Sm. No, Sir, it has been twenty Years in my Lord's Family, but *Quare* lately put a new Case and Dial-Plate to it.

Nev. Why, that's for all the World like the Man, who swore he kept the same Knife for forty Years, only he sometimes changed the Haft, and sometimes the Blade.

Lord Sm. Well, *Tom*, to give the Devil his due, thou art a right Woman's Man.

Col. Od so, I have broke the Hinge of my Snuff-Box, I'm undone, beside the Loss.

Miss. A-lack-a-Day, Colonel, I vow I had rather have found forty Shillings.

Nev. Why, Colonel; all I can say, to comfort you, is, that you must mend it with a new one.

[*Miss laughs.*]

Col. What, Miss, you can't laugh, but you must shew your Teeth.

Miss. I'm sure, you shew your Teeth, when you can't bite. Well, thus it must be, if we sell Ale.

Nev. Miss, you smell very sweet: I hope, you don't carry Perfumes.

Miss. Perfumes! No, Sir, I'd have you to know, it is nothing but the Grain of my Skin.

Lord Sp. So, Ladies, and Gentlemen, methinks you are very witty upon one another: Come, box it about, 'twill come to my Father at last.

Col. Why, my Lord, you see Miss has no Mercy, I wish she were marry'd; but I doubt, the grey Mare would prove the better Horse.

Miss. Well, God forgive you for that Wish.

Lord Sp. Never fear him, Miss.

Lord Sm. What have you to say to that, Colonel?

Nev. O, my Lord, my Friend, the Colonel, scorns to set his Wit against a Child.

Miss. Scornful Dogs will eat dirty Puddens.

Col. Well, Miss, they say, a Woman's Tongue is the last Thing about her that dyes: Therefore, let's kiss and Friends.

Miss. Hands off.

Lord Sp. Faith, Colonel, you are in for Ale, and Cakes. But, after all, Miss, you are too severe; you would not meddle with your Match?

Miss. All they can say, goes in at one Ear, and out at t'other for me, I can assure you; only, I wish they would be quiet, and let me drink my Tea.

Nev. What, I warrant you think all is lost that goes beside your own Mouth.

Miss. Pray, Mr. *Neverout*, hold your Tongue for once, if it be possible. Women! One would think you were a Woman in Men's Cloaths, by your prating.

Nev. No, Miss, it is not handsome to see one hold one's Tongue; besides, I should slobber my Fingers.

Col. Miss, did you never hear, that three Women, and a Goose, are enough to make a Market.

Miss. I'm sure, if Mr. *Neverout*, or you, were among them, it would make a Fair.

[*Footman comes in.*]

Lady Sm. Here, take away the Tea-Table, and bring up Candles.

Lady Ans. O, Madam, no Candles yet, I beseech you; don't let us burn Day-Light.

Nev. I dare swear; Miss, for her Part, will never burn Day-Light, if she can help it.

Miss. Lord, Mr. *Neverout*, one can't hear ones own Ears for you.

Lady Sm. Indeed, Madam, it is blind Man's Holiday, we shall soon be all of a Colour.

Nev. Why then, Miss, we may kiss where we like best.

Miss. Fogh, these Men talk of nothing but kissing.

[*She spits.*]

Nev. What, Miss, does it make your Mouth water?

Lady Sm. It is as good to be in the Dark, as without Light; therefore, pray bring in Candles. They say, Women, and Linnen, shew best by Candle-Light. Come, Gentlemen, are you for a Party at *Quadrille?*

Col. I'll make one, with you three Ladies.

Lady Ans. I'll sit down, and be a Stander-by.

Lord Sm. [*To Lady* Answerall]. Madam, does your Ladyship never play?

Col. Yes, I suppose, her Ladyship plays sometimes for an Egg at *Easter.*

Never. Ay, and a Kiss at *Christmas.*

Lady Ans. Come, Mr. *Neverout*, hold your Tongue, and mind your Knitting.

Nev. With all my Heart. Kiss my Wife, and welcome.

[*The Colonel, Mr.* Neverout, *Lady* Smart, *and Miss*, go to Quadrille, *and sit 'till Three in the Morning.*] [*They rise from Cards.*]

Lady Sm. Well, Miss, you'll have a sad Husband, you have such good Luck at Cards.

Nev. Indeed, Miss, you dealt me sad Cards; if you deal so ill by your Friends, what will you do with your Enemies?

Lady Ans. I'm sure, 'tis Time for all honest Folks to go to Bed.

Miss. Indeed, my Eyes draw Straws. [*she's almost asleep.*]

Nev. Why, Miss, if you fall asleep, some Body may get a Pair of Gloves.

Col. I'm going to the Land of Nod.

Nev. Faith, I'm for *Bedfordshire.*

Lady Sm. I'm sure, I shall sleep without rocking.

Nev. Miss, I hope you'll dream of your Sweetheart.

Miss. O, no doubt of it: I believe, I shan't be able to sleep for dreaming of him.

Col. [*To Miss.*] Madam, I shall have the Honour to escorte you.

Miss. No, Colonel, I thank you. My Mama, has sent her Chair, and Footmen. Well, my Lady *Smart*, I'll give you Revenge whenever you please.

[*Footman comes in.*]

Footman. Madam, the Chairs are waiting.

[*They all take their Chairs, and go off.*]

FINIS.

A Modest Defence of
Punning

A MODEST DEFENCE OF PUNNING;

Or a compleat Answer to a scandalous and malicious
Paper called

GOD'S REVENGE AGAINST PUNNING.

In a Letter to a Member of Parliament.

Punica mala leges. Virg.

Cambridge Nov^{br} 8th 1716.

S^r

THAT Gentleman (whoever he was) who lately under
the Name of *J. Baker Knight*, thought fit to publish
a Discourse entitled God's Revenge against Punning
seems to have *founded* his whole Discourse upon one
grand Mistake: And therefore his whole Discourse will be
founddead as soon as I have removed that Mistake; which is,
that He condemns the whole Art in generall without distinguishing Puns into Good and Bad, whereby it appears how
ignorant he is in Antiquity. The antient Romans very well
understood the Difference between the *fine* or *pretty* Pun,
and the *bad* Pun: hence we read so often of the *bellum Punicum*,
and the *malum Punicum*. Of which our Author is as ignorant
as a certain Gentleman who reading of a *Roman Scholar*,
thought *Roman* was a *Waterman* and *Scholar* a *Sculler*.

The Word *Pun* appears to be of Greek Originall. Some
derive it from Πύνδαξ, which signifyes either *Fundum*, a Bottom,
or *Maniebrium gladij*, the handle of a Sword. From the former,
because this kind of Wit is thought to lye *deeper* than any other.
I will produce an Instance in this very word, *Fundum*. When
a young Parson marryed Mrs *Sarah* —— and got a Living,
which is called Smock Simony, one of our Fraternity most
surprisingly said, *Sera est in Fundo Per-Simonia.* (Anglice)
Sarah was at the *Bottom by Simony.* Secondly, from the Handle
of a Sword: Because whoever *wields* it will shew something
Bright and *sharp* at the *End*: Another and more probable

Opinion is that the word *Pun* comes from Πυνθάνομαι; because without *Knoledge*, *hearing* and *Enquiry*, this Gift is not to be obtained.   There is a more modern Etymology which I cannot altogether approve, tho' it be highly ingenious: For, the Cantabrigians derive the Word from *Ponticulus* Quasi, *Pun tickle us*, which signifyes a *little Bridge*, as ours over *Cam*, where this Art is in highest Perfection.   Again; others derive it from *Pungo*; because whoever lets a *Pun go* will be sure to make his Adversary *smart*.   And to include this Head, I shall not conceal one Originall of this Word assigned by our Adversaryes, from the French word *Punaise*, which signifyes a little stinking Insect that gets into the Skin, provokes continual *Itching*, and is with great Difficulty removed.   These Gentlemen affirm the same Evils to be in punning, that it is very offensive to company, that the *Itch* of it is hardly to be cured, and that the Custom of *Scratching* a man when he makes a Pun, (which is a Rudeness much practised by Abhorrers) came from the same Originall.

To come now to our Author, *J. Baker Knight*, who usually passeth for a *Spaniard* and by the *Quarter* he meets with among certain Lords may be a *Quarter* longer, I mean a Spani - *ell*. I thought *Punnado* had been a Spanish Dish that his Stomach would *Digest*, and his *Jest dy*.   I am considering what Sort of Knight he should be; when he is among his Equalls he is a Knight of *Malt*-a, when he travels, he is a Knight of *Rhodes*, or if we allow him to be a Knight of the *Post* it must be the *Foot-post*; But being a Spaniard, perhaps he may be Knight of St *Jakes*, or if he hath been in France, they may have conferred upon him the Order of *Sans Esprit*.   But for my own Part, I am apt to think that having so much in him of the Spaniard, he may be descended from the famous *Fonseca*, and that he is the Chevalier de *Fond Sec*.

I shall now with as much Care and Candor as I am master of examine his Discourse.   But I think I may let pass his *Petty* Accounts of the great Plague, where five Millions as he says were *Swept* away, which indeed Mr. Alexander *Broom* records, tho' there *be some* who deny it, and think it a *Whisker* yet every body allows it to have been a terrible *Brush*, and that it made *clean* work, especially in *Birchin* Lane. In this Pestilence he mentions the Woman and the Jews by themselves, because indeed it was the worst of *Maladyes* for the *Mall Ladyes*, and there is no doubt but the *Jews* were put to their *Trumps*.

Neither shall I *touch* the Fire he mentions, that burnt our *Metropolis* which hath already been recorded in never dying Puns by *Poor Robin* a member of our Fraternity. London was still a *Metropolis* even after it was burnt, *mais trop aux Lis* as the French express it, or rather in our Author's own Words, when the Houses were gone it was a *Few-nest* place indeed.

The next Judgment our Author mentions is an *Inundation* of Obscenity, wherein I care not to *dip* my *Fingers*; and whoever cannot behold these Obscenityes upon our Walls with *chast eyes* he may justly *chastise* them. Yet Travellers inform us, the same Abominations are seen in *Italy* (though he may think *It a Ly*) and even in Rome itself, to such a degree, that, many believe there is hardly a virtuous Woman in that City, according to our English Proverb, *Rome* for Cuckolds; wherein we *allude* to *a lewd* Town. However, it is plain by this wicked Practice in London that we are more addicted to *Whetstonism* than *Whistonism*.

He proceeds next to the Visitation of the *nine Comets* seen *so high* as *So Ho* by Mrs *Wadlingtun* of which Appellation there may be as many women in London as there are *fat overgrown* Bawds, which Circumstance made me first suspect the Fact, and that to make it Truth we must resolve it into a *Pun*: For the Number *nine* was only the *nine* of *Diamonds*, which happens to be the best Card at *Comet*. Or was this perhaps a various Reading crept from the Margin to the Text by the Ignorance of some Copyer. If I were *Bent t' lye*, what an Air of Erudition could I give my self upon such an Occasion! After the same Manner when this Author assures us that the Sky did *Coruscat*, it was onely a *Chorus* of *Cats* on the Tyles in *Soho* whose Eyes glistning in the Night made Mrs *Wadlington* mistake them for Stars. Had she been a Scholar she might probably have thought their Meawling to have been the Musick of the Sphears.

I have now with some difficulty traced our Author Step by

Step till he is got to his Relation of severe Judgments upon Punsters. The Maxim he lyes down amounts to this: that wherever a *Pun is meant*, there certainly follows a *Punishment*, whereof he pretends to produce severall Instances. The first is of a certain Lord, whom he onely hints at; for he leaves a blank and does not make him *A peer*. This Noble Person our Author is pleased to call a *Reprobat*, sed non *re probat*. He Claps as a Chastisement upon this Noble *Hero*, a *wry Nose*, as if he would make him a *Rinoseros*. In short the Writer was determined to bring in his Lordships *wry* nose by *Hook or by Crook*, for which he deserves to be *hisst* whether my Lord were *clapt* or no: However I confess I should be sorry for the affirmative, to think he had changed his *Bristow stones* for *Carbuncles*, and his future certainty of a *Coronet* for the present possession of a *Corona* Veneris.

But pray S^r, be pleased to observe how little consistent this Writer is with Himself. His first Instance you see is of a young Lord who got a *Wry Nose* as a Judgment upon Punning, and immediatly forgetting what he had said, He now produceth a Second of another young Noble who lost his ready *Rino's* for the same Crime, and as he expresseth it, by the Box and Dice. So it seems what is got by the *Pox* is lost by the *Box* (according to the Proverb). But here is another Mistake in Fact, For it is well known how this second young Lord came to *Cinque* his Fortune at Dice, by some who were not his *Cater*-cousins, and that there are sharpers allways ready to se*duc*e and Be*tray* young Men of Quality and will not bate them an *Ace*: And thus it fell out that this young *Noble* was brought to a *Nine-pence*.

The third Nobleman he mentions would never have fallen into the Arms of a Dalilah, if His Lordship had not been as the Poet says *Var vecûm in patriâ crassoq. sub aere natus.* However if this Dalilah should ever have the *Barba*rity to cutt of His Lordships *Hair* (which our modern Dalilahs can do without Scissors) his comfort is, that in spight of her he will be allways *Rich*, and therefore he may defy the *Philistins* and *Go ly a* bed.

The grave antient Collonell deserves better Treatment. He

was formerly a great *Support* to our Fraternity, two or three of them used to *Sup Port* with him as often as He thought fit to afford it. But since he is grown a *supporter* of Poets, I am informed they only *Sup Porter*.

As for Thomas *Pickle*, the true Reason why he went to Minorca, was because he had not a *Sowse*. To let pass his Instances of Muley Hamet and Eustace, which upon Enquiry would be found to *budge ill* as any of the rest I dare engage that Daniel *Button* will find a *Loop-hole* to creep out of whenever this Writer is pleased to *Quote* him if I be not mistaken in his *Mold*.

We are come at *Length* to a Gentleman stunted in *Stature* for attempting to Pun. But that Person cannot be called a *proper* Instance. 'Tis true, some are *longer* and some *shorter* at Punning, and if a *Pig may* Pun as our Detractors affirm, then certainly a *Pigmay* can.

The worst that can be said of George *Simmons* is that he *gave all the Shoes in his Shop* to be a Punster, and so would many a better Man do, and not think it *Simmony*.

As to the Reflection he is pleased to cast on our University Clergymen for being Drunkards and Toryes, I think it will be allowed that Punning is the *dryest* of all Joking, and therefore whether those Gentlemen he hints at (if there be any such) learned their *Tope*ography here we appele to the World: I know some have affirmed that we sit up at *Supper late* in the *Eve*ning, which is false in the *Supperlative* Degree. For his other Reflection, in calling us Toryes, thus much we declare, that His Majesty's *Liber*ality in that noble Present of *Books*, as it will make us *Lettered*, so it *Leaves* us *bound* to Him for ever, and we should be *covered* with *Gilt*, and deserve to be *bound* as Slaves in *Turkey*, if we failed in our Loyalty; and we hope the *No-Tory*-ety of our Behavior will appear by this further Declaration against all *indefesable Titles* and *Lines* except in His Majesty's *Family* and the *Books* he hath been pleased to give us.

Our Author concludes with a Fact entirely false, relating to a Devonshire Man of Wit. That this Gentleman fell from his Horse down a *Precipice* and broke his Neck, by which he would *press a piece* of History upon us without any *good Ground*; He likewise recites the Pun which brought on this Judgment, and had his *Horse punnd* no better, he deserved to be drownd in a *Horse-pond*. But the Story is all mistold; a Pun indeed there was, and with some Relation to a Horse; For it seems this Man of Wit happened to call the maid of the House where he lodged a *Sow*; and thn he told a Friend, that it was the *Poets Horse*, for he had called *Peg a Sus*; which was a very happy Turn of what we call the Remote or longinque kind. Neither did the Gentleman break his Neck (for the Author allows him to be a *Devonshire* man, and not from *Brecknock*) but is alive, and Hearty at this present writing. So that although I cannot affirm this Writer is a Conjurer, yet I think from publishing so premeditate a falshood he may justly be called a *Neck-Romancer*.

I am with great Respect

Sᵣ

Yᵣ &c.

On Good-Manners and Good-Breeding

ON

GOOD-MANNERS

AND

GOOD-BREEDING.

GOOD-Manners is the Art of making those people easy with whom we converse.

Whoever makes the fewest persons uneasy is the best bred in the company.

As the best law is founded upon reason, so are the best manners. And as some lawyers have introduced unreasonable things into common law; so likewise many teachers have introduced absurd things into common good-manners.

One principal point of this art is to suit our behaviour to the three several degrees of men; our superiors, our equals, and those below us.

For instance, to press either of the two former to eat or drink is a breach of manners; but a farmer or a tradesman must be thus treated, or else it will be difficult to persuade them that they are welcome.

Pride, ill-nature, and want of sense, are the three great sources of ill-manners; without some one of these defects, no man will behave himself ill for want of experience; or of what, in the language of fools, is called, knowing the world.

I defy any one to assign an incident wherein reason will not direct us what we are to say or to do in company, if we are not misled by pride or ill-nature.

Therefore I insist that good sense is the principal foundation of good manners: but because the former is a gift which very few among mankind are possessed of, therefore all the civilized nations of the world have agreed upon fixing some rules for common behaviour, best suited to their general customs, or fancies, as a kind of artificial good sense to supply the defects of reason. Without which, the *gentlemenly* part of dunces would be perpetually at cuffs, as they seldom fail when they happen to be drunk, or engaged in squabbles about women, or play. And, God be thanked, there hardly happens a duel in a year, which may not be imputed to one of those three motives. Upon which account, I should be exceedingly sorry to find the legislature make any new laws against the practice of duelling; because the methods are easy, and many, for a wise man to avoid a quarrel with honour, or engage in it with innocence. And I can discover no political evil in suffering bullies, sharpers, and rakes, to rid the world of each other by a method of their own; where the law hath not been able to find an expedient.

As the common forms of good-manners were intended for regulating the conduct of those who have weak understandings; so they have been corrupted by the persons for whose use they were contrived. For these people have fallen into a needless and endless way of multiplying ceremonies, which have been extremely troublesom to those who practise them; and insupportable to every body else: insomuch that wise men are often more uneasy at the over civility of these refiners, than they could possibly be in the conversations, of peasants or mechanicks.

The impertinencies of this ceremonial behaviour are no where better seen than at those tables, where ladies preside; who value themselves upon account of their good-breeding; where a man must reckon upon passing an hour without doing any one thing he has a mind to; unless he will be so hardy to break thorough all the settled decorum of the family. She determines what he loves best, and how much he shall eat; and if the master of the house happens to be of the same disposition, he proceeds in the same tyrannical manner to prescribe in the drinking part: at the same time, you are under the necessity of answering a thousand apologies for your entertainment. And although a good deal of this humour is pretty well worn off among many people of the best fashion, yet too much of it still remains, especially in the Country. Where an honest gentleman assured me, that having been kept four days, against his will, at a friend's house, with all the circumstances of hiding his boots, locking up the stable, and other contrivances of the like nature; he could not remember from the moment he came into the house, to the moment he left it, any one thing, wherein his inclination was not directly contradicted: as if the whole family had entered into a combination to torment him.

But besides all this, it would be endless to recount the many foolish and ridiculous accidents I have observed among these unfortunate proselytes to ceremony. I have seen a dutchess fairly knock'd down by the precipitancy of an officious cox-comb, running to save her the trouble of opening a door. I remember, upon a birth-day, at court, a great Lady was utterly desperate by a dish of sauce let fall by a page directly upon her headdress, and brocade; while she gave a sudden turn to her elbow upon some point of ceremony with the person who sat next her. Monsieur BUYS, the *Dutch* Envoy, whose politicks and manners were much of a size, brought a son with him, about thirteen years old, to a great table at court. The boy, and his father, whatever they put on their plates, they first offered round in order, to every person in the company; so that we could not get a minute's quiet during the whole dinner. At last, their two plates happened to encounter, and with so much violence, that being china, they broke in twenty pieces; and stained half the company with wet sweet meats and cream.

There is a pedantry in manners, as in all arts and sciences; and sometimes in trades. Pedantry is properly the overrating any kind of knowledge we pretend to. And if that kind of knowledge be a trifle in itself, the pedantry is the greater. For which reason, I look upon fidlers, dancing-masters, heralds, masters of the ceremony, &c. to be greater pedants, than LIPSIUS, or the elder SCALIGER. With these kind of pedants, the court, while I knew it, was always plentifully stocked: I mean from the gentleman-usher (at least) inclusive, downward to the gentleman-porter: who are generally speaking, the most insignificant race of people, that this island can afford, and with the smallest tincture of good-manners; which is the only trade they profess. For being wholly illiterate, and conversing chiefly with each other, they reduce the whole system of breeding within the forms and circles of their several offices: and as they are below the notice of ministers, they live and die in court under all revolutions, with great obsequiousness to those who are in any degree of favour or credit: and with rudeness or insolence to every body else. From whence I have long concluded, that good-manners are not a plant of the court growth: for if they were, those people who have understandings directly of a level for such acquirements, and who have served such long apprentiships to nothing else, would certainly have picked them up. For as to the great officers who attend the prince's person or councils, or preside in his family, they are a transient body, who have no better a title to good-manners, than their neighbours, nor will probably have recourse to gentlemen-ushers for instruction. So that I know little to be learnt at court upon this head, except in the material circumstance of dress; wherein the authority of the maids of honour must indeed be allowed, to be almost equal to that of a favourite actress.

I remember a passage my Lord BOLINGBROKE told me, that going to receive Prince EUGENE of *Savoy* at his landing, in order to conduct him immediately to the Queen; the Prince said, he was much concerned that he could not see her Majesty that night; for Monsieur HOFFMAN (who was then by) had assured his highness, that he could not be admitted into her presence with a tied-up periwig: that his equipage was not arrived, and that he had endeavoured in vain to borrow a long one among all his valets and pages. My Lord turned the matter to a jest, and brought the Prince to her Majesty: for which he was highly censured by the whole tribe of gentlemen-ushers: among whom Monsieur HOFFMAN, an old dull resident of the Emperor's, had picked up this material point of ceremony; and which, I believe, was the best lesson he had learned in five and twenty years residence.

I make a difference between good-manners, and good-breeding; although in order to vary my expression, I am sometimes forced to confound them. By the first, I only understand the art of remembring, and applying certain settled forms of general behaviour. But good-breeding is of a much larger extent; for besides an uncommon degree of literature sufficient to qualify a gentleman for reading a play, or a political pamphlet, it takes in a great compass of knowledge; no less than that of dancing, fighting, gameing making the circle of *Italy*, riding the great horse, and speaking *French*; not to mention some other secondary, or subaltern accomplishments, which are more easily acquired: so that the difference between good-breeding, and good-manners, lies in this; that the former cannot be attained to by the best understandings, without study and labour: whereas a tolerable degree of reason will instruct us in every part of good-manners, without other assistance.

I can think of nothing more useful upon this subject, than to point out some particulars, wherein the very essentials of good-manners are concerned, the neglect or perverting of which, doth very much disturb the good commerce of the world; by introducing a traffic of mutual uneasiness in most companies.

First, a necessary part of good-manners, is a punctual observance of time at our own dwellings, or those of others, or at third places; whether upon matter of civility, business, or diversion; which rule, tho' it be a plain dictate of common reason, yet the greatest minister I ever knew, was the greatest trespasser against it; by which all his business doubled upon him, and placed him in a continual arrear. Upon which I often used to rally him, as deficient in point of good-manners. I have known more than one ambassador, and secretary of state, with a very moderate portion of intellectuals, execute their offices with good success and applause by the mere force of exactness, and regularity. If you duly observe time for the service of another, it doubles the obligation; if upon your own account, it would be manifest folly, as well as ingratitude, to neglect it. If both are concerned, to make your equal or inferior attend on you, to his own disadvantage, is pride and injustice.

Ignorance of forms cannot properly be stiled ill-manners; because forms are subject to frequent changes; and consequently, being not founded upon reason, are beneath a wise man's regard. Besides, they vary in every country; and after a short period of time, very frequently in the same. So that a man who travels must needs be at first a stranger to them in every court, through which he passes. And perhaps at his return, as much a stranger in his own; and after all, they are easier to be remembered, or forgotten, than faces, or names.

Indeed among the many impertinencies that superficial young men bring with them from abroad, this bigotry of forms is one of the principal, and more prominent than the rest. Who look upon them, not only as if they were matters capable of admitting of choice, but even as points of importance, and therefore zealous upon all occasions to introduce, and propagate the new forms and fashions they have brought back with them. So that usually speaking, the worst bred person in the company, is a young traveller just returned from abroad.

Hints on Good-Manners

H I N T S

O N

G O O D   M A N N E R S.

GOOD MANNERS is the art of making every reasonable person in the company easy, and to be easy ourselves. What passeth for good manners in the world, generally produceth quite contrary effects.

Many persons of both sexes, whom I have known, and who passed for well-bred in their own and the world's opinion, are the most troublesome in company to others and themselves.

Nothing is so great an instance of ill manners as flattery. If you flatter all the company, you please none; if you flatter only one or two, you affront the rest.

Flattery is the worst, and falsest way of shewing our esteem.

Where company meets, I am confident the few reasonable persons are every minute tempted to curse the man or woman among them, who endeavours to be most distinguished for their good manners.

A man of sense would rather fast until night, than dine at some tables, where the lady of the house is possessed with good manners; uneasiness, pressing to eat, teazing with civility; less practised in England than here.

Courts are the worst of all schools to teach good manners.

A courtly bow, or gait, or dress, are no part of good manners. And therefore every man of good understanding is capable of being well-bred upon any occasion.

To speak in such a manner as may possibly offend any reasonable person in company, is the highest instance of ill manners.

Good manners chiefly consist in action, not in words. Modesty and humility the chief ingredients.

OF THE

EDUCATION

OF

LADIES.

THERE is a subject of controversy which I have frequently met with in mixt and select companies of both sexes, and sometimes only of men; whether it be prudent to chuse a wife, who hath good natural sense, some taste of wit and humour, sufficiently versed in her own natural language, able to read and to relish history, books of travels, moral or entertaining discourses, and be a tolerable judge of the beauties in poetry. This question is generally determined in the negative by the women themselves, but almost universally by the men.

We must observe that, in this debate, those whom we call men and women of fashion, are only to be understood, not merchants, tradesmen, or others of such occupations, who are not supposed to have shared in a liberal education. I except likewise all ministers of state, during their power, lawyers and physicians in great practice, persons in such employments as take up the greater part of the day, and perhaps some other conditions of life which I cannot call to mind. Neither must I forget to except all gentlemen of the army, from the general to the ensign; because those qualifications above-mentioned, in a wife, are wholly out of their element and comprehension; together with all mathematicians, and gentlemen lovers of music, metaphysicians, virtuosi, and great talkers, who have all amusements enough of their own. All these put together, will amount to a great number of adversaries, whom I shall have no occasion to encounter, because I am already of their the university, about treble that number. The sons of clergy-men bred to learning with any success, must, by reason of their parents poverty, be very inconsiderable, many of them being only admitted servitors in colleges, (and consequently proving good for nothing:) I shall therefore count them to be not above fourscore. Bit, to avoid fractions, I shall suppose there may possibly be a round number of two thousand male human creatures in England (including Wales), who have a tolerable share of reading and good sense. I include in this list all persons of superior abilities, or great genius, or true judg-ment and taste, or of profound literature, who, I am cofident, we may reckon to be at least five and twenty.

I am very glad to have this opportunity of doing an honour to my country, by a computation which I am afraid foreigners may conceive to be partial; when, out of only fifteen thousand families of lords and estated gentlemen, which may probably be their number. I suppose one in thirty to be tolerably educated, with a sufficient share of good sense. Perhaps the censure may be just. And therefore, upon cooler thoughts, to avoid all cavils, I shall reduce them to one thousand; which, at least, will be a number sufficient to fill both Houses of Parliament.

The daughters of great and rich families, computed after the same manner, will hardly amount to above half the number of the male: Because the care of their education is either left entirely to their mothers, or they are sent to boarding-schools, or put into the hands of English or French governesses, and generally the worst that can be gotten for money. So that, after the reduction I was compelled to, from two thousand to one, half the number of well-educated nobility and gentry must either continue in a single life, or be forced to couple themselves with women for whom they can possibly have no esteem; I mean fools, prudes, coquettes, gamesters, saunterers, endless talkers of nonsense, splenetic idlers, intriguers, given to scandal and censure,   *   *   *   *   *   *   *   *   *   *   *
*   *   *

A Discourse to Prove the Antiquity of the English Tongue

A

DISCOURSE,

To prove the Antiquity of the

ENGLISH TONGUE.

Shewing, from various Instances, that HEBREW, GREEK, *and* LATIN, *were derived from the* ENGLISH.

DURING the reign of parties, for about forty years past, it is a melancholy consideration to observe how *Philology* hath been neglected, which was before the darling employment of the greatest authors, from the restoration of learning in Europe. Neither do I remember it to have been cultivated, since the revolution, by any one person with great success, except our illustrious modern star, Doctor Richard Bentley, with whom the republic of learning must expire; as mathematics did with Sir Isaac Newton. My ambition hath been gradually attempting, from my early youth, to be the holder of a rush-light before that great luminary; which, at least, might be of some little use during those short intervals, while he was snuffing his candle, or peeping with it under a bushel.

My present attempt is to assert the antiquity of our English Tongue; which, as I shall undertake to prove by invincible arguments, hath varied very little for these two thousand six hundred and thirty-four years past. And my proofs will be drawn from etymology; wherein I shall use my readers much fairer than Pezron, Skinner, Vorstigan, Camden, and many other superficial pretenders have done. For I will put no force upon the words, nor desire any more favour than to allow for the usual accidents of corruption, or the avoiding a cacophonia.

I think I can make it manifest to all impartial readers, that our language, as we now speak it, was originally the same with those of the Jews, the Greeks, and the Romans, however corrupted in succeeding times by a mixture of barbarisms. I shall only produce, at present, two instances among a thousand from the Latin tongue. *Cloaca*, which they interpret a *necessary-house*, is altogether an English word, the last letter *a* being, by the mistake of some scribe, translated from the beginning to the end of the word. In the primitive orthography it is called *a cloac*, which had the same signification; and still continues so at Edinburgh in Scotland; Where a man in *a cloac*, or cloak, of large circumference and length, carrying a convenient vessel under it, calls out, as he goes through the streets, *Wha has need of me?* Whatever customer calls, the vessel is placed in the corner of the street, the *cloac*, or a cloak, surrounds and covers him, and thus he is eased with decency and secrecy.

The second instance is yet more remarkable. The Latin word *Turpis* signifieth *nasty*, or *filthy*. Now this word *Turpis* is a plain composition of two English words; only by a syncope, the last letter of the first syllable, which is *d*, is taken out of the middle, to prevent the jarring of three consonants together: And these two English words express the two most unseemly excrements that belong to man.

But although I could produce many other examples, equally convincing, that the Hebrews, the Greeks, and the Romans originally spoke the same language which we do at present; yet I have chosen to confine myself chiefly to the proper names of persons, because I conceive they will be of greater weight to confirm what I advance; the ground and reason of those names being certainly owing to the nature, or some distinguishing action or quality in those persons, and consequently expressed in the true antient language of the several people.

I will begin with the Grecians, among whom the most antient are the great leaders on both sides in the siege of Troy. For it is plain, from Homer, that the Trojans spoke Greek as well as the Grecians. Of these latter, *Achilles* was the most valiant. This Hero was of a restless, unquiet nature, never giving himself any repose, either in peace or war; and therefore, as Guy of Warwick was called a Kill-cow, and another terrible man a Kill-devil, so this General was called *A Kill-ease*, or destroyer of ease; and at length, by corruption, *Achilles*.

Hector, on the other side, was the bravest among the Trojans. He had destroyed so many of the Greeks, by *hacking* and *tearing* them, that his soldiers, when they saw him fighting, would cry out, 'Now the enemy will be *hackt*, now he will be *tore*.' At last, by putting both words together, this appellation was given to their leader, under the name of *Hack-tore*; and, for the more commodious sounding, *Hector*.

Diomede, another Grecian captain, had the boldness to fight with Venus, and wound her; whereupon the Goddess, in a rage, ordered her son Cupid to make this Hero be hated by all women, repeating it often that he should *die a maid*; from whence, by a small change in orthography, he was called *Diomede*. And it is to be observed, that the term *Maiden-head* is frequently, at this very day, applied to persons of either sex.

Ajax was, in fame, the next Grecian general to Achilles. The derivation of his name from *A Jakes*, however asserted by great authors, is, in my opinion, very unworthy both of them and of the Hero himself. I have often wondered to see such learned men mistake in so clear a point. This Hero is known to have been a most intemperate liver, as it is usual with soldiers; and, although he were not old, yet by conversing with camp-strollers, he had got pains in his bones, which he pretended to his friends were only *Age-aches*; but they telling the story about the army, as the vulgar always confound right pronunciation, he was afterwards known by no other name than *Ajax*.

The next I shall mention is *Andromache*, the famous wife of Hector. Her father was a Scotch gentleman, of a noble family still subsisting in that antient kingdom. But, being a foreigner in Troy, to which city he led some of his countrymen in the defence of Priam, as *Dictys Cretensis* learnedly observes; Hector fell in love with his daughter, and the father's name

S

was *Andrew Mackay*. The young lady was called by the same name, only a little softened to the Grecian accent.

Astyanax was the son of Hector and Andromache. When Troy was taken, this young Prince had his head cut off, and his body thrown to swine. From this fatal accident he had his name; which hath, by a peculiar good fortune, been preserved entire, *A sty, an ax.*

Mars may be mentioned among these, because he fought against the Greeks. He was called the God of War; and is described as a swearing, swaggering companion, and a great giver of rude language. For, when he was angry, he would cry, 'Kiss *my a—se, My a—se* in a band-box, *My a—se* all over:' which he repeated so commonly, that he got the appellation of *My-a—se*; and, by a common abbreviation, *M'as*; from whence, by leaving out the mark of elision, *Mars*. And this is a common practice among us at present; as in the words D'anvers, D'avenport, D'anby, which are now written Danvers, Davenport, Danby, and many others.

The next is *Hercules*, otherwise called *Alcides*. Both these names are English, with little alteration; and describe the principal qualities of that Hero, who was distinguished for being a slave to his mistresses, and at the same time for his great strength and courage. Omphale, his chief mistress, used to call her lovers *Her cullies*; and, because this Hero was more and longer subject to her than any other, he was in a particular manner called the chief of *her cullies*; which, by an easy change, made the word *Hercules*. His other name, *Alcides*, was given him on account of his prowess; for, in fight, he used to strike on *all sides*; and was allowed on *all sides* to be the chief hero of his age. For one of which reasons, he was called *All sides*, or *Alcides*; but I am inclined to favour the former opinion.

A certain Grecian youth was a great imitator of Socrates; which that philosopher observing, with much pleasure, said to his friends, 'There is an *Ape o' mine own days.*' After which the young man was called *Epaminondas*, and proved to be the most virtuous person, as well as the greatest general of his age.

Ucalegon was a very obliging inn-keeper of Troy. When a

guest was going to take horse, the landlord took leave of him with this compliment, 'Sir, I shall be glad to see *you call again.*' Strangers, who knew not his right name, caught his last words; and thus, by degrees, that appellation prevailed, and he was known by no other name, even among his neighbours.

Hydra was a great serpent which Hercules slew. His usual outward garment was the *raw hyde* of a lion, and this he had on when he attacked the serpent; which, therefore, took its name from the skin: The modesty of that Hero devolving the honour of his victory upon the lion's skin, calling that enormous snake the *Hyde-raw* serpent.

Leda was the mother of Castor and Pollux; whom Jupiter embracing in the shape of a swan, she *laid a* couple of eggs; and was therefore called *Laid a,* or *Leda.*

As to Jupiter himself: It is well known that the statues and pictures of this Heathen God, in the Roman-catholic countries, resemble those of St. Peter, and are often taken the one for the other. The reason is manifest: For, when the emperors had established Christianity, the Heathens were afraid of acknowledging their heathen idols of the chief God, and pretended it was only a statue of the *Jew Peter.* And thus the principal Heathen God came to be called by the antient Romans, with very little alteration, *Jupiter.*

The *Hamadryades* are represented by mistaken antiquity as Nymphs of the Groves. But the true account is this: They were women of Calabria, who dealt in bacon; and, living near the sea-side, used to pickle their bacon in salt-water, and then set it up to dry in the sun. From whence they were properly called *Ham-a-dry-a-days,* and, in process of time, mispelt *Hamadryades.*

Neptune, the God of the sea, had his name from the *Tunes* sung to him by tritons, upon their shells every *neap* or *nep* tide. The word is come down to us almost uncorrupted, as well as that of the *Tritons,* his servants, who, in order to please their master, used to *try* all *tones,* until they could hit upon that he liked.

Aristotle was a Peripatetic philosopher, who used to instruct his scholars while he was walking. When the lads were come, he would *arise to tell* them what he thought proper; and was therefore called *Arise to tell*. But succeeding ages, who understood not this etymology, have, by an absurd change, made it *Aristotle*.

Aristophanes was a Greek comedian, full of levity, and gave himself too much freedom; which made a graver people not scruple to say, that he had a great deal of *airy stuff in his* writings: And these words, often repeated, made succeeding ages denominate him *Aristophanes*. Vide *Rosin. Antiq. l.* iv.

Alexander the Great was very fond of eggs roasted in hot ashes. As soon as his cooks heard he was come home to dinner or supper, they called aloud to their under-officers, *All eggs under the Grate:* Which, repeated every day at noon and evening, made strangers think it was that Prince's real name, and therefore gave him no other; and posterity hath been ever since under the same delusion.

Pygmalion was a person of very low stature, but great valour, which made his townsmen call him *Pygmy lion:* And so it should be spelt; although the word hath suffered less by transcribers than many others.

Archimedes was a most famous mathematician. His studies required much silence and quiet: But his wife having several maids, they were always disturbing him with their tattle or their business; which forced him to come out every now and then to the stair-head, and cry, '*Hark ye maids*, if you will not be quiet, I shall turn you out of doors.' He repeated these words, *Hark ye maids*, so often, that the unlucky jades, when they found he was at his study, would say, There is *Hark ye maids*, let us speak softly. Thus the name went through the neighbourhood; and, at last, grew so general, that we are ignorant of that great man's true name to this day.

Strabo was a famous geographer; and, to improve his knowledge, travelled over several countries, as the writers of his life inform us; who likewise add, that he affected great niceness and finery in his cloaths: From whence people took occasion to call him the *Stray beau*; which future ages have pinned down upon him, very much to his dishonour.

Peloponnesus, that famous Grecian peninsula, got its name from a Greek colony in Asia the Less; many of whom going for traffic thither, and finding that the inhabitants had but one well in the town of * * * *, from whence certain porters used to carry the water through the city in great pails, so heavy that they were often forced to set them down for ease; the tired porters, after they had set down the pails, and wanted to take them up again, would call for assistance to those who were nearest, in these words, *Pail up, and ease us*. The stranger Greeks, hearing these words repeated a thousand times as they passed the street, thought the inhabitants were pronouncing the name of their country, which made the foreign Greeks call it *Peloponnesus*, a manifest corruption of *Pail up and ease us*.

Having mentioned so many Grecians to prove my hypothesis, I shall not tire the reader with producing an equal number of Romans, as I might easily do. Some few will be sufficient.

Cæsar was the greatest captain of that empire: The word ought to be spelt *Seiser*, because he *seised* on not only most of the known world, but even the liberties of his own country: So that a more proper appellation could not have been given him.

Cicero was a poor scholar in the unversity of Athens, wherewith his enemies in Rome used to reproach him; and, as he passed the streets, would call out, *O Ciser, Ciser o!* A word still used in Cambridge, and answers to a servitor in Oxford.

Anibal was sworn enemy of the Romans, and gained many glorious victories over them. This name appears at first repeating to be a metaphor drawn from tennis, expressing a skilful gamester, who can take *any ball*; and is very justly applied to so renowned a commander. Navigators are led into a strange mistake upon this article. We have usually in our fleet some large men of war, called the *Anibal* with great propriety, because it is so strong that it may defy *any ball* from a cannon. And such is the deplorable ignorance of our seamen, that they miscal it the *Honey-ball*.

Cartago was the most famous trading city in the world;

where, in every street, there was many a *cart a going*, probably laden with merchants goods. Vide *Alexander ab Alexandro*, and *Suidas* upon the word *Cartago*.

The word *Roman* itself is perfectly English, like other words ending in *man* or *men*, as Hangman, Drayman, Huntsman, and several others. It was formerly spelt *Row-man*, which is the same with *Water-man*. And therefore, when we read of *Jesta*, (or, as it is corruptly spelt, *Gesta*) *Romanorum*, it is to be understood of the rough manner of *jesting* used by watermen; who, upon the sides of rivers, would *row man or'um*. This, I think, is clear enough to convince the most incredulous.

Misanthropus was the name of an ill-natured man, which he obtained by a custom of catching a great number of *mice*, then shutting them up in a room, and throwing a cat among them. Upon which his fellow citizens called him *Mice and throw puss*. The reader observes how much the orthography hath been changed without altering the sound: But such depravations we owe to the injury of time, and gross ignorance of transcribers.

Among the antients, fortune-telling by the stars was a very beggarly trade. The professors lay upon straw, and their cabins were covered with the same materials: Whence every one who followed that mystery was called *A straw lodger*, or a lodger in straw; but in the new-fangled way of spelling, *Astrologer*.

It is remarkable that the very word *Dipthong* is wholely English. In former times, school-boys were chastised with thongs fastened at the head of a stick. It was observed that young lads were much puzzled with spelling, and pronouncing words where two vowels came together, and were often corrected for their mistakes in that point. Upon these occasions the master would *dip* his *thongs* (as we now do rods) in p—, which made that difficult union of vowels to be called *Dipthong*.

Bucephalus, the famous horse of Alexander, was so called because there were many grooms employed about him, which *fellows* were always *busy* in their office; and, because the horse had so many *busy fellows* about him, it was natural for those who went to the stable to say, 'Let us go to the *busy fellows*'; by which they meant to see that Prince's horse. And, in process of time, these words were absurdly applied to the animal itself, which was thenceforth styled *Busy-fellows*, and very improperly *Bucephalus*.

I shall now bring a few proofs of the same kind, to convince my readers that our English language was well known to the Jews.

Moses, the great leader of those people out of Egypt, was in propriety of speech called *Mow seas*, because he *mowed* the *seas* down in the middle, to make a path for the Israelites.

Abraham was a person of strong bones and sinews, and a firm walker, which made the people say, He was a man (in the Scotch phrase, which comes nearest to the old Saxon) of *a bra ham*; that is, of a brave strong ham, from whence he acquired his name.

The man whom the Jews called *Balam* was a shepherd; who, by often crying *Ba* to his *lambs*, was therefore called *Baalamb*, or *Balam*.

Isaac is nothing else but *Eyes ake*; because the Talmudists report that he had a pain in his eyes. Vide *Ben-gorion* and the *Targum* on *Genesis*.

Thus I have manifestly proved, that the Greeks, the Romans, and the Jews, spoke the language we now do in England; which is an honour to our country that I thought proper to set in a true light, and yet hath not been done, as I have heard, by any other writer.

And thus I have ventured (perhaps too temerariously) to contribute my mite to the learned world; from whose candour, if I may hope to receive some approbation, it may probably give me encouragement to proceed on some other speculations, if possible, of greater importance than what I now offer; and which have been the labour of many years, as well as of constant watchings, that I might be useful to mankind, and particularly to mine own country.

Thoughts on Various
Subjects

THOUGHTS

ON

Various SUBJECTS.

ALTHOUGH Men are accused for not knowing their own Weakness; yet perhaps as few know their own Strength. It is in Men as in Soils, where sometimes there is a Vein of Gold, which the Owner knows not of.

SATYR is reckoned the easiest of all Wit; but I take it to be otherwise in very bad Times: For it is as hard to satyrize well a Man of distinguished Vices, as to praise well a Man of distinguished Virtues. It is easie enough to do either to People of moderate Characters.

INVENTION is the Talent of Youth, and Judgment of Age; so that our Judgment grows harder to please when we have fewer Things to offer it: This goes through the whole Commerce of Life. When we are old, our Friends find it Difficult to please us, and are less concerned whether we be pleased or no.

NO wise Man ever wished to be younger.

AN idle Reason lessens the Weight of the good ones you gave before.

THE Motives of the best Actions will not bear too strict an Enquiry. It is allowed, that the Cause of most Actions, good or bad, may be resolved into the Love of our selves: But the Self-Love of some Men inclines them to please others; and the Self-Love of others is wholly employed in pleasing themselves. This makes the great Distinction between Virtue and Vice. Religion is the best Motive of all Actions; yet Religion is allowed to be the highest Instance of Self-Love.

WHEN the World hath once begun to use us ill, it afterwards continues the same Treatment with less Scruple or Ceremony; as Men do to a Whore.

OLD Men view best at Distance with the Eyes of their Understanding, as well as with those of Nature.

SOME People take more Care to hide their Wisdom than their Folly.

ARBITRARY Power is the natural Object of Temptation to a Prince; as Wine or Women to a young Fellow, or a Bribe to a Judge, or Avarice to old Age, or Vanity to a Female.

Anthony Henly's Farmer dying of an Asthma, said: Well, if I can get this Breath once *out*, I will take care it shall never get *in* again.

THE Humour of exploding many Things under the Names of Trifles, Fopperies, and only imaginary Goods, is a very false Proof either of Wisdom or Magnanimity; and a great Check to virtuous Actions. For Instance, with Regard to Fame: There is in most People a Reluctance and Unwillingness to be forgotten. We observe, even among the Vulgar, how fond they are to have an Inscription over their Grave. It requires but little Philosophy to discover and observe that there is no intrinsick Value in all this; however, if it be founded in our Nature, as an Incitement to Virtue, it ought not to be ridiculed.

COMPLAINT is the largest Tribute Heaven receives; and the sincerest Part of our Devotion.

THE common Fluency of Speech in many Men, and most Women, is owing to a Scarcity of Matter, and Scarcity of Words; for whoever is a Master of Language, and hath a Mind full of Ideas, will be apt in speaking to hesitate upon the Choice of both: Whereas common Speakers have only one Set of Ideas, and one Set of Words to cloath them in; and these are always ready at the Mouth. So People come faster out of a Church when it is almost empty, than when a Crowd is at the Door.

FEW are qualified to *shine* in Company; but it is in most Mens Power to be *agreeable*. The Reason, therefore, why Conversation runs so low at present, is not the Defect of Understanding; but Pride, Vanity, ill Nature, Affectation, Singularity, Positiveness; or some other Vice, the Effect of a wrong Education.

To be vain, is rather a Mark of Humility than of Pride. Vain Men delight in telling what Honours have been done them, what great Company they have kept, and the like; by which they plainly confess, that these Honours were more than their Due; and such as their Friends would not believe if they had not been told: Whereas a Man truly proud, thinks the greatest Honours below his Merit, and consequently scorns to boast. I therefore deliver it as a Maxim; that whoever desires the Character of a proud Man, ought to conceal his Vanity.

LAW in a free Country, is, or ought to be the Determination of the Majority of those who have Property in Land.

ONE Argument used to the Disadvantage of Providence, I take to be a very strong one in its Defence. It is objected, that Storms and Tempests, unfruitful Seasons, Serpents, Spiders, Flies, and other noxious or troublesome Animals, with many more Instances of the like Kind, discover an Imperfection in Nature; because human Life would be much easier without them: But the Design of Providence may clearly be perceived in this Proceeding. The Motions of the Sun and Moon; in short, the whole System of the Universe, as far as Philosophers have been able to discover and observe, are in the utmost Degree of Regularity and Perfection: But wherever God hath left to Man the Power of interposing a Remedy by Thought or Labour, there he hath placed Things in a State of Imperfection, on purpose to stir up human Industry; without which Life would stagnate, or indeed rather could not subsist at all: *Curis acuens mortalia corda.*

PRAISE is the Daughter of present Power.

HOW inconsistent is Man with himself!

I HAVE known several Persons of great Fame for Wisdom in publick Affairs and Counsels, governed by foolish Servants.

I HAVE known great Ministers distinguished for Wit and Learning, who preferred none but Dunces.

I HAVE known Men of Valour, Cowards to their Wives.

I HAVE known Men of the greatest Cunning, perpetually cheated.

I KNEW three great Ministers, who could exactly compute

and settle the Accounts of a Kingdom; but were wholly ignorant of their own Oeconomy.

THE Preaching of Divines helps to preserve well-inclined Men in the Course of Virtue; but seldom or never reclaims the Vicious.

PRINCES usually make wiser Choices than the Servants whom they trust for the Disposal of Places: I have known a Prince more than once chuse an able Minister; but I never observed that Minister to use his Credit in the Disposal of an Employment to a Person whom he thought the fittest for it. One of the greatest in this Age owned and excused the Matter to me; from the Violence of Parties, and the Unreasonableness of Friends.

SMALL Causes are sufficient to make a Man uneasy, when great ones are not in the Way: For want of a *Block* he will stumble at a *Straw*.

DIGNITY, high Station, or great Riches are in some sort necessary to old Men, in order to keep the younger at a Distance; who are otherwise too apt to insult them upon the Score of their Age.

EVERY Man desires to live long: but no Man would be old.

LOVE of Flattery in most Men proceeds from the mean Opinion they have of themselves: In Women from the contrary.

IF Books and Laws continue to increase as they have done for fifty Years past; I am in some Concern for future Ages, how any Man will be learned, or any Man a Lawyer.

KINGS are commonly said to have *long Hands*; I wish they had as *long Ears*.

PRINCES in their Infancy, Childhood and Youth, are said to discover prodigious Parts and Wit; to speak Things that surprize and astonish: Strange, so many *hopeful* Princes, and so many *shameful* Kings! If they happen to die young, they would have been *Prodigies* of Wisdom and Virtue: If they live, they are often *Prodigies* indeed; but of *another Sort*.

POLITICKS, as the Word is commonly understood, are nothing but Corruptions; and consequently of no Use to a good King, or a good Ministry: For which Reason, Courts are so over-run with Politicks.

SILENUS, the Foster-Father of *Bacchus*, is always carried by an *Ass*, and hath Horns on his Head. The Moral is; that Drunkards are led by Fools, and have a great Chance to be Cuckolds.

VENUS, a beautiful good-natured Lady, was the Goddess of Love; *Juno*, a terrible Shrew, the Goddess of Marriage; and they were always mortal Enemies.

THOSE who are against Religion, must needs be Fools: And therefore we read, that, of all Animals, GOD refused the *First-born* of an Ass.

A VERY little Wit is valued in a Woman; as we are pleased with a few Words spoken plain by a Parrot.

A NICE Man is a Man of nasty Ideas.

APOLLO was held the God of Physick, and Sender of Diseases: Both were originally the same Trade, and still continue.

OLD Men and Comets have been reverenced for the same Reason; their long Beards, and Pretences to foretel Events.

I WAS asked at Court, what I thought of the *French* Ambassador and his Train; who were all Embroidery and Lace; full of Bows, Cringes, and Gestures? I said, it was *Solomon*'s Importation; *Gold and Apes*.

THERE is a Story in *Pausanias*, of a Plot for betraying a City, discovered by the Braying of an *Ass*: The Cackling of *Geese* saved the *Capitol*: And *Cataline*'s Conspiracy was discovered by a *Whore*. These are the only three Animals, as far as I remember, famous in History for *Evidences* and *Informers*.

MOST Kinds of Diversion in Men, Children, and other Animals, are an Imitation of Fighting.

AUGUSTUS meeting an *Ass* with a *lucky Name*, foretold himself good Fortune. I meet many *Asses*, but none of them have lucky Names.

IF a Man makes me keep my Distance; the Comfort is, he keeps his at the same Time.

WHO can deny that all Men are violent Lovers of Truth, when we see them so positive in their Errors; which they will maintain out of their Zeal to Truth, although they contradict themselves every Day of their Lives?

THAT was excellently observed, say I, when I read a Passage in an Author, where his Opinion agrees with mine. When we differ, there I pronounce him to be *mistaken*.

VERY few Men, properly speaking, *live* at present; but are providing to *live* another Time.

As universal a Practice as Lying is, and as easy a one as it seems; I do not remember to have heard three good Lyes in all my Conversation; even from those who were most celebrated in that Faculty.

LAWS penned with the utmost Care and Exactness, and in the vulgar Language, are often perverted to wrong Meanings; then why should we wonder that the Bible is so?

ALTHOUGH Men are accused for not knowing their Weakness, yet perhaps, as few know their own Strength.

A MAN seeing a Wasp creeping into a Phial filled with Honey, that was hung on a Fruit-tree, said thus: Why, thou sottish Animal, art thou mad to go into that Phial, where you see many hundred of your kind there dying in it before you? The Reproach is just, answered the Wasp, but not from you Men, who are so far from taking Example by other Peoples Follies, that you will not take Warning by your own. If after falling several Times into this Phial, and escaping by Chance, I should fall in again, I should then but resemble you.

AN old Miser kept a tame Jack-daw, that used to steal Pieces of Money, and hide them in a Hole, which the Cat observing, asked, Why he would hoard up those round shining Things that he could make no use of? Why, said the Jack-daw, my Master hath a whole Chest-full, and maketh no more Use of them than I.

MEN are content to be laughed at for their Wit, but not for their Folly.

IF the Men of Wit and Genius would resolve never to complain in their Works of Criticks and Detractors, the next Age would not know that they ever had any.

AFTER all the Maxims and Systems of Trade and Commerce,

a Stander-by would think the Affairs of the World were most ridiculously contrived.

THERE are few Countries, which, if well cultivated, would not support double the Number of their Inhabitants, and yet fewer where one Third of the People are not extremely stinted even in the Necessaries of Life. I send out twenty Barrels of Corn, which would maintain a Family in Bread for a Year, and I bring back in return a Vessel of Wine, which half a Dozen good Fellows would drink in less than a Month, at the Expence of their Health and Reason.

A MOTTO for the Jesuits:

Quæ regio in terris nostri non plena laboris?

A MAN would have but few Spectators, if he offered to shew for Three-pence how he could thrust a red-hot Iron into a Barrel of Gunpowder, and it should not take Fire.

Query, Whether Churches are not Dormitories of the Living as well as of the Dead?

Harry Killigrew said to Lord *Wharton*, 'You would not swear at this Rate, if you thought you were doing GOD Honour.'

A COPY of Verses kept in the Cabinet, and only shewn to a few Friends, is like a Virgin much sought after and admired; but when printed and published, is like a common Whore, whom any body may purchase for half a Crown.

Lewis the XIVth of *France* spent his Life in turning a Good Name into a Great.

THE *Epicureans* began to spread at *Rome* in the Empire of *Augustus*, as the *Socinians*, and even the *Epicureans* too, did in *England*, towards the End of King *Charles* the Second's Reign; which is reckoned, although very absurdly, our *Augustan* Age. They both seem to be Corruptions occasioned by Luxury and Peace, and by Politeness beginning to decline.

SOMETIMES I read a Book with Pleasure, and detest the Author.

AT a Bookseller's Shop, some Time ago, I saw a Book with this Title; *Poems by the* * *Author of the Choice*. Not enduring to read a dozen Lines, I asked the Company with me, whether they had ever seen the Book, or heard of the Poem from

* The Reverend Mr. *Pomfret*, a Dissenting Minister.

T

whence the Author denominated himself? They were all as ignorant as I. But I find it common with these small Dealers in Wit and Learning, to give themselves a Title from their first Adventure, as *Don Quixot* usually did from his last. This ariseth from that great Importance which every Man supposeth himself to be of.

ONE *Dennis*, commonly called *the Critick*, who had written a three Penny Pamphlet against the Power of *France*, being in the Country, and hearing of a *French* Privateer hovering about the Coast, although he was twenty Miles from the Sea, fled to Town, and told his Friends, they need not wonder at his Haste; for the King of *France*, having got Intelligence where he was, had sent a Privateer on Purpose to catch him.

DR. *Gee*, Prebendary of *Westminster*, who had written a small Paper against *Popery*, being obliged to travel for his Health, affected to disguise his Person, and change his Name, as he passed through *Portugal*, *Spain*, and *Italy*; telling all the *English* People he met, that he was afraid of being murdered, or put into the Inquisition. He was acting the same Farce at *Paris*, until Mr. *Prior* (who was then Secretary to the Ambassy) quite disconcerted the Doctor, by maliciously discovering the Secret, and offering to engage, Body for Body, that not a Creature would hurt him, or had ever heard of him or his Pamphlet.

A CHAMBER-MAID to a Lady of my Acquaintance, thirty Miles from *London*, had the very same Turn of Thought, when talking with one of her Fellow-Servants, she said, 'I hear it is all over *London* already, that I am going to leave my Lady.' And so had a Footman, who being newly married, desired his Comrade to tell him freely what the Town said of it. When somebody was telling a certain great Minister, that the People were discontented: 'Poh, said he, half a dozen Fools are prating in a Coffee-house, and presently think their own Noise about their Ears is made by the World.'

I

WHENCE comes the Custom of bidding a Woman look upon her Apron-strings to find an Excuse? Was it not from the Apron of Fig-leaves worn by *Eve*, when she covered her-self; and was the first of her Sex who made a bad Excuse for eating the forbidden Fruit?

I NEVER wonder to see Men wicked, but I often wonder to see them not ashamed.

Do not we see how easily we pardon our own Actions and Passions, and the very Infirmities of our Bodies; why should it be wonderful to find us pardon our own Dulness?

DIGNITY and Station, or great Riches, are in some Sort necessary to old Men, in order to keep the younger at a Distance, who are otherwise too apt to insult them upon the Score of their Age.

THERE is no Vice or Folly that requireth so much Nicety and Skill to manage, as Vanity; nor any which, by ill Manage-ment, maketh so contemptible a Figure.

OBSERVATION is an old Man's Memory.

POLITICKS are nothing but Corruptions, and are conse-quently of no Use to a good King, or a good Ministry; for which Reason all Courts are so full of Politicks.

ELOQUENCE smooth and cutting, is like a Razor whetted with Oil.

IMAGINARY Evils soon become real ones, by indulging our Reflections on them; as he, who, in a melancholy Fancy, seeth something like a Face on the Wall or the Wainscot, can, by two or three Touches with a leaden Pencil, make it look visible and agreeing with what he fancied.

MEN of great Parts are often unfortunate in the Management of publick Business; because they are apt to go out of the common Road, by the Quickness of their Imagination. This I once said to my Lord *Bolingbroke*, and desired he would observe, that the Clerks in his Office used a sort of Ivory Knife, with a blunt Edge, to divide a Sheet of Paper, which never failed to cut it even, only requiring a strong Hand; whereas, if they should make use of a sharp Penknife, the Sharpness would make it go often out of the Crease, and disfigure the Paper.

He who doth not provide for his own House, St. *Paul* sayeth, *is worse than an Infidel*. And I think, he who provideth *only* for his own House, is just equal with an Infidel.

JEALOUSY like Fire may shrivel up Horns, but it makes them stink.

A FOOTMAN'S Hat should fly off to every Body; and therefore *Mercury*, who was *Jupiter*'s Footman, had Wings fastened to his Cap.

WHEN a Man pretendeth Love, but courteth for Money, he is like a Juggler, who conjureth away your Shilling, and conveyeth something very indecent under the Hat.

ALL Panegyricks are mingled with an Infusion of Poppy.

2

ONE Top of *Parnassus* was sacred to *Bacchus*, the other to *Apollo*.

MATRIMONY hath many Children; Repentance, Discord, Poverty, Jealousy, Sickness, Spleen, Loathing, *&c.*

VISION is the Art of seeing Things invisible.

THE two Maxims of any great Man at Court are, always to keep his Countenance, and never to keep his Word.

I ASKED a poor Man how he did? He said, he was like a Washball, always in Decay.

Hippocrates, *Aph*. 32. *Sect*. 6. observeth, that stuttering People are always subject to a Looseness. I wish Physicians had Power to remove the Profusion of Words in many People to the inferior Parts.

A MAN dreamt he was a Cuckold; a Friend told him it was a bad Sign, because when a Dream is true, *Virgil* sayeth, it passeth through the horned Gate.

LOVE is a Flame, and therefore we say, Beauty is attractive; because Physicians observe, that Fire is a great Drawer.

Civis, the most honourable Name among the *Romans*; a Citizen, a Word of Contempt among us.

A LADY who had Gallantries, and several Children, told her Husband, he was like the austere Man, who reaped where he did not sow.

WE read that an Ass's Head was sold for eighty Pieces of Silver; they have been lately sold ten thousand times dearer, and yet they were never more plentiful.

I MUST complain the Cards are ill shuffled, until I have a good Hand.

VERY few Men do properly live at present, but are providing to live another Time.

WHEN I am reading a Book, whether wise or silly, it seemeth to me to be alive and talking to me.

WHOEVER live at a different End of the Town from me, I look upon as Persons out of the World, and only myself and the Scene about me to be in it.

WHEN I was young, I thought all the World as well as myself was wholly taken up in discoursing upon the last new Play.

MY Lord *Cromarty*, after fourscore, went to his Country House in *Scotland*, with a Resolution to stay six Years there and live thriftily, in order to save up Money, that he might spend in *London*.

IT is said of the Horses in the Vision, that their Power was in their Mouths and in their Tails. What is said of Horses in Vision, may be said of Women in reality.

ELEPHANTS are always drawn smaller than the Life, but a Flea always larger.

WHEN old Folks tell us of many Passages in their Youth, between them and their Company, we are apt to think how much happier those Times were than the present.

WHY does the elder Sister dance bare-foot when the younger is married before her? Is it not that she may appear shorter, and consequently be thought younger than the Bride?

No Man will take Counsel, but every Man will take Money; therefore Money is better than Counsel.

I NEVER yet knew a Wag (as the Term is) who was not a Dunce.

A PERSON reading to me a dull Poem of his own making, I prevailed on him to scratch out six Lines together: In turning over the Leaf, the Ink being wet, marked as many Lines on the other Side; whereof the Poet complaining, I bid him be easy, for it would be better if those were out too.

At *Windsor* I was observing to my Lord *Bolingbroke*, that the Tower where the Maids of Honour lodged (who at that Time were not very handsome) was much frequented with Crows. My Lord said, it was because they smelt Carrion.

APPENDIXES

I

A DIALOGUE IN THE CASTILIAN LANGUAGE

L.L. Dr Swift, You know, Gemelli says ——

Tom A. (Interrupting quick) Jemmi Lee, My Lord, Jemmi Lee, I know him very well, a very honest Gentleman.

Dr H. My Ld, there is a great Dispute in Town, whether this Parliament will be dissolved by your Excellency or onely prorogued.

L.L. D^r, I did not see you at the Society last meeting.

D^r. H. My Ld, Your Excellency I hope is pleased with their Proceedings this Session.

L.L. Dr Swift, won't you take another Cup of Coffee.

Tom A. Pray, D^r which is the way to dissolve a Parliament, should it be done in Vinegar or Aqua fortis?

Dr M.^olnx My Lord, I do not think Coffee so proper to help those who are troubled with a lacochymia, or dyspepsia, as the Concha of testaceary Fishes pulverized. I mean not onely those to which Nature has denyed Motion, but all that move in armatura articulata, or Crustaceous, as the Astacus major and minor, which latter I take to be the Crafish, and both are indeed but a Species of the cancer marinus, in all which the chelae or acetabula, that is the extremity of the Forceps (improperly called Crabs Eyes) reduced to Powder, Paracelsus recommends as a noble Alcali.

D^r. H. Chalk or powderd Eggshells are full as good.

Tom A. Dr What do you think of powderd Bief.

D^r. H. Mr Ash if I had an Engine to shut your Mouth I should value it more than that we make use of to stretch open the Mouths of our Patients.

Sr A. F. The D^r says that I suppose by way of OS—tentation.

Dr H. Well, but a, why, ay, why, but Oysters, as for Oysters, My Ld, Pliny seems to prefer those of Brundisium. Martial thinks the best come from the Lacus Lucrinus,

Richard Nobel was hanged on March 29, 1713. The above was circulated by Swift, Arbuthnot and Lady Masham on the eve of All Fools' Day as an April 1st joke: but Swift reported in the Journal to Stella for that day:

> We had no success in our story, though I sent my man to several houses, to inquire among the footmen, without letting him into the secret; but I doubt my colleagues did not contribute as they ought.

On the same page there follows:

> Is the story of the Baker bran new? I shall sift it to day. *Yea*sterday I heard no such thing. pray keep a*loaf* from such tittle-tattle. I suppose it was told you by my Ld Crum-arty, O-vain man to believe it. if Miles had told it me I would have said to Him *Rot you low rum*.

P. 32   If Bp Cloyn* cozes, what vomit? Crow-Cuz
   Enemy burn London, Qu —— bid not, what Plaister.
     Spair my city.
  If I say to you, Honey, what meddcine for Clap,—
    Call you mel   (calomel)
    All bum Grecum
    Ox a Meal of's Quells. (Oxymel of squills)
    Asaph et Ida   (Asafoetida)
    A Medecine a Farthing, A bolus Obolus.
    Ratify, Rot a Fee, Ratify.
    Die of drinking sack, what Plaister, Dia palma.
    Gang-green. Newcastle's woodmen
    Iliac Ill I act passion
    Mary Snow Mollynix   (Molyneux, Mullinix)
    Her Majesty's Eye. Queenseye. (*deleted*)
  A Man has a sore throat, why will he be a Favorite.
    He has the Queen's Eye upon him
  You sued her I feck, went to law with her in troth. (sudorific)
(*Added in another hand*: made lick on through Pye. Liconthropy)

* Charles Crow

III

TO MY LORD HIGH ADMIRALL.
THE HUMBLE PETITION OF THE DOCTOR, AND
THE GENTLEMEN OF IRELAND

Humbly Sheweth, That since your Lordship is new *deckt* for the sea, your petitioners have been excluded as *Ig-navi* or cast-aways; whereof they cannot *fathom* the cause. Your Lordship is the Doctor's peculiar governor, since he that is Admiral of the *Fleet* must be so of the *Swift*. You were not used to look Stern upon your visitants, nor to keep *abaft* while we were *afore*. Pray, my Lord, have a *car'-in-a* new office, not to disoblige your old friends. Remember, be-*fore-castle* puns, you never heard any in your life. We are content to be used as the *second rate*, as becomes men of our *pitch*. If Tom Ash were here, he would never keep at land, but *pump* hard for a new sea pun. I designed to have Mr. *Keel-hawld* to your Lordship yesterday, but you saw no company. Thus we are kept under *hatches*, and cannot *compass* our *point*. I have a *Deal* of stories to tell your Lordship, and tho' you may have heard them before, I should be glad to *Chatt'em* over again; but I am now sick, tho' I hope not near *Grave's-end*. But your Lordship must give me leave to say that if we lose the sight of you in England as well as in Ireland, Fortune who is a Gray, and not a Green-witch, is much in our Dept-for't. But how can your friends of Ireland approach, while the seamen *punch* us away, to get at you. But, while you canvas their affairs, *can* they not drink their *canvas*, to your health at home; and swallow Ph'lip at a sup; and when they see your Lordship's *flag-on*, toss up another of their own? But your petitioners with humble submission can not see why you should be much pleased with your new office, considering the mischiefs likely to happen under your administration. First, the seamen in complaisance to my Lady, will take a young *Arundel* into every ship, whom they begin to call by a diminutive name,

Arundelet. Then, upon your Lordship's account, the merchant will turn gamester, and be ready to venture all upon any *Main*, without fearing a *Cinque*. Again, while your Lordship is Admiral, I doubt we shall lose all our *sea-faring* Men, for, as you are likely to manage it, every seaman that has any merit, will soon be *landed*. What a confusion must this cause! and more still, when our boats must be all troubled with a *Wherry-go-nimble*, and our ships new-trimmed must all dance *Rigg-i'-Downs*. We agree your Lordship will certainly beat the French: but what honour is that? Alas they are all *Galli-slaves* already. My Lord; your petitioners beg one hour a week to attend, for which they shall ever pray; that after your Lordship has subdued the French and Spaniard, and given us an honourable Peace, you may retire many years hence from the wett to the dry *Downs*; from the boat-*swains* looking to their *ship* to the *swains* looking to their *sheep*, and, that my meaning may not be mistaken, from those Downs where *Sails* are hoist and rais'd to those of *Sails*bury (Wilton by Salisbury).

TO THE
EARL of PEMBROKE.
The DYING SPEECH of TOM ASHE*

TOm Ashe died last night. It is conceived he was so puffed up by my Lord Lieutenant's *favour*, that it struck him into a *fever*. I here send you his dying speech, as it was exactly taken by a friend in short-hand. It is something long, and a little incoherent; but he was several hours delivering it, and with several intervals. His friends were about the bed, and he spoke to them thus:

MY FRIENDS,

IT is time for a man to look *grave*, when he has one foot there. I once had only a *pun*nick fear of death, but of late, have *pun*dred it more seriously. Every fit of *coffing* hath put me in mind of my *coffin*; though *dissolute* men seldomest think of *dissolution*. This is a very great alteration: I, that supported myself with good *wine*, must now be myself supported by a *small bier*.——A fortune-teller once looked on

---

* Thomas Ashe, Esq; descended from an antient family of that Name in Wiltshire, was a gentleman of fortune in Ireland. He was a facetious pleasant companion, but the most eternal unwearied punster that perhaps ever lived. He was thick and short in his Person, being not above five feet high at the most, and had something very droll in his appearance. He died about the year 1719, and left his whole estate, of about a thousand pounds a year, to his intimate friend and kinsman Richard Ashe of Ashefield, Esq. There is a whimsical story, and a very true one, of Tom Ashe, which is well remembered to this day. It happened, that, while he was travelling on horseback, and at a considerable distance from any town, there burst from the clouds such a torrent of rain as wetted him through. He galloped forward; and, as soon as he came to an inn, he was met instantly by a drawer: 'Here,' said he to the fellow, stretching out one of his arms 'Take off my coat immediately.' 'No, Sir, I won't,' said the drawer. 'Pox confound you,' said Ashe, 'take off my coat this instant.' 'No, Sir, (replied the drawer) I dare not take off your coat; for it is felony to strip an ASH.' Tom was delighted beyond measure, frequently told the story, and said he would have given fifty guineas to have been the author of that pun. This little tract of Dr. Swift's, intituled *The Dying Words of Tom Ashe*, was written several years before the decease of Tom, and was merely designed to exhibit the manner in which such an eternal punster might have expressed himself on his death-bed.

my hand, and said, This man is to be a great traveller: He will soon be at the *Diet* of *Worms*, and from thence go to *Rat-is-bone*. But now I understand his double meaning.— I desire to be privately *buried*, for I think a public funeral looks like *Bury* Fair; and the *rites* of the dead too often prove *wrong* to the living. Methinks the word itself best expresses the number, neither *few nor all*.—A dying man should not think of *obsequies*, but *ob se quies*.—Little did I think you would so soon see poor *Tom stown* under a *tomb stone*. But, as the *mole* crumbles the *mold* about her, so a man of my small *mold*, before I a*m old*, may *molder* away.—Sometimes I've *rav'd* that I should *revive*; but physicians tell me, that when once the great *artery* has drawn the *heart awry*, we shall find the *cor die all*, in spite of the highest *cordial*.—Brother, you are fond of *Daffy*'s elixir; but, when Death comes, the world will see that in spite of *Daffy-down-Dilly**.—Whatever doctors *may design* by their *medicines*, a man in a *dropsy drops he* not, in spite of Goddard's *drops*, though none are reckoned such high *drops*.——I find Death smells the blood of an Englishman: A *fee faintly fum*bled out, will be a weak defence against his *fee-fa-fum*.—*P.T.* are no letters in Death's *alphabet*; he has not *half a bit* of either: He moves his *sithe*, but will not be moved by all our *sighs*.—Every thing ought to put us in mind of death: Physicians affirm that our very food breeds it in us, so that in our *dieting*, we may be said to *di eating*.—There is something ominous, not only in the names of diseases, as *di*-arrhœa, *di*-abetes, *di*-sentery, but even in the drugs designed to preserve our lives; as *di*-acodium, *di*-apente, *di*-ascordium.——I perceive Dr. *Howard* (and I feel *how hard*) *lay thumb* on my *pulse*, then *pulls* it back, as if he saw *Lethum* in my face. I see as bad in his; for sure there is no *physick* like a *sick phiz*. He thinks I shall *decease* before the *day cease*; but, before I die, before the bell hath *toll'd*, and *Tom Tollman* is *told* that little *Tom*, though not *old*, has paid nature's *toll*, I do desire to give some advice to those that survive me. First, Let gamesters consider that death is *hazard* and *passage*,

* A nickname of Tom Ashe's brother.

upon the turn of a *die*. Let Lawyers consider it is a hard *case*. And let punners consider how hard it is to *die jesting*, when death is so hard in *digesting*.

As for my Lord-Lieutenant the Earl *Mungomerry*, I am sure he *be-wales* my misfortune; and it would move him to stand by, when the carpenter (while my friends grieve and make an odd *splutter*) *nails* up my coffin. I will make a short *affidavi*-t, that, if he makes my *epitaph I* will take it for a great honour; and it is a plentiful subject. His Excellency may say, that the art of punning is dead with Tom. Tom has taken all puns away with him: *Omne tulit pun-Tom.*—May his Excellency long *live tenant* to the Queen in Ireland. We never *Herberd* so good a governor before. Sure he *mun-go-merry* home, that has made a kingdom so happy.——I hear my friends design to publish a collection of my puns. Now I do confess, I have let many a *pun go*, which did never *pungo*; therefore the world must read the bad as well as the good. Virgil has long foretold it: *Punica mala leges.*——I have had several forebodings that I should soon die: I have, of late, been often at committees, where I have sate de *die* in *diem.*——I conversed much with the *Usher* of the *black rod:* I saw his *medals*; and woe is *me dull s*oul, not to consider they are but dead mens faces *stampt over* and *over* by the living, which will shortly be my condition.

Tell Sir Andrew *Fountain* I *ran* clear to the *bottom*, and wish he may be a late *a-river* where I am going. He used to *brook* my compliments. May his *sand* be long a *running*; not *quicksand*, like mine. Bid him avoid *poring* upon monuments and books, which is in reality but *running* among *rocks* and *shelves*, to *stop* his *course*. May his *waters* never be *troubled* with *mud* or *gravel*, nor *stopt* by any *grinding stone*. May his friends be all true *trouts*, and his enemies laid flat as *flounders*. I look upon him as the most *fluent* of his *race*; therefore let him not des*pond*. I foresee his black *rod* will *advance* to a *pike*, and destroy all our *ills*.

But, I am going; my *wind in* lungs is turning to a *winding* sheet. The thoughts of a *pall* begin to *a-pall* me. Life is but a

U

vapour, car elle *va pour* la moindre cause. Farewel: I have lived ad amicorum *fastidium*, and now behold how *fast I di um!*

Here his breath faileth him, and he expired. There are some false spellings here and there, but they must be pardoned in a dying man.

April Fool's Joke in LONDON POST-BOY, March 31, 1709
The Post-Boy, Number 2165. From Tuesday March 29 to
Thursday March 31

ADVERTISEMENTS

Tomorow, being Friday between the Hours of 3 and 5,
Afternoon, will be sold, by Auction, at Mr. Doily's in The
Strand, a small Collection of about a Hundred Books, of the
choicest Kinds and Editions, all fair; as, Victorinus's Tully;
Tully's Offices, suppos'd of the first that ever was printed;
several Classicks, of Aldus and Elzevir; a Volume of French
Pamplets, [*sic*] writ in the Time of the League. Ovid's
Epistles, by Mezeriac; Dialogues of Vannius, &c. as likewise
7 Marc-Antonio Prints; proof Plates, a Porphiry Urn; two
browze [*sic*] Lamps; and a small Parcel of Medals, some very
rare.

In the following Number, 2166, From Thursday March 31 to
Saturday April 2 appeared the following:

N.B. . . . whereas an Advertisement was inserted in our last,
of a pretended *Auction*, to have been as yesterday, at Mr.
Doily's in the Strand; This is to give Notice, That there was
no such Auction design'd; and that the said Advertisement was
taken in, and inserted by the Printer's Boy's Inadvertency.

MISCELLANIES IN PROSE AND VERSE 1711

THE PUBLISHER TO THE READER.

TO Publish the Writings of Persons without their Consent, is a Practice, generally speaking, so unfair, and has so many times proved an unsufferable Injury to the Credit and Reputation of the Authors, as well as a shameful Imposition on the Publick, either by a Scandalous Insertion of Spurious Pieces, or an Imperfect and Faulty Edition of such as are Genuine; that though I have been Master of such of the following Pieces as have never yet been Printed, for several Months, I could never, though much importuned, prevail on my self to Publish them, fearing even a Possibility of doing an Injury in either of those two Respects to the Person who is generally known to be the Author of some; and, with greater Reason than I am at present at Liberty to give, supposed to be the Author of all the other Pieces which make up this Collection. But as my own Unwillingness to do any thing which might prove an Injury to the supposed Author's Reputation, to whom no Man pays a juster Esteem, or bears a greater Respect than my self, has hitherto kept me from giving the World so agreeable an Entertainment as it will receive from the following Papers, so the Sense I had that he would really now suffer a much greater in both Instances from other hands, was the Occasion of my determining to do it at present; since some of the following Pieces have lately appeared in Print, from very imperfect and uncorrect Copies. Nor was the Abuse like to stop here; for these, with all the Defects and Imperfections they came out under, met with so much Applause, and so universal a good Reception from all Men of Wit and Taste, as to prompt the *Booksellers*, who had heard that other of these Tracts were in Manuscript in some Gentlemens Hands, to seek by any means to procure them, which should they compass, they would, without Question, publish in a manner as little to the Author's Credit and Reputation, as they have already done those few which unfortunately have fallen into their Possession. This being a known Fact, I hope will be sufficient to make this Publication, tho' without the Author's Consent or Knowledge, very consistent with that Respect I sincerely bear him: Who, if it should not appear to be perfectly without Fault, can with little Justice complain of the Wrong he receives by it, since it has prevented his suffering a much greater; no more than a Man who is pushed down out of the way of a Bullet, can with Reason take as an Affront, either the Blow he falls by, or the Dirt he rises with.

But indeed I have very little Uneasiness upon me for fear of any Injury the Author's Credit and Reputation may receive from any Imperfection or Uncorrectness in these following Tracts, since the Persons from whom I had them, and in whose Hands I have Reason to believe the Author left them, when his Affairs called him out of this Kingdom, are of so much Worth themselves, and have so great a Regard for the Author, that I am confident they would neither do, nor suffer any thing that might turn to his Disadvantage. I must confess I am upon another account under some Concern, which is, lest some of the following Papers are such as the Author perhaps would rather should not have been Published at all; in which Case, I should look upon my self highly obliged to ask his Pardon: But even on this Supposition, as there is no Person named, the supposed Author is at liberty to disown as much as he thinks fit of what is here Published, and so can be chargeable with no more of it than he pleases to take upon himself.

From this Apology I have been making, the Reader may in part be satisfied how these Papers came into my Hands; and to give him a more particular Information herein, will prove little to his Use, tho' perhaps it might somewhat gratify his Curiosity, which I shall think not material any farther to do, than by assuring him, that I am not only my self sufficiently convinced that all the Tracts in the following Collection, excepting Two, before both of which I have in the Book expressed my Doubtfulness, were wrote by the same Hand, but several Judicious Persons, who are well acquainted with the supposed Author's Writings, and not altogether Strangers to his Conversation, have agreed with me herein, not only for the Reasons I have before hinted at, but upon this Account also, that there are in every one of these Pieces some particular Beauties that discover this Author's Vein, who excels too much not to be distinguished, since in all his Writings such a surprizing Mixture of Wit and Learning, true Humour and good Sense, does every-where appear, as sets him almost as far out of the Reach of Imitation, as it does beyond the Power of Censure.

THE Reception that these Pieces will meet with from the Publick, and the Satisfaction they will give to all Men of Wit and Taste, will soon decide it, whether there be any Reason for the Reader to suspect an Imposition, or the Author to apprehend an Injury: The former, I am fully satisfied, will never be; and the latter, I am sure, I never intended. In confidence of which, should the Author, when he sees these Tracts appear, take some Offence, and know where to place his Resentment, I will be so free as to own, I could without much Uneasiness sit down under some degree of it, since it would be no hard Task to bear some Displeasure from a single Person, for that for which one is sure to receive the Thanks of every Body else.

A CONSULTATION *of* FOUR PHYSICIANS *upon a* LORD
that was dying.

First Doctor

IS his Honor sic? Præ lætus felis Puls. It do es beat veris loto de.

Second Doctor. No notis as qui caffi e ver fel tu metri it. Inde edit is as fastas an alarum, ora fire bellat nite.

Third Doctor. It is veri hi.

Fourth Doctor. Noto contra dictu in mi juge mentitis veri loto de. Itis as orto maladi sum callet. [Here e ver id octo reti resto a par lori na mel an coli post ure.]

First Doctor. It is a me gri mas I opi ne.

Second Doctor. No docto rite quit fora quin si. Heris a plane sim tomo fit. Sorites Para celsus; Præ re adit.

First Doctor. Nono Doctor I ne ver quo te aqua casu do.

Second Doctor. Sum arso: Mi autoris no ne.

Third Doctor. No quare lingat præ senti de si re. His honor is sic offa Colli casure as I sit here.

Fourth Doctor. It is æther an atro phi ora colli casu sed: Ire membri re ad it in Doctor me ades Esse, here itis.

Third Doctor. I ne ver re ad apage init, no re ver in tendit.

Second Doctor. Fer ne is offa qui te di ferent noti o nas i here.

First Doctor. Notis ab ludi fluxit is veri plene.

Second Doctor. I fitis a fluxit me re qui re ac lis ter.

Third Doctor. I a ver his casis venere alas i disco ver edit in as hanc cor; an da poli pus in his no se. An di fit be as I cetis, ago no rea me en sue.

First Doctor. It is ad ange rus casas ani.

Fourth Doctor. Imus tellure alitis ago uti humor in his Bel li. Hi sto macto is empti.

First Doctor. It me bea pluri si; avo metis veri pro per fora manat his age.

Second Doctor. Ure par donat præfenti des ire; His dis eas is a cata ride clare it.

Third Doctor. Atlas tume findit as tone in his quid ni es.

Fourth Doctor. Itis ale pro si fora uti se. Præ hos his a poti cari? cantu tellus? Ab lis ter me bene cessa risum decens. Itis as ure medi in manicas es.

Third Doctor. I findit isto late tot hinc offa reme di; fori here his Honor is De ad.

Second Doctor. His ti meis cum.

First Doctor. Is it trudo ut hinc?

Fourth Doctor. Itis veri certa in. His Paris his Belli sto ringo ut foris de partu re.

Third Doctor. Næ, i fis Ecce lens is de ad lætus en dum apri esto præ foris sole. His Honor has bina Cato liquor a de isti here.

First Doctor. Alor dis sum times as tingi as an usu reris.

Second Doctor. Api stolis alligo time a verbi mi at endans for a forte nite.

Third Doctor. O mei ne vera tendo na nil ordinis sic nes ani more.

Fourth Doctor. Api stolis ne a quin in a nil ordo fis qua liti; sum pes fore times more. It istos mala fito a Doctor o fis hic.

Second Doctor. Lætus paco fitis time.

First Doctor. Abigo ditis hi time, inde editis, forus alto fallas campe ringo fas fastas arato ut offa da iri; fori fera bea tinge veri minute; bimi solido. His lac quis, an das turdis aussi sto ut valet is rea di forus.

Second Doctor. Ali feris ab ast in a do; fori here ano is at adis stans.

A
Hiſtory of Poetry,

In a LETTER to a Friend.

By the Rev^{d.} D---- *S----t.*

SIR,

IN *Obedience to your Commands,* I *here send You the following short* Essay *towards a History of Poetry in* England *and* Ireland.

AT first it was a *Science* we only began to CHAW S^{r.} a hundred Years after we attempted to Translate out of the Psalms, but could not our STERNHOLD. In Queen *Elizabeth*'s Reign I think there was but one DI-SPENCER of good Verses, for his Patron, though a great Man, IS HID NIGH by the length of Time. Yet a little before her Death, we attempted to deal in Tragedy, and began to SHAKE SPEARS; which was pursu'd under King *James* the First, by three great Poets, in one of them many a Line so strong, that you might make a BEAM-ONT; the second indeed, gives us some times but FLAT-CHEER, and the third is BEN-ding a little to stiffness.

In the Reign of King *Charles* the First there was a new succession of Poets; one of Them though seldom read I am very fond of, he has so much Salt in his Compositions that you would think, he had been used to SUCK-LING: As to his Friend the Author of *Gondibert,* I'D' AVE AN AUNT write better. I say nothing against your Favourite, though some censure him for writing too COOLY; but he had a Rival

273

whose happier Genius made him stand like a WALL OR a Pillar against Censure.

During the *Usurpation* we fell into Burlesque, and I think whoever reads *Hudibrass* cannot BUT LEER. I have COT ONE more, who Travesty'd *Virgil*, though not equal to the Former.

After the Restauration Poets became very Numerous, the Chief whose fame is louder than a MILL-TONE, must never be forgot. And here I must observe, that Poets in those Days lov'd Retirement so much, that sometimes they liv'd in Dens, One of them in a DRY-DEN; Another call'd his Den his Village, of DEN-HAM; and I am inform'd that the sorry Fellow, who is now Laureat, affects to USE-DENS still: But to return from this Digression, we were then famous for Tragedy and Comedy; the Author of *Venice Preserv'd* is seldom O'T AWAY; yet he who writ the *Rival Queens* before he lost his Senses, some times talk'd MAD LEE. Another who was of this Kingdom, went into *England*, because it is more SOUTHERN, and he writ tolerably well, I say nothing of the Satyrist, with his OLD-DAM Verses. As for Comedy, the *Plain Dealer* W'ICH EARLY came into Credit, is allow'd on all hands an excellent Piece : He had a dull Co-temporary, who some times shew'd Humour, but his colouring was bad, and he could not SHADE-WELL Sir *George* in my opinion out-did them All, and was sharp at EITHER EDGE. The Duke is also excellent who took a BOOKIN GAME, and turn'd it into ridicule, under the name of the *Rehearsal*. It is indeed no wonder to find Poetry thrive under the Reign of that Prince, when by one of his great Favourites, who was likewise an excellent Poet, there was a DORE SET open for all Men of Wit. Perhaps you WILL-MUTT-er that I have left out the Earl of *Rochester*; but I never was one of his Admirers.

Upon the Revolution Poetry seem'd to decline, however, I shall PRYO'R as many Poets as I can remember. Mr. *Montague* affected to be a Patron of Wit, and his House was the Poets HALL I FACKS for several Years, which one of them us'd to STEP NIGH every Day. Another of them who was my old Acquaintance, succeeded well in Comedy, but failed when he began to CON GRAVE Subjects. The rest came in a ROW.

The Author of the *Dispensary* has Writ nothing else valuable, and therefore is too small in the GARTH: But may not a Man be allow'd to ADD-IS-OWN Friend to the number? I mean the Author of *Cato*.

To mention those who are now alive, would be endless; I will therefore only venture to lay down one Maxim, That, a good Poet, if he designs to TICKLE the World, must be GAY and YOUNG; but if he proposes to give us rational Pleasure, he must be as grave as a POPE.

I am, Sir, Yours, &c.

I

NOTES FOR POLITE CONVERSATION
from Huntington MS. 14341 and Forster MS. 530

1. Tomorrows a new day. To morrow come never.

    cf. Forster, 530, p. 158: Tomo rosa nudae

    Nev. No, Miss, I'll send it you To-morrow.

    Miss. Well, well, To-morrow's a new Day: But I suppose,
    you mean, To-morrow come never.

2. It's one a Clock. Ans.: What that among all us.

    Ld. Sp. (looking at his Watch.) 'Tis past twelve a Clock.

    Lady Smart. Well, what is that among us all.

3. You may put it into yr. Eye, and see never the worse.

    Nev. Faith, Madam, all he gets by her, he may put into his
    Eye, and see never the worse.

4. May you live 100 years. Ans. pray dont stint me.

    Nev. Come, all Quarrels laid aside: Here, Miss, may you
    live a thousand Years. (*He drinks to her.*)

    Miss. Pray, Sir, don't stint me.

5. Sings as a Man may say.

    Ld. Sp. Pray Madam, does not Miss sing very well?

    Lady Ans. She sings, as one may say; my lord.

6. At your Service in a civil way.

    Col. And pray, Sir John, how does your Lady unknown?

    Sir John. My wife's well, Colonell; and at your service in a
    civil way.

This and other phrases collected for *Polite Conversation* may
also be found in Anglo-Angli or Latino-Angli forms in
HM14338, and in Forster 530.

1. Mi la de is at ure cervice.

    Suis me de armis tres, at are cervice, Ime an, as far as ani
    fine vir tuus laedis civi litigo es.

2. Mi dans cinge des aro ver.

    Mi des aro verto cingor dans (Forster 530, p. 37).

Lady Answ. She did; but, I doubt, her dancing days are over.

3. More Saxon them ill (HM14338).
Nev. Colonel, come sit down on my Lap; more Sacks upon the Mill.

4. Mi co at isto os horti Ime an (F. 530, p. 48).
Lady Smart. Colonel, methinks your coat is too short.

5. Mollis as imple tonas ani in tuenti miles o fano ac (F. 530, p. 13).
Nev. Why, one that lives within a mile of an oak.

6. Ano ulli nae nivibus (F. 530, p. 60).
Justus ano lina nivibua has (F. 530, p. 164).
Col. Look? Egad he look'd for all the world like an owl in an ivy-bush.

7. Y es as asso ubi comes as adde lis it notas Ise? (F. 530, p. 103).
Sir John. Ay; and it became him, as a saddle becomes a sow.

II

A DIALOGUE IN HIBERNIAN STYLE BETWEEN A AND B

A. *Is* not [*deleted*] *Them* Apples is very good?
B. I am *again* you in that.
A. Lord I was so bodderd tother day with that prating fool Tom.
B. Pray, how does he *get* his Health?
A. He's often very *unwell*. [Lord, he had He always keeps half a Dozen Pet Dogs. *deleted*]
B. [I] hear he was a great Pet of Yours. Where does he live?
A. Opposite the red Lyon.
B. I think he behaved very ill the last Sessions.
A. [Pray will you give me a Drink of your small beer *deleted*].
A. That's true but I cannot forbear loving his Father's child: Will you tast a glass of my Ale?
B. No, I thank you, I took a drink of small bear at home before I came here.
A. I always brew with my own Bear: You have a Country-house, are you [?a] Planter.

B. Yes, I have planted a great many Oak trees, and Ash trees, and some Elm-trees round a Lough.

A. And a good warrant you have: It is kind Father for you. And what Breakfast do you take in the Country?

B. Why, sometimes Sowins, and sometimes Stirabout, and in Summer we have the best Fraughauns in all the Country.

A. What kind of Man is your Neighbor, Squire Doll?

B. Why, a meer Buddogh. He sometimes coshers with me; And once a month I take a Pipe with him, and we strole it about for an hour together.

A. Well, I'd give a Cow in Connaugh to see you together. I hear he keeps good horses.

B. None but Garrauns, and I have seen him often riding on a Sougawn. In short, he is no better than a Spawleen; a perfect Monaghen. When I was there last, we had nothing but a Maddor to drink out of; and the Devil a Night-gown but a Caddow. Will you go see him when you come into our Parts.

A. Not *without* you go with me:

B. Will you lend me your Snuff-box, *till* I take a pinch of Snuff?

A. Do you make good Cheese and Butter.

B. yes, when we can get milk; But our Cows will never keep a drop of milk without a Puckaun.

III

IRISH ELOQUENCE

From Huntington MS. 14343. A single sheet of notepaper.

I hope you will come and take a drink of my Ale. I always brew with my own Beare. I was at your Cozen Tom's house in the County of Fermanagh. He has planted a great many Oak trees, and Elm trees round his Lough: And, a good Warrant he had; it is kind Father for him. I stayd with him a

Week. At Breakfast we had sometimes Sowins, and sometimes Stirabout, and sometimes Fraughauns and milk; but his Cows (will not *deleted*) would hardly give a drop of Milk (without a *deleted*) For his herd had lost the Puckaun. His Neighbor Squire Doll is a meer Buddough. I'd give a Cow in Canaught You could see him. He keeps none but Garrauns, and he rides on a Soogaun with nothing for his Bridle but Gadd. In short, he is a meer Spawleen. and a perfect Monaghen, and a Munster Crack into the Bargain. Without you saw him on Sunday you would take him for a Brogadeer and a Spanel. (*Inserted above the line:* His cook did not know how to draw Butter.) We drank Balcan and Whisky out of Maddors. And the Devil a Nightgoun had but a Caddow. (*Deleted:* Pray lend me a lone of your last news paper till I read it over. I could hardly get a Drop of milk in the Country, for your Cousin Tom's herd had lost the Puckaun.) I wonder your Cozen does not learn him better manners. (He *deleted*) Your cousin desires you will buy him some Cheney Cups. I remember he had a great many; I wonder what is gone with them. I coshered on him for a week (*deleted:* and twice [or] three times a Day we shoh't a Pipe together:) He has a fine Haggard of Corn. Miss Molly is his chief Pet. His Lady has been very Unwell. I was sorry that any thing should ayl her Fathers child.

Pray lend me a Loan of your last News-paper, till I read it over

Firing is very dear thereabout, The Turf is drawn two miles in Kishes. And they send new rounds from the Mines, nothing comes in the Cleeves but Slack.

(*The next sentence is crossed out:* We had (bief *deleted*) once a foreroan of Bief, and once a Rump for Dinner)

APPENDIX H

ON

BARBAROUS DENOMINATIONS

IN IRELAND.

I HAVE been lately looking over the advertisements in some of your Dublin newspapers, which are sent me to the country, and was much entertained with a large list of denominations of lands, to be sold or let. I am confident they must be genuine; for it is impossible that either chance, or modern invention, could sort the alphabet in such a manner, as to make those abominable sounds, whether first invented to invoke, or fright away the Devil, I must leave among the curious.

If I could wonder at any thing barbarous, ridiculous, or absurd among us, this should be one of the first. I have often lamented that Agricola, the Father-in-law of Tacitus, was not prevailed on by that petty King from Ireland, who followed his camp, to come over and civilize us with a conquest, as his countrymen did Britain, where several Roman appellations remain to this day; and so would the rest have done, if that inundation of Angles, Saxons, and other northern people, had not changed them so much for the worse, although in no comparison with ours. In one of the advertisements just mentioned, I encountered near a hundred words together, which I defy any creature in human shape, except an Irishman of the savage kind, to pronounce; neither would I undertake such a task, to be owner of the lands, unless I had liberty to humanize the syllables twenty miles round. The Legislature may think what they please, and that they are above copying the Romans in all their conquests of barbarous nations; but I am deceived, if any thing hath more contributed to prevent the Irish from being tamed, than this encouragement of their language, which might easily be abolished, and become a dead one in half an age, with little expence, and less trouble.

How is it possible that a gentleman, who lives in those parts, where the Town-lands (as they call them) of his estate produce such odious sounds from the mouth, the throat, and the nose, can be able to repeat the words, without dislocating every muscle that is used in speaking, and without applying the same tone to all other words, in every language he understands? As it is plainly to be observed, not only in those people, of the better sort, who live in Gallway and the Western parts, but in most counties of Ireland.

It is true, that in the city-part of London, the trading people have an affected manner of pronouncing; and so, in my time, had many ladies and coxcombs at Court. It is likewise true, that there is an odd provincial cant in most counties of England, sometimes not very pleasing to the ear: and the Scotch cadence, as well as expression, are offensive enough. But none of these defects derive contempt to the speaker; whereas, what we call the Irish Brogue is no sooner discovered, than it makes the deliverer, in the last degree, ridiculous and despised; and, from such a mouth, an Englishman expects nothing but bulls, blunders, and follies. Neither does it avail whether the censure be reasonable or not, since the fact is always so. And, what is yet worse, it is too well known that the bad consequence of this opinion affects those among us who are not the least liable to such reproaches, further than the misfortune of being born in Ireland, although of English parents, and whose education hath been chiefly in that kingdom.

I have heard many gentlemen among us, talk much of the great convenience to those who live in the country, that they should speak Irish. It may possibly be so: But, I think, they should be such who never intend to visit England, upon pain of being ridiculous. For I do not remember to have heard of any one man that spoke Irish, who had not the accent upon his tongue, easily discernible to any English ear.

But I have wandered a little from my subject, which was only to propose a wish, that these execrable denominations were a little better suited to an English mouth, if it were only for the sake of the English lawyers; who, in trials upon appeals to the House of Lords, find so much difficulty in repeating the

x

names, that, if the plaintiff or defendant were by, they would
never be able to discover which were their own lands. But,
beside this, I would desire, not only that the appellations of
what they call Town-lands were changed, but likewise of
larger districts, and several towns, and some counties; and,
particularly, the seats of country-gentlemen, leaving an *alias*
to solve all difficulties in point of law. But I would by no
means trust these alterations to the owners themselves; who,
as they are generally no great clerks, so they seem to have no
large vocabulary about them, nor to be well skilled in prosody.
The utmost extent of their genius lies in naming their country-
habitation by a hill, a mount, a brook, a burrough, a castle,
a bawn, a ford, and the like ingenious conceits. Yet these are
exceeded by others, whereof some have continued anagram-
matical appellations, from half their own and their wives
names joined together, others only from the lady. As, for
instance, a person, whose wife's name was Elizabeth, calls his
seat by the name of *Bessborow*. There is likewise a famous
town, where the worst iron in the kingdom is made, and it is
called *Swandlingbar*. The original of which name I shall explain,
lest the antiquaries of future ages might be at a loss to derive it.
It was a most witty conceit of four gentlemen, who ruined
themselves with this iron project. *Sw.* stands for *Swift*, *And.*
for *Sanders*, *Ling.* for *Darling*, and *Bar.* for *Barry*. Methinks I
see the four loggerheads sitting in consult, like Smectimnius,
each gravely contributing a part of his own name to make up
one for their place in the iron-work; and could wish they had
been hanged, as well as undone, for their wit. But I was most
pleased with the denomination of a town-land, which I lately
saw in an advertisement of Pue's Paper: 'This is to give notice,
that the lands of Douras, *alias* W HIG-*borow*, &c.' Now this
zealous proprietor, having a mind to record his principles in
religion or loyalty, to future ages within five miles round him,
for want of other merit, thought fit to make use of this expedient; wherein he seems to mistake his account: For this
distinguishing term, *Whig*, had a most infamous original,
denoting a man who favoured the Fanatic sect, and an enemy
to kings, and so continued 'till the idea was a littled softened,

some years after the Revolution, and during a part of her late Majesty's reign. After which it was in disgrace until the Queen's death: Since which time it hath, indeed, flourished with a witness: But how long it will continue so, in our variable scene, or what kind of mortal it may describe, is a question which this courtly landlord is not able to answer. And therefore, he should have set a date on the title of his burrough, to let us know what kind of creature a Whig was in that year of our LORD.—I would readily assist nomenclators of this costive imagination; and therefore I propose, to others of the same size in thinking, that, when they are at a loss about christening a country-seat, instead of straining their invention, the would call it *Booby-burrow*, *Fool-brook*, *Puppy-ford*, *Coxcomb-hall*, *Mount-loggerhead*, *Dunce-hill*; which are innocent appellations proper to express the talents of the owners. But I cannot reconcile myself to the prudence of this Lord of WHIG-*borow*, because I have not yet heard, among the Presbyterian squires, how much soever their persons and principles are in vogue, that any of them have distinguished their country-abode by the name of *Mount-regicide*, *Covenant-hall*, *Fanatic-hill*, *Roundhead-bawn*, *Canting-brook, or Mount-rebel*, and the like; because there may, possibly, come a time when those kind of sounds may not be so grateful to the ears of the kingdom. For I do not conceive it would be a mark of discretion, upon supposing a gentleman, in illusion to his name, or the merit of his ancestors, to call his house *Tyburn-hall*.

But the scheme I would propose, for changing the denominations of land into legible and audible syllables, is by employing some gentlemen in the University; who, by the knowledge of the Latin-tongue, and their judgment in sounds, might imitate the Roman way, by translating those hideous words into their English meanings, and altering the termination, where a bare translation will not form a good cadence to the ear, or be easily delivered from the mouth. And, when both these means happen to fail, then to name the parcels of land from the nature of the soil, or some peculiar circumstance belonging to it; as in England, Farn-ham, Oat-lands, Black-heath, Cornbury, Rye-gate, Ash-burnham, Barn-elms, Cole-ortum, Sand-wich, and many others.

I am likewise apt to quarrel with some titles of Lords among us, that have a very ungracious sound, which are apt to communicate mean ideas to those who have not the honour to be acquainted with their persons, or their virtues, of whom I have the misfortune to be one. But I cannot pardon those gentlemen, who have gotten titles since the judicature of the peers among us hath been taken way, to which they all sub-mitted with a resignation that became good Christians, as undoubtedly they are. However, since that time, I look upon a graceful harmonious title to be, at least, forty *per cent.* in the value intrinsick of an Irish peerage: And, since it is as cheap as the worst, for any Irish law hitherto enacted in England to the contrary, I would advise the next sett, before they pass their patents, to call a consultation of scholars, and musical gentle-men, to adjust this most important and essential circumstance. The Scotch noblemen, though born almost under the North Pole, have much more tuneable appellations, except some very few, which, I suppose, were given them by the Irish, along with their language, at the time when that kingdom was conquered, and planted from hence; and, to this day, retain the denominations of places, and surnames of families, as all historians agree.

I should likewise not be sorry, if the names of some bishops sees were so much obliged to the alphabet; that, upon pro-nouncing them, we might contract some veneration for the order and persons of those reverend peers, which the gross ideas sometimes joined to their titles, is very unjustly apt to diminish.

TEXTUAL NOTES

1. A PROPOSAL FOR CORRECTING THE ENGLISH TONGUE

First printed May 17, 1712. See facsimile of title-page, p. 3.

The Second Edition, 1712. Mainly reset from the first edition, with minor corrections; some pages are either remainder sheets of the first edition or from the same setting of type.

Miscellanies in Prose and Verse. The First Volume, 1727, pp. 316–48.

Miscellanies in Prose and Verse. London Printed and Dublin Reprinted, 1728, pp. 184–203. This is a reprinting of Motte's *Miscellanies*, 1727, by Samuel Fairbrother, whom Swift called 'an arrant rascal'. It has no textual authority. See Teerink, *Bibliography*, No. 33.

Works, Faulkner, 1735, I, 186–207. Although the copy of the *Miscellanies*, 1727, containing Swift's corrections (now in the possession of Lord Rothschild), has only three marginal corrections, Faulkner's text, which was set from the *Miscellanies*, shows careful revision, including a number of substantive changes, probably made in proof.

A manuscript in the hand of an amanuensis is in the Harleian Collection (P. 33845, Harl. 6386), apparently copied from the manuscript which Swift sent to Harley in Feb. 1711–12 (see Introduction, p. xi). The scribe was careless, but his copy is close enough to the first printed version to reveal much concerning Swift's revision of his original draft for the printer. He made numerous stylistic changes as well as some excisions and additions. Two of the interesting excisions I have restored to the present text, within square brackets, and I have included other substantive changes in the textual variants.

The present text is printed from Faulkner's edition of the *Works* (35), and is collated with the first edition (12a), the second edition (12b), the *Miscellanies* (27), and the Harleian copy (MS). Faulkner includes the following preliminary statement, probably by Swift:

It is well known, that if the Queen had lived a Year or two longer, the following Proposal would in all Probability have taken Effect. For the Lord Treasurer had already nominated several Persons without Distinction of Quality or Party, who were to compose a Society for the Purposes mentioned by the Author; and resolved to use his Credit with Her Majesty, that a Fund should be applyed to support the Expence of a large Room, where the Society should meet, and for other Incidents. But this Scheme fell to the Ground, partly by the Dissentions among the great Men at Court; but chiefly by the lamented Death of that glorious Princess.

Page	Line	PRESENT TEXT	VARIANTS
5	*h.t.*	A | PROPOSAL | &c.	Dr. *SWIFT*'s | LETTER | TO THE | Lord High Treasurer. 12a, 12b
	3f.b.	on such like	on the like 12a, 12b, 27, MS
6	2	are	were 12a, 12b, 27, MS
	21	complain	conplain (*misprint in* 12b)
	7f.b.	Island	Island₃ (*misprint in* 12a)
	last line	*Britons*	*Britains* 12a, 12b, 27, MS
7	3	*Britons*	*Britains* 12a, 12b, 27, MS
	12	appears	seems MS

Page	Line	Present Text	Variants
	20	This ... Court 12a, 12b, 27	(*not in* MS)
	25	thither	there 12a, 12b, 27
	9 f.b.	Years 12a, 12b, 27, MS	Year (*misprint in* 35)
	8 f.b.	with the *French*	with *French* 12a, 12b, 27, MS
	2 f.b.	the several	several MS
8	1	into a wide Field	into a Field too wide MS
	6	manifest	certain MS
	23	wholly turned into	turned wholly to MS
	10 f.b.	arrived	seems to have arrived MS
	9 f.b.	decay: *The French*	decay: And the *French* 12a, 12b, 27, MS
	7 f.b.	People, as well as the Affectation	People, and the Affectation 12a, 12b, 27, MS
	3 f.b.	many new Terms 27	many hundred new Terms 12a, 12b, MS
9	1	as, upon that Account, to make us apprehend	as to make us apprehend 12a, 12b, 27, MS
	3	Ways to fix it	Ways found out to fix it 12a, 12b, 27, MS
	9	are, I think, less subject	are less subject MS
	12	above a Thousand Years	about – – – hundred Years MS
	15	to the *Northern* Parts	to Northern Parts MS
	17	where	were (*misprint in* 27; *corrected in margin in Lord Rothschild's copy*)
	18	after	till MS
	19	and till they were over-run	or were over runne MS
	22	Conquests	Conquests Conquests (*misprint in* 12a); Contests (*misprint in* 27; *corrected in margin in Lord Rothschild's copy*)
	7 f.b.	the great Rebellion	The Civill War MS
	2 f.b.	From that great Rebellion	From the Civil War 12a, 12b, 27, MS
10	4	as was not shaken off	as was not shook off 12a, MS
	7	Which last, was	which was MS
	16	be taken	is taken MS
	6 f.b.	neither Humour nor Significancy	neither Wit, Humour, nor Significancy MS
	4 f.b.	Scribbles	Scribblers (*misprint in* 27; *corrected in margin in Lord Rothschild's copy*)
11	10	could endure	can endure MS
	12	And their Taste in Time became	And at length their Taste became MS
	17	full of those Manglings	Stuffed with those kinds of Manglings MS
	19	*Drudg'd, Disturb'd, Rebuk'd, Fledg'd*	*Disturb'd Rebuk't Fledg'd Entomb'd* MS
	9 f.b.	Counties	Countries 12a, 12b, 27
	4 f.b.	entirely confound	make vile work in MS
	3 f.b.	[It ... bodyes] MS	(*omitted in all printed texts*)

Page	Line	PRESENT TEXT	VARIANTS
13	3	Fruits	Fruit 12a, 12b, 27, MS
	7	who have no need	who think they have no need MS
	20	of the Women	of Women MS
	9 f.b.	*High-Dutch* 12a, 12b, 27	*High-Duth* (*misprint in* 35)
	8 f.b.	Vowels	Bowels (*misprint in* 27)
14	4	fix on Rules	fix on some Rules MS
	10	a little Envy	some Envy MS
	25	that it is better	that is better 12b, MS
	27	one Time or other, or at length	one Time, or at length 12a, 12b, 27, MS
	9 f.b.	meet	find MS
	6 f.b.	usually	equally MS
	5 f.b.	limited in *Time* as much as *Place*	limited likewise in Time MS
	3 f.b.	if it were not	if were not 12b
15	1	Hundred Years 12a, 12b, 27, MS	hundred Year (*misprint in* 35)
	7	greatest	true MS
	11	that	those MS
	10 f.b.	find	have MS
16	20	an ingenious *Gentleman Fn. *Mr.* Addison (See Swift's *Corr.*, ed. Ball, II, 139, where Swift identifies Steele as the 'ingenious Gentleman')	an ingenious Gentleman 12a, 12b, 27, MS
	24	[In . . . Deserve] MS	(*omitted in all printed texts*)
17	8	Felicity	blessing MS
	28	of	or (*misprint in* 27)
19	4	deserves to be treated with Ability and Care	deserves a much better Pen MS
	10	if Genius and Learning	if Learning MS
	24	Besides . . . Lives	(*not in* MS)
20	25	and loudly celebrated to the World	(*not in* MS)
	9 f.b.	might	would MS

2. MR. COLLINS'S DISCOURSE OF FREE-THINKING

First printed Jan. 25, 1712–13. For facsimile of title-page see p. 25.

Reprinted in *A Supplement to Dr. Swift's Works*, ed. John Nichols, London, 1776, pp. 249–306.

The present text is printed from a photostat of the Bodleian Library copy of the first edition. Marginal glosses referring to pages in Collins's *Discourse of Free-Thinking* are omitted. A few obvious errors have been silently corrected.

3. SOME THOUGHTS ON FREE-THINKING

First printed in 1767, in *Volume XVI. Containing Letters to and from Dr. Jonathan Swift, Dean of St. Patrick's, Dublin, from the Year 1703, to 1743. With Notes Explanatory and Historical, By the Rev. Thomas Birch, D.D.F.R.S., John*

Hawkesworth, L.L.D. and the Editor, Mr. Thomas Wilkes. With an Appendix, Containing many original Pieces. Dublin: Printed by George Faulkner, 1767.

Reprinted in *An Appendix to Dr. Swift's Works and Literary Correspondence. Improved from an Edition Printing by Mr. Faulkner: And now First Published, April, 1767.* London: Printed for W. B. and sold by S. Bladon, in Paternoster Row, MDCCLXVII, pp. 14–16.

The present text is printed from Faulkner's Vol. XVI, 1767, Appendix, pp. 26–8, where this fragment is designated Letter XIV and has the following superscription: '*Some thoughts on Free-thinking, by the same Author, written in* England, *but left unfinished: Copied from the original.*' Two misprints have been silently corrected.

4. A PREFACE TO THE BISHOP OF SARUM'S INTRODUCTION

First published Dec. 7, 1713. See facsimile of title-page, p. 53.

The Second Edition. Same title, except for *The Second Edition* between single rules following the Latin quotation. For a few pages Morphew used either remainder sheets or the same setting of type; otherwise this edition was reset line for line from the first edition. Published Dec. 25, 1713.

A Preface to the B – – p of S – r – m's Introduction to the Third Volume of the History of the Reformation of the Church of England. By Gregory Misosarum. Dublin: Printed by D. Tompson for John Henly at the Black-Moor's Head, in Castle Street, 1714. In addition to some minor revisions, this edition has a significant textual change for which Swift was undoubtedly responsible (see *Introduction*, pp. xxiv-xxviii).

Swift's *Works*, Faulkner, 1738, VI, 53–93. The title-page of the tract is dated 1737. Faulkner's edition was set from the Dublin edition of 1714, with corrections and revisions for stylistic purposes. The tract was reprinted from Faulkner in *Political Tracts. By the Author of Gulliver's Travels.* Printed for C. Davis in Paternoster Row, 1738, II, 53–93.

The present text is printed from Faulkner (38) and collated with the first edition (13a), the second edition (13b), and the Dublin edition (14).

Names and titles appearing with initials only or omitted letters have been given in full and a few obvious misprints silently corrected.

Page	Line	PRESENT TEXT	VARIANTS
55	15	Your humble Servant	Your most Humble Servant 13a, 13b, 14
	16	G. Misosarum 13a, 13b, 14	(*omitted in* 38)
57	*h.t.*	A | PREFACE | To the RIGHT REVEREND | Dr. B – – – T, &c.	A | PREFACE | TO THE | B – – – p of S – – – m's | INTRODUCTION, &c. 13a, 13b, 14
	13	*The English Man Fn. Mr.* Steele	(*Fn. not in earlier editions*)
58	26	appeared several Times	appeared at several times 13a, 13b, 14
	9f.b.	after all, we were some Times	after all, were (*misprint in* 13b) sometimes 13a, 13b, 14
59	5	*Editions*	*Edition* 13a, 13b, 14
	15	the other	t'other 13a, 13b, 14

Page	Line	PRESENT TEXT	VARIANTS
60	14	who	that 13a, 13b, 14
	20	mentioning a peculiar Method which this	giving Notice of a peculiar Method this 13a, 13b; giving a peculiar Method 14
	22	*Bishop of *Rochester* *Fn. Dr.* Atterbury	(*Fn. not in earlier editions*)
62	3	were of any Advantage	were any advantage 13b
	9	this Nation's	the Nation's 13a, 13b
	17	Writing	Writings 13a, 13b
	10*f.b.*	*that*	*who* 13a, 13b
	last line	Principles	Principle 13b
63	14	King *James* the Second	King *James* 13a, 13b, 14
	21	a thousandth Part 13a, 13b	the thousandth Part 14, 38
	23	a Paper	the Paper 13a, 13b, 14
	28	happen	happens 13a, 13b, 14
	6*f.b.*	otherways	otherwise 13a, 13b
	2*f.b.*	upon all those	on those 13a, 13b
64	23	here is	is here 13a, 13b
65	2	who	that 13a, 13b, 14
	15	destitute	destituted 13a, 13b, 14
	19	these Means	this Means 13a, 13b, 14
	23	above 100	above 200 13a, 13b, 14
	3*f.b.*	would	will 13a, 13b, 14
66	16	these 13a, 13b, 14	those 38
	19	*Beside; that engaging*	*Besides that, the engaging* 13a, 13b, 14
	20	*this*	*that* 13a, 13b, 14
	25	never to consent to	never consent to 13a, 13b, 14
	7*f.b.*	as a Means	as means 13a, 13b, 14
	6*f.b.*	Whereas, the Continuance	The Continuance 13a, 13b, 14
67	2	Ground 13a, 13b, 14	Gound (*misprint in* 38)
	4	Inclination to Popery Lay	Inclination towards Popery lay 13a, 13b; Inclination lay 14
	14	L – – – p's 13a, 13b, 14	L – – – p (*misprint in* 38)
68	3	Reasons	Reason 13a, 13b, 14
	15	Mercy, he assures them 13a, 13b, 14	Mercy. He assures them (*misprint in* 38)
	17	must be infallibly	must infallibly be 13a, 13b, 14
	3*f.b.*	that whole Reverend Body	all that Reverend Body 13a, 13b, 14
69	7	*their*	*the* 13a, 13b
	28	*procure*	*produce* 13b
70	5	Whoremongers	Whoremasters 13a, 13b
	12	*Toland, Asgil, Molesworth, Collins, Tindal*	*Toland, Collins, Tindal* 13a, 13b; *Toland, Asgil, M . . . th, Collins, Tindal* 14; *Toland, Asgil, Monmouth, Collins, Tindal* (*see Introduction, pp.* xxiv-xxviii)
	24	he so much despiseth	he despises 13a, 13b
	6*f.b.*	Majority	Mojority (*misprint in* 13b)
71	20	he 13a, 13b, 14	we (*misprint in* 38)
73	15	throughout	thro' 13a, 13b

Page	Line	PRESENT TEXT	VARIANTS
75	11	Man	Men 13a, 13b
	14	one	it 13a, 13b
		be	are 13a, 13b, 14
	19	Cause; when 13a, 13b, 14	Cause. When (*misprint in* 38)
	9 f.b.	Religion: *Popery*	Religion: That *Popery* 13a, 13b
76	12	thinks 13a, 13b, 14	think (*misprint in* 38)
	16	God to enlighten	God either to enlighten 13a, 13b
	23	*Liberty*	*Liberties* 13a, 13b
77	15	*Depths*	*Depth* 13a, 14
	25	in Disputes	in the Disputes 13a, 13b
78	10	Popery	Propery (*misprint in* 13b)
79	11	really just	real and just 13a, 13b; real just 14
	13	*Danger*	*Dangers* 13a, 13b
	19	*Priests*	*Papists* 13a, 13b
	26	be the Author	be Author 13a, 13b
82	2	nor can they ever	nor can ever 13a, 13b
	15	suppose it to be true	suppose it be true 13a, 13b, 14
	18	Queen and Monarchy	Queen, the Monarchy 13a, 13b, 14
	5 f.b.	in the Choice	in his Choice 13a, 13b, 14
83	6	an	a 13a, 13b
	10	going 13a, 13b	a going 14, 38
	14	the Tories not to *light*	the Clergy and Laiety of the Tory Side, not to *light* 13a, 13b; the Tory, not to *light* (*misprint in* 14)
	27	ignominious	ignominous (*misprint in* 13a, 13b)
	10 f.b.	had Picklocks	had his Picklocks 13a, 13b, 14
84	7	already	lately 13a, 13b

5. HINTS TOWARDS AN ESSAY ON CONVERSATION

First printed by Faulkner in Vol. X of the *Works*, Dublin, 1763, pp. 163–77, from which the present text is taken.

Reprinted in *Works*, London, 1764, Vol. VII, Pt. I, pp. 178–87.

Page	Line	PRESENT TEXT	VARIANTS
87	9	to be so much to be said	so much to be said
92	6	Uneasiness at being	uneasiness of being

6. POLITE CONVERSATION

In a letter of July 23, 1737, from London, Lord Orrery writes to Swift (*Corr.* vi, 39):

> Your commands are obeyed long ago; Dr. King has his cargo, Mrs. Barber her conversation, and Mr. Pope his letters.

From this it is evident that Swift had agreed to Mrs. Barber's request that she might have the benefit of the London publication of his *Polite Conversation* (*Corr.* v, 390) and this duly appeared as *A Complete Collection*, etc. (see facsimile of t.p.) in 1738, an octavo of 215 pages. [M]

But at the same time Swift had himself arranged for the book to be published in Dublin, and Faulkner printed it in the spring of the same year as a separate publication, and also reprinted it from the same type in the *Works*, Vol. VI,

TEXTUAL NOTES

pp. 213–344. In a letter of March 8, 1737–8 (*Corr.* vi, 67–8) to Faulkner, he had complained of his delay:

> when you so often desired that I should hasten to correct the several copies you sent me, which, as ill as I have been, and am still, I dispatched as fast as I got them. I expect you will finish it immediately, and send it to me. I hope you have observed all the corrections. I hear you have not above four or five pages remaining. I find people think you are too negligent, and, if you delay longer, what you fear may come to pass, that the English edition may come over before you have your own ready.

It is clear from this that Swift was responsible for the Dublin edition and corrected the proofs. I have no hesitation therefore in choosing Faulkner's edition as my copy-text. [F] It contains certain passages, which either Mrs. Barber or her printer thought it advisable to omit in the London edition; they are now restored here. Other variants in the London edition are noted below, and in a few minor cases, it will be seen that they have been embodied in the text. (For t.p. see facsimiles pp. 97, 127.)

On the verso of the title, of the Dublin eds. in 1738, is the following:

ERRATA,

To the following Treatise.

Page 231, line 12 *for* Direction, *read* Discretion
Page 234, line 11 *for* I have therefore, by the chief Patterns, *read* Wherein I follow the chief Patterns.

(These *Errata* were corrected in the Dublin ed. of 1741.)

AN INTRODUCTION TO THE FOLLOWING TREATISE

Page	Line	PRESENT TEXT	VARIANTS
99	20	these Materials	those Materials
100	3–4	we all ought	we ought
	20	happened at any Time	happened
	22	in my own	at my own
101	12	enrich	inrich
	20	(paying the Postage)	(they paying the Postage)
	5 f.b.	Assembly	Assemblee
102	16	the whole	that whole
	8 f.b.	ought in Justice	in Justice ought
103	17	Dialogues M	Dialogue F
	22	Word they deliver M	Word she delivers F
104	5	Heavings	turnings
105	3	infinite more	infinitely more
	23	reacheth M	reached F
	27	And these	And those
	9 f.b.	strowed	strewed
	4 f.b.	these Terms	those Terms
106	1	succeed better	succeed much better
	13	to advance Politeness	towards Politeness
	23	Clubs and Coffee-Houses	Clubs of Coffee-houses
107	15	until after	till after
108	12	Besides,	And besides,
	27–28	famous Court-Chaplain	infamous Court-Chaplain

Page	Line	PRESENT TEXT	VARIANTS
109	10	charged for	charged with
110	15–16	Female Acquaintance	several Acquaintance
	last line	primitive natural	natural
111	5	as now	as are now
	17	my Readers	my male Readers
112	5	so easily acquired	so easy an Acquirement
	12	hardly falls	hardly fall
	14	neither, perhaps hath	neither hath
	27	slackness	slowness
		Tones	Turns
113	1	Pattern	Patterns
	24	pronounced. Wherein I follow (*see Errata*)	pronounced by M pronounced. I have therefore, by F
	9*f.b.*	hav'n't	han't M; ha'v't F
	6*f.b.*	now pared	not pared
	4*f.b.*	Lard	*Lierd*
	3*f.b.*	Larnin	*Larnen*
114	21–22	great a Variety	great Variety
	9–8*f.b.*	nicer Ears	nice Ears
	last line	until	till
115	8–9	Black-pudding	Black Pudden
	5–4*f.b.*	few, ... Custom; no ... Wit. M	few; ... Custom. No ... Wit, F
116	6	these Meetings	those Meetings
	14	dismissed	dismiss
	17	contriving	continuing
117	9	where	when
	23	or brangling	nor Brangling
	10–9*f.b.*	Left and Right, until he be	Left to the Right, till he is
	8*f.b.*	likewise made	made
118	1	for this	for which
	17	*Charles Gildon* M	*Cha. Gildon* F
	24	And, I	And here, I
	27	*Stevens* M	Stephens F
	28	Eminency	Eminence
120	9	after I have exhausted	after having exhausted
	11	into the	in the
	26	instil only	instil early
	30–33	the never-to-be-too-much admired *Lord H——*, in his truly sublime Poem, called, *Loyalty defined*.	

> Who's not polite, for the Pretender, is;
> A Jacobite, I know him by his Phizz.
>
> *Fn.* **It is erroneously printed in the* London *Edition,*
> *Mr.* Stephen Duck.

(This passage is omitted in M. There are no signs of a cancel, but p. lxxv contains only 16 instead of the usual 20 lines. I do not understand this footnote in F unless some copies were issued with the above lines attributed to Stephen Duck.)

Page	Line	PRESENT TEXT	VARIANTS
121	1	In the like Manner, the	the
	5	Hear M	Here F
	23–25	may perhaps, resolve not to read my Book; chusing, from a want of true Taste or by strong Affectation, rather	from a Want of true Taste, or by strong Affectation, may perhaps resolve not to read my Book; chusing rather
	25	shining M	sharing F
122	3–2f.b.	in the Mint, at the Tower	at the Mint, in the Tower
123	15	shaped	formed
127		(Full title)	(Half-title)
130	1–13	The Argument	(*not in* M)
131	1–4	A compleat COLLECTION Of genteel and Ingenious Conversation, &c.	Polite Conversation, &c.
	18–19	it? what, . . . trees?	it, that . . . Trees?
	8–7f.b.	Nev.	(*order reversed in* M)
	6–5f.b.	Col.	
132	11	Porter	*the* Porter
	19	Smart, *and Lady Answerall* M	Smart, *Lady* Answerall, *Miss* Notable F
133	10	Lord Sp.	Lady Smart
		go to	come to
	15	so well	so much
	20	heard 'em say that	heard say
	26–27	good Condition	in good Conditions
	8f.b.	Here's poor Miss	Here's Miss M
	7f.b.	Thought	Thoughts
134	4	promise	promise him
	19	thou art	you are
	20	this Cream	the Cream
	21	Betty M	Lady Smart F
	22	run Girl	you Girl
	23	the Cat	a Cat
	9f.b.	and Silver	Silver
	8f.b.	*Miss*	*Neverout.* Miss,
135	23	(*Here a loud Laugh*)	(—*Laugh*—)
	9f.b.	fill me	fill me out
	5f.b.	she's an	'tis an
136	2	the *Philistians*	*Philistines*
	5	Well, 'tis	'Tis
	6	your Manners	your good Manners
	8	for when	When
	9f.b.	Maids, they say,	they say, Maids
137	1	stuck	sick
	8–9	upon poor	on poor
	13	please to favour	be so good as to favour
	15	I have got	for I have
	21	there you	you
138	18	thinks, the Bell chinks	thinks—
	20	upon it	on it

Page	Line	PRESENT TEXT	VARIANTS
	27	Wit	the Wit
	5 f.b.	*Col.* Ods so! . . . can't cry	*This passage comes after* Well, Miss, and so can I. M
139	1		
	9–10	*Miss.* No Madam . . . grow apace	*Not in* M
	20	the last Dish	the last
	26	even her	her
	9 f.b.	if you don't like it, dy'e see,	do you see, if you don't much like it,
	6 f.b.	Sir *John Bearish*	Sir *John Brisk*
	last line	Ay, some	Ay, ay, some
140	2	ay, Madam, as	ay, as
	3	say he	say that he
	11	Well, ay, but scornful Dogs, they say, will	Well; but scornful Dogs will
	14	upon	on
	23–24	*Col.* Why, if Things do not break or wear out, how should	*Col.* 'Tis a Folly to cry for spilt Milk. *Lady Smart.* Why, if Things did not break or wear out, how would
	25	Well, I'm very sick, if any Body cared for it. (*She spits.*) I believe I shall dye, for I can't spit from me.	Well, I am . . . body car'd for it. M. *Rest of speech omitted in* M *and given to* C*olonel at p.* 156, 7 *f.b. thus—* (Colonel *spits*) Lord. I shall die; I cannot spit from me. M
141	10	Mr. *Neverout*, now you are up	Now you are up, Mr. *Neverout*,
	17	he could	it would
	23	knife	Penknife
	9 f.b.	seen him often	often seen him
142	1	I find you are pleased	you are pleas'd
	4 ff.	*Lady Smart.* Ah, Miss, Love will creep where it can't go: They say, touch a gall'd Horse, and he'll wince. *Miss.* I'd hold	*Lady Smart.* Touch a gall'd Horse, and he'll wince: Love will creep where it dare not go: I'd hold
	10	seen her	been here
143	1	struck M	stuck F
	29	lend	send
	7 f.b.	*whole Face*	*Face*
144	5	a new Pleasure	one Pleasure
	10	a Word and	a Bit and
145	17	*Dimple*	*Snuff*
	19	and that's all	well enough
	7 f.b.	*Nev.* I hear, my Lord what d'ye call 'um is courting her.	*Wrongly given to* Lady Answerall M I hear, my Lord What-d'you-call-him is courting her.

Page	Line	PRESENT TEXT	VARIANTS
146	17	Pye-Crusts, they say, are	Pye-crusts are
	18	Carrilye's	Carry-lye's
	19	tell my	tell you my
	6 f.b.	If you	You
	last line	*Water	(no footnote in M)
147	1	Miss, Never fear:	Never fear, Miss;
	16	here's some	there's some
	21	all goes	goes all
	25–26	I let	I have let
148	5	self.	self. *Lady Smart.* So they pray'd
		Nev. Well;	me to tell you. *Nev.* Well,
	5 f.b.	Days	Reign
149	22	Years	Year.
	23	Miss, and you	Miss, you
150	18	I can assure you, there	there
	28	Lady	my Lady
		were walking	was walking
151	8	pray, where	where
	18	there's	here's
	8 f.b.	*Strut*	*Brag*
	4 f.b.	is not he	is he not
152	16–21	*Col.* Well, I must be plain …	(later, after l.8 f.b. in M)
		Miss. … a very good poor	Colonel. … a very bad poor Man's
		man's Sow. But,	Sow.
	25	come you hither,	come hither,
152	11 f.b.	*Nev.* I assure you, Miss	*Neverout.* Miss I assure you
	8 f.b.	into	in
	3 f.b.	another	more
153	25	What, you are	What! you are
154	12	you are grown as	you are as
	24	Why, Madam,	Why, indeed, Madam
	7 f.b.	Pride should	Pride wou'd
155	3	They said you	They said, that you
	2 f.b.	Have a Care, Miss,	Have a Care;
156	1	one wrinkle	a Wrinkle
	6	for using	to use
	7	go to that,	go, that,
	8	that there's	there's
	9	every one	every body
157	5	one can't	we can't
	11	possible that she	possible, she
	19	Friends	Friend
	25–26	Man nor Boy	a Man nor a Boy
158	28	does not	do not
159	8	that just at	that at
	4 f.b.	a true	the true
161	3	I mean	I meant
	12	(not in F)	*Nev.* Faith, Miss, you have mended it, as a Tinker mends a Kettle; stop one Hole, and make two.

Page	Line	Present Text	Variants
161	20	the Black Ox has	the Black has
	23	he is	her Husband
	26	*Nev.* (Fn. added by *Swift*)	(*not in* M)
	27	in Cog?	*incog?*
162	1	you to hold	you hold
	5	and you	and then you
	8	have no	has no
	10	hang them	hang him
	11	Well, but I don't like such Jesting	(*omitted in* M)
	15	you would wish	you wish
	16–17	Truth for once,	Truth,
	22	Garter	Garters
	24	Bite, Miss,	Pretty Miss
	29	Back-Bone	Back
163	8	forget	forgot
	6*f.b.*	*a Thimble*	*her Thimble*
165	19	that once	that
	26	Women	Woman
165	10*f.b.*	I'gad	Egad M
	9*f.b.*	(*not in* F	*Ld. Sparkish.* Well, Colonel, there's one Comfort, that you need not fear a Cannon-Bullet.
			Col. Why so, my Lord?
			Ld. Sparkish. Because they say, he was curs'd in his Mother's Belly, that was kill'd by a Cannon-Bullet.
166	20	I am sure, I have seen	I've seen
	25	was naughty	a naughty Pack
167	11	you may——	you may kiss——
		strives	*tries*
168	1	*Door*	*Closet Door*
	10	Word spoken	Word's spoke
	17	This it is	This is it
	20	among us all	among all us
	21	Leave.	Leave: Come, Gentlemen, are you for a March?
169	1	Second CONVERSATION	Polite Conversation, *&c.*

DIALOGUE II

	9	into	to
170	6*f.b.*	Grace to them.	Grace.
	last line	pleases	please
171	3–4	*Nev.* Ay, here's etc.	*Nev.* Ay, here's cut and come again, Miss, But pray etc. F
		Miss. But Pray, etc. M	
	10	*Lady Smart.* Beef is Man's Meat	*Ld. Sparkish.* Beef etc. M, F

Page	Line	PRESENT TEXT	VARIANTS
172	16	killing that would 41	killing that, that would
	22	Bit	Piece
173	*last line*	sorry	very sorry
175	2	*Miss.*	*Lady Sm.*
		this Finger, (God bless the Mark)	which Finger? (God bless the Mark)
after 16		(*not in* F)	*Nev.* Faith, my Lord, I pledged myself, for I drank twice together without thinking.
	20	old Maid	old Woman
176	6–7	I have	I'll have
	8	good Broth	very good Broth
177	4–6	*Col.* I am . . . Chaplain. I can . . . all.	(*These sentences reversed in* M)
	13	and burns	*and it burns*
	4f.b.	Lady *Answerall*, M	Lady *Sparkish* F
	2f.b.	Lady *Answ.* M	Lady *Sp.* F
179 *after* 2		(*not in* F, *here, but inserted in its proper place below*)	*Colonel tasting the Wine.*
	3	Lord *Sm.* M	Lady *Sm.* F
	4	Peak M	Park F
	7	Lord *Sm.* M	Lady *Sm.* F
	11	knew	know
	17	drunk M	drank F
180	7	such	so much
	10	Nay,	I own
	11	wou'd have	had
	13	*Nev.* Miss, I'll tell you one thing. M	(*omitted in* F)
	28	Wont M	Want F
181	15	(*not in* F)	*Col.* Well, this Eating and Drinking takes away a body's Stomach, as Lady *Answerall* says.
	18	but I find, my	but my
	8f.b.	this Part	that Part
182	16	twenty wise Men	the wisest body
	21	I'faith	faith
	9f.b.	so you	if you
	5f.b.	Caudle	Candle
184	1	Why, take it	Why I'll take it,
	2	Well, you're	You are
	2f.b.	brings	brings up
	last line	Lordship	Ladyship
185	1	Lord *Sm.*	Lady *Sm.*
186	27	*long*	*large*
	3f.b.	*Footman brings in*	*A Footman brings*
187	1	brosten	rosten
	16	Miss, you	Miss; faith you
	7–6f.b.	weary with	weary of
	5f.b.	I fear	fear
188	7	besides,	And besides,

Y

Page	Line	Present Text	Variants
189	19	*Sir John*	(*omitted in* M)
190	2–3	*Derbyshire.*	*Darbyshire.* Come, sit down; let us
		Sir John. Not a Drop more.	put off the evil Hour as long as
			we can.
			Sir John. Faith, I could not drink a
			Drop more, if the House was full.
	14	takes his Leave	takes Leave
	21	had been	were
	27	Nose M	Hose F
	3*f.b.*	*Nev.* Pray, Miss	*Neverout.* Faith, he's a true
			Country Put. Pray, Miss
191	8–9	Why, he dyed, because	Why, because
	25	is Sawce for	is for
	8*f.b.*	Don't be mauming and gau-	Don't be so teizing! You plague
		ming a Body so	a body so!
192	16	*Neverout.* I hear	*Neverout* my Lord and I intend to
			beat up your Quarters one of
			these Days: I hear
	last line	wash Glasses M	wash the Glasses F
193	1	Third CONVERSATION	Polite Conversation, *&c.*

DIALOGUE III

	10	Well, but	But
194	3	claw thee	claw thou
	17	——	A ——
195	7	my Bed-fellow	Bed-fellows
	8	Left-Hand	Right Hand
	9*f.b.*	her. ——	her as the Devil loves Holy Water
196	12	rises	ris'
		——	A ——
	20	*a Spoon.*	*the Spoon*
	5*f.b.*	a little thinner,	thinner
197	19	Miss, come be	come, Miss; be
	23–24	but once look . . . Apron	but look . . . Apron-String
		Strings	
	27	*Neverout*, no Offence	*Neverout*, I beg your Diversion;
			no Offence,
	4*f.b.*	loud and	loud
198	18	lately put	put
	20	for forty	forty
	28	all I	all that I
198	*last line*	(*cut out because used before,*	*Col.* Tom, you have a good Nose
		p. 152, *ll.* 20–21)	to make a poor Man's Sow.
199	8	*Miss.* What, my Lord, do	(*omitted in* F)
		you think I was born in a	
		Wood, to be afraid of an	
		Owl? M	
	15	Hands off.	Hands off! that's Meat for your
			Master.

Page	Line	Present Text	Variants
	16	are in for	are for
	25–26	possible. Women ! One . . . Men's	possible; one . . . Man's
200	8–7f.b.	all honest Folks to go to Bed.	honest Folks to be a-bed.
	6f.b.	Eyes draw Straws	Eyes draws Straw
201	4	I shall have	shall I have

7. A MODEST DEFENCE OF PUNNING

The text is printed from the original autograph now in the Pierpont Morgan Library in New York, with kind permission. The manuscript seems to be a fair copy set out ready for printing, and written on the first three pages of a large folded sheet, in the form of a Letter to a Member of Parliament, dated from Cambridge, Nov. 8, 1716.

The following corrections are made in the manuscript all in the hand of the author.

Page	Line	Passages deleted	Corrected readings
205	16	By which	whereby
	21	one of his Fraternity	a certain Gentleman
206	20	Knight	*Spaniard*
208	8	inflicts[?] as a	Claps as a
209	27	whether we be Toryes or no	in calling us Toryes
	10–9f.b.	covers us with Gratitude(?)	we should be *covered* with *Gilt,*

It may be added that in the Bodleian copy of *God's Revenge against Punning*, the three noblemen referred to are said to be (1) Lord Hervey, (2) Lord Stanhope, (3) Lord Warwick (Rich) and the rest, Col. Frowd, Tom Earle, Col. Lambard, *Eustace*, an Irishman, *Samuel* Mollineaux.

8. TREATISE ON GOOD MANNERS AND GOOD BREEDING

First printed by Dr. Delany as an appendix to his *Observations upon Lord Orrery's Remarks etc.*, London, 1754, pp. 293–308. Reprinted by Faulkner in *Works*, Dublin, 1758, IX, Supplement, pp. 37–47, where he has followed his usual practice in capitalization and in the use of the ending -eth.

The text is printed from Dr. Delany's Appendix, 1754.

Page	Line	Present Text	Variants
213	17	farmer or a tradesman	Tradesman or a Farmer
214	4f.b.	as to break through 58	to break thorough 54
215	20	desperate	disconsolate
216	12	favour or credit	Credit or Favour
218	7	prominent	predominant

9. HINTS ON GOOD MANNERS

First printed by Deane Swift in 1765 in *Works*, London, 4to, Vol. VIII, pt. I, 238–9.

Reprinted by Faulkner in *Works*, Dublin, Vol. XII, 361–4.

The text is taken from Deane Swift. There are no variants.

10. OF THE EDUCATION OF LADIES

First printed by Deane Swift in 1765 in *Works*, London, 4to, Vol. VIII, pt. I, 265–8.

Reprinted by Faulkner in *Works*, Dublin, Vol. XII, 407–13.

The text is taken from Deane Swift. There are no variants.

11. A DISCOURSE TO PROVE THE ANTIQUITY OF THE ENGLISH TONGUE

First printed by Deane Swift in 1765 in Swift, *Works*, London, 4to, Vol. VIII, pt. I, p. 269.

Reprinted by Faulkner in Swift, *Works*, Dublin, 1765, 8vo, Vol. XII, p. 415.

The text is taken from Deane Swift.

Page	Line	PRESENT TEXT	VARIANTS
234	4 f.b.	*Epaminondas*	*Epaminondes* S and F
237	20	*Seiser*	*Seiseher* F

12. THOUGHTS ON VARIOUS SUBJECTS

See Vol. I of this edition, pp. 241–5, where those only were reprinted which Swift had included in his *Miscellanies in Prose and Verse*, 1711, pp. 235 f., with the title: *Various Thoughts*, Moral and Diverting. Written October the 1st. 1706. These were reprinted in *Miscellanies in Prose and Verse. The First Volume*, 1727, pp. 388–98, with additions, pp. 398–408, the whole reprinted again in Swift's *Works*, Faulkner, Vol. I, 1735, pp. 297–310, from which the present text is taken.

Further Thoughts, that is the different collection beginning 'Laws penned with the utmost Care', was first printed by Dodsley in *Works*, 1745, Vol. X, pp. 232–47, and reprinted by Faulkner in 1746, *Works*, Vol. VIII, pp. 282–93. It was later included by him in his *Works*, Dublin, 1752, Vol. VIII, pp. 351–9, and reprinted in the Hawkesworth London edition in 1755, Vol. VI, pt. II, pp. 178–84, with this note:

These *Thoughts* and the *Bons Mots de Stella* that follow, seem to be part of *Sheridan's* collection of *Contes à rire* and *Bons Mots*, mentioned in Swift's letter to Sheridan, March 27, 1733:

I am confident (it) will be much the best extant; but you are apt to be terribly sanguine about the profits of publishing; however it shall have all the pushing I can give.

Even if Sheridan collected these *Thoughts*, they must have been taken down from Swift's telling. The stories that come from London and those that contain remarks made to and about Dr. Gee, Prebendary of Westminster, Prior, Dennis, Wharton and Bolingbroke, must have been told by Swift.

The present text is taken from Faulkner, 1752, to conform with most of the volume in spelling, punctuation and capitalization. It has been collated with Dodsley and Hawkesworth.

Page	Line	PRESENT TEXT	VARIANTS
243	11	It is 27	It it 35
244	7	Female	Woman 27
245	28	*Curis acuens mortalia corda* 27	*Curis acuens mortalia Concordia* 35

Page	Line	Present Text	Variants
	4 *f.b.*	of Valour	of great valour 27

(N.B.—'great' occurs in preceding sentence and 'greatest' in the following: this correction not made in Swift's own copy of *Miscellanies*, but certainly made by him in the proofs.)

Page	Line	Present Text	Variants
246	11–12	Matter to me; from	Matter from 27
247	21–23	I was . . . I thought . . . I said,	A Person . . . he thought . . . He said 27
	8 *f.b.*	are S	(MS. correction of 'is' in 27)
248	17	Phial	vial (*throughout* D *and* H)
	20	hundred . . . there dying in it	hundreds . . . dying H
	6 *f.b.*	content	contented D, H
249 *fn. to* 3 *f.b.*	The Reverend Mr. *Pomfret*, a Dissenting Minister	The Rev. Mr. *Pomfret*. H
250	2 *f.b.*		The death of a private man is generally of so little importance in itself; and yet I do not ob-observe from the practice of mankind, that either philosophy or nature have sufficiently armed us against the fears which attend it. Neither do I find any thing able to reconcile us to it, but extreme pain, shame, or despair; for poverty, imprisonment, ill fortune, grief, sickness, and old age, do generally fail. (*only in* D *and* H)
251	25	leaden	lead H
252	11		I have known men happy enough at ridicule, who upon grave subjects were perfectly stupid; of which Dr. *Echard* of *Cambridge*, who writ *The contempt of the clergy*, was a great instance. (*only in* H)
253	22	may be said of women in reality.	in reality it may be said of women. H.

APPENDIX A

These three short pieces are reprinted from the MS. volume of *Poems and Letters* in the Pierpont Morgan Library, New York, They had been formerly printed by Elrington Ball, see *Corr.* i, 375–7 and 380, and ii, 407–8.

APPENDIX B

The Dying Speech of Tom Ashe

First printed by Faulkner in *Works*, Vol. XIII, pp. 223f., with a note that it was the pretended DYING SPEECH of TOM ASHE, whose brother, the Reverend Dillon Ashe, was nicknamed Dilly. 'Given to Dr. Monsey by Sir Andrew Fountaine, and communicated to the Editor of these Volumes by that ingenious, learned, and very obliging Gentleman.'

APPENDIX C

Swift was at this time with Sir Andrew Fountaine in London, and this joke may well have been concerted between them. It is reprinted from a copy of the *Post-Boy*.

APPENDIX D

Printed from the first edition of the *Miscellanies in Prose and Verse*, 1711. Swift had made all the arrangements for the publication of the *Miscellanies* with Benjamin Tooke (see *Corr.* i, 185–6) and there can be no doubt that he himself wrote this Publisher's Preface.

APPENDIX E

Printed from Faulkner's edition of the *Works*, Vol. VIII, pp. 387f. It was reprinted with slight modifications in the London edition of the *Works*, 4to, Vol. VI, pt. II, pp. 162f.

APPENDIX F

Printed from a photostat of a copy of the original half-sheet, printed by Waters, Dublin, 1726, in the National Library, Dublin.

APPENDIX G

Printed from the original MSS. in the Huntington Library, HML4341,2,3. The first, *Notes for Polite Conversation*, was kindly copied for me by George P. Mayhew. In the third, *Irish Eloquence*, I am indebted to Professor David Nichol Smith and Mr. Myles Dillon of the Dublin Institute for Advanced Studies for their help with a difficult manuscript. *Sowins*, a thin porridge; *Fraughauns*, bilberries; *Puckaun*, a he-goat, kept with cows to prevent abortion (information from Seán ó Suilleabháin, Registrar of the Irish Folklore Commission); *Buddough*, churl; *Canaught*, purchase; *Garrauns*, geldings; *Soogaun*, plaited straw; *Gadd*, withe; *Balcan*, spirits distilled from black oats; *Maddors*, wooden cups.

APPENDIX H

Printed from the text of Deane Swift in *Works*, 4to, Vol. VIII, pt. II, pp. 261f.; reprinted by Faulkner, *Works*, Vol. XIII, p. 234.

ADDITIONAL VARIANTS for *POLITE CONVERSATION*

Page,	line	Present text		Variants
101,	5	foresee		foretel
102,	18	Reader		Readers
103,	23	Cadencies		Cadences
108,	5	until		till for
109,	4	Reason		Reasons
109,	5	from		who, from
113,	19	every such School		every School
113,	2fb	Positively		Positive
115,	8fb	Consequences		Consequence
117,	1	confine		compute
118,	15	commanded		commended
120,	7	true		and true
	22	the Fountain		the very Fountain
121,	6	poetick Quire		whole Poetick Choir
122,	27	inhumanly		inhumanely

ADDITIONAL VARIANTS for *A PROPOSAL FOR CORRECTING THE ENGLISH TONGUE*

8,	16	into 12		to 35
11,	9	unharmonious 12		unharmonius 35
19,	b	Credit 12		credit, 35

MINOR CORRECTIONS IN THE TEXT

9,	24	changes	*read*	Changes
17,	6	Princes:		Princes;
20,	4fb	Conveniences		Conveniencies
100,	18	higest		highest
101,	3fb	want:		want;
117,	25	surpizing		surprizing
118,	8	Persons;		Persons:
122,	20	*Czar of*		*Czar* of

I am indebted for the above corrections to Professor Maurice Johnson, and am very grateful to him for his very careful review. See *P.Q.* XXXVII, III, July, 1958.

A closer study of the Huntington Manuscripts 14342 and 14343 has led me to accept the following readings, as suggested to me by Professor George Mayhew:

P. 277, last line	*for*	[? a] Planter	*read*	Planted
P. 278, l. 7	*for*	Country	*read*	County
l. 8		Doll		Dolt
l. 11		strole		shoh (cf. shoh't p. 279)
l. 15		Spawleen		Spawlpeen
P. 279, l. 5	*for*	Doll	*read*	Dolt
l. 10		Spanel		Spaned

Also on page 277, insert after title, A DIALGOUE etc.
From Huntington MS, 14342.

INDEX

Academy, French, xiv, 14
Adam, 46
Addison, Joseph, 16
Agricola, 280
Alexander the Great, xxxviii, 45, 236
Amos, 45
Anne, Queen of England, xxiii, 75, 283; and the dating of *Polite Conversation*, xxix; and Prince Eugène, xxxvii, 216
Apollo, 46, 252
Arbuthnot, Dr. John, xxxii, 118, 260
Asgill, John, his *Letter to the . . . Bishop of Sarum*, xxii; and the Molesworth controversy, xxv f.
Ashe, Captain Thomas, 261; his '*Dying Speech*', *see* Swift
Atheism and Free-Thinking, *see* Free-Thinkers
Athens, 237
Atterbury, Dr. Francis, Bishop of Rochester and Dean of Carlisle, xi, 31, 36, 43–4; his 'Ingratitude', 60
Ault, Norman, his *Prose Works of Alexander Pope* cited, xxxiv

Bacon, Francis, Lord Chancellor, 46
'Baker, Sir John, Kt.', *see* Ford
Barber, Mrs. Mary, and *Polite Conversation*, xxix, xxxiii
Bathurst, Allen, 1st Baron and Earl, and Sheridan's *Contes à rire*, xxxix
Bentinck, William, Earl of Portland, 58
Bentley, Dr. Richard, his *Remarks upon a Late Discourse of Free-Thinking*, pt. 2, attacks deism, x, xvii; Swift's irony on him, xxxviii, 207, 231
Bible, The, xxvi; its literary influence, 14–15; *Old Test.*, 45, 48; *New Test.*, 45, 48; *Genesis*, 239
Bickerstaff, Isaac, his *Index Expurgatorius*, xi, *see also* Swift
Bolingbroke, Viscount, *see* St. John
Bouffleurs, Monsieur, 58
Britain, Roman literary influence on, 6–7, 280

British Academy, The, and Swift's *Proposal*, xiii, xiv
British Mercury, The, and Molesworth, xxvii
'Bristow-stones', xxxv, 208
Brown, Thomas, *Works* of, 118
Budgell, Eustace, xxxv, 209
Bull, George, Bishop of St. David's, 34
Burnet, Gilbert, Bishop of Salisbury, his *Introduction to the Third Volume of the History of the Reformation of the Church of England*, ix, x, xi, xxi f.; xxv; *see* Swift's *Preface, passim*; his *History of his own Times*, xxiv, 107; his *History of the Reformation*, vols. I and II, xxi, xxiii, 60 f.; his *Pastoral Care*, xxi; *Some Sermons*, xxii; his literary style, xxiii, 69–70, 82–3
Butler, Samuel, *Hudibras*, 274
Button, Daniel, xxxv, 209
Buys, Monsieur de, Dutch envoy, 215

Caesar, Julius, xv
Cain, 45–6
Calvinism, and Collins's *Discourse*, xviii
Cambridge, University of, 206, 237; and George I's present of books, xxxiv, 209
Camden, William, 231
Cant-words, 8, 105, 110, 146, 161
Catholicism, Roman, and Burnett's 'Nose' for it, xxiii, 61 f., 74–6; and Henry VIII, 72 f.; compared with Dissent, 77–8
Cervantes, *Don Quixote*, 250
Charles I, King of England, literary influence of women in his reign, xxxi, 94–5; poetry in his reign, 273–4
Charles II, King of England, 62; 68; 103; 109; 'our Augustan Age', 249, 274
Charles XII, King of Sweden, 122
China, permanence of its language, xx
Church of England, its clergy criticized, xviii, xx f., 29, 27–8, 39 f., 47,

303